THE DAMAGED SELF

Exploring the Psychopathology
of a Diminished Life

by John H. Morgan

John H. Morgan

THE DAMAGED SELF
Exploring the Psychopathology
of a Diminished Life
(studies in child personality development)

John H. Morgan
Ph.D., Psy.D. (FH/Oxford), D.Sc.(CAS/London)

ISBN 978-155605-521-8 Paperback
ISBN 978-155605-522-5 Ebook

Wyndham Hall Press

Levering, MI

John H. Morgan

Table of Contents

John H. Morgan

ACKNOWLEDGMENTS

I wish to acknowledge with deep gratitude my appointment as Senior Fellow in Behavioral Science at Foundation House/Oxford (UK) during which time for 20 years I was privileged to teach a doctoral-level seminar in the International Summer Program of Oxford University. Of special mention are Dr. Vincent Strudwick, Fellow of Kellogg College/Oxford, the late Dr. Angus Hawkins, Fellow of Keble College/Oxford, and Dr. Jane Shaw, Principal of Harris Manchester College/Oxford and Pro-Vice-Chancellor of Oxford University, for without their collegial support my efforts in this regard would not have come to fruition.

Preface

Consider the diminished child, he or she who whose life spirit has been squelched, whose growth potential put on hold, whose process toward self-actualization frustrated. What does life have in store for that child?

Take a step back now and ask: How did that child become diminished? What was absent in that child's growth and development? What initiatives are needed now to reverse the direction of that child's life? And who's responsible—both for the diminishment and for the healing? These are the questions that undergird John Morgan's *The Damaged Self: Exploring the Psychopathology of a Diminished Life.*

Dr. Morgan, a scholar of multiple disciplines, explores these questions through the wisdom of eleven men and women who confronted the roots of childhood pathology during the foundational years of psychotherapy, roughly the 1930s through the 1980s. Through a variety of philosophical backgrounds, academic specialties, and hands-on approaches, each theorist, from Sigmund Freud to Anna Freud, identifies pathways through which a healthy self-concept, the opposite of the diminished self, might be attained.

Now, no one would argue that Sigmund Freud left us, among his other revolutionary insights, a viable plan for raising children. But with his theorizing about childhood, specifically related to the psychosexual development of the child as the origin of adult symptomology, he opened the door to child psychology, one his daughter Anna would hasten to enter. Others would follow in rapid succession—Alfred Adler, Melanie Klein, Erik Erikson, Karen

Horney—taking Freud's initial insights, rejecting this, further developing that, and leaving a solid foundation for all those who work in child and family psychology today. Anna, who would often eavesdrop on her beloved father's therapy sessions, was among the first to make alterations in the strict Freudian routine by ditching the iconic couch—the children with whom she worked, like children today, couldn't *sit* still, much less *lie* still. Besides, their free play, like the free associations of adults, opened a window to their inner worlds for those intuitive and patient enough to take notice. Erikson, whom Anna trained in the psychoanalytic method her father had pioneered, would become a master at interpreting child play.

In these pages we learn how each thinker built upon those who came before, expanding their collective vision in the process. Freud's initial emphasis on the psychosexual etiology of child pathology, with intensive psychoanalysis as the sole pathway to healing, has through the years almost entirely given way to more direct, face-to-face, person-to-person approaches championed by humanistically oriented theorists like Carl Rogers, Abraham Maslow, and Harry Stack Sullivan. The social scientists Charles Horton Cooley and George Herbert Meade took this an important step further by emphasizing the broader social perspective, one that recognizes the great truth eternalized by John Donne over three centuries previously that "no man is an island, entire of itself." We are not solitary creatures; each of us is part of something greater than ourselves, the social context in which we struggle and, hopefully, find healing. It is true: It takes a whole village to raise a child into adulthood.

Within that social context, Adler, Horney, and Sullivan gave precedence to the quality of the parent/child relationship, an insight that led to the development of a plethora of parent education programs starting in the 1960s, largely drawing upon Adler's work. From Freud's initial insights drawn from the unconscious realm of his patients, a tradition of psychotherapy that addresses the needs of adults and children alike was born, and all of us who work with families in any capacity are indebted to these men and women.

In *The Damaged Self,* John Morgan masterfully demonstrates how eleven theorists and practitioners from the psychological and social sciences addressed both the causes of child diminishment and the various pathways to healing during the formative years of the counseling profession. Whether the men and women featured herein are old friends or relative newcomers, our understanding and appreciation of their importance to both the development of contemporary psychotherapy and the specific identification of more affirming, encouraging, and growth-oriented opportunities for the young will be much enhanced. If the future of our children is important to us, this is a book that matters.

Michael L. Brock, PhD, LPC

Carl Ranson Rogers Professor of Counseling Psychology

Graduate Theological Foundation

John H. Morgan

INTRODUCTION: THE SELF CONCEPT AND PERSONALITY DEVELOPMENT

By investigating the social and psychological contexts within which the self is damaged resulting in the diminishment of an individual's potential for a meaningfully fulfilling life, the self-*concept which has been developed by leading behavioral and social* scientists such as Abraham Maslow, Alfred Adler, and Carl Rogers will be framed here within the interpersonal theory of psychotherapy developed by Harry Stack Sullivan and subsequent theorists such as Anna Freud, Melanie Klein, and Karen Horney. The development of the self-concept is composed of a balancing integration of self-image and self-esteem and these are directly developed and nurtured through the maturation process in childhood. In clinical cases of a diminished sense of self (demeaned self-image and/or self-esteem), there is evidence of a failure within the family matrix of nurturing the child's sense of self, whether that failure is due to a self-conscious disregard of the child or an inadvertent failure to assume parental oversight in the child's development. A diminished life is the result of this failure to foster a positive and healthy self-concept in childhood and it is the intention of this study to explore the psychopathology resulting from this failure in what is being called here the diminished self.

The psychopathology of a diminished life producing a mental injury is characterized by the downward spiral in an individual's self-concept (self-image and self-esteem) brought on by a diminished opinion of one's self resulting from negative interpersonal experiences especially from childhood. This approach is based on the work of Harry Stack Sullivan, M.D., and is explored within the context of the traditional orientation of psychoanalysis developed by Sigmund Freud, M.D. A damaged self is evidenced in a variety of personality disorders described in the DSM-5 and is

11

treatable using a variety of psychotherapeutic modalities of intervention which will be explored here. The reconstituting of a healthy self-concept is the assessment and treatment focus employed in the use of both Sullivan's *Interpersonal Psychiatry* and Freud's *Psychodynamic Psychoanalysis*. A comprehensive understanding of the concept of the self is integrated into this psychopathological disorder incorporating a range of diagnostic and treatment protocols with special use of Carl Rogers' concept of *unconditional positive regard* as well as Abraham Maslow's concept of *self-actualization*. Rogers' extensive development of the theory of the self-concept is complimented with Maslow's development of the self-actualized personality. Both Rogers and Maslow concurred with Sullivan in the conviction that the human psyche has implicit within it the capacity, if nurtured and not stifled, to reach a level of cognitive integration of the personality such that the individual can lead a productive and meaningful life. Alfred Adler's contribution to the discussion of the relationship between negative child-rearing practices and the development of mental disorders in early childhood will be carefully considered in our attempt to understand human nature's drive towards self-actualization in the face of the experience of inferiority. Erik Erikson's concept of personal identify in the maturation of the child is linked to the work of Charles Horton Cooley (*the looking-glass self*) and George Herbert Mead (*the social self*) which provides the matrix within which the psychodynamic social interactive development of the self-concept is understood. A significant component of this research will incorporate the pioneering work in child psychotherapy developed by Anna Freud, Karen Horney, and Melanie Klein within the context of classical psychoanalytic theory and constructs.

In this study, we will begin with an overview of the concept of self (image and esteem) wherein damage to the individual self-concept presented and manifested as a mental injury in child development is explicated. Then we will summarize each theorist's approach by providing an overview of each theorist's concept of "the self" and suggest ways in which their approach addresses the psychopathological developments occurring in a damaged or diminished self-concept (image and esteem).

The human community has been concerned with and reflective upon the nature and meaning of life and our place within the matrix of all reality from our earliest consciousness. "Who am I?" is the enduringly abiding occupation of the reflective individual. Though the origin of the concept of the "self," is disputed by social historians, there is little doubt that the "self-concept" is credited to the humanistic school of psychotherapy, particularly with Carl Rogers and Abraham Maslow. The self-concept functions essentially as that aspect of our self-awareness embodying our notion of whom we are including thoughts and feelings involving the triadic matrix of physical, personal, and social characteristics. It also comprises our self's proper comportment and abilities all of which begin to emerge very early in infancy and continue a trajectory towards maturity through the self-discovery process of maturation. Affected by heredity and one's life situation, both physical and social, the self-concept is susceptible to life changes experienced in the maturation process of self-reflection and real circumstances. Such circumstances can be productive or counter-productive and in the latter case damage to the self can be profound, the origin commonly of mental disorders in adolescence and adulthood.

According to social psychologists, there are three fundamental components of the self-concept, viz., one's self-image, self-esteem, and the ideal self. Since our concern in this study is that of the "damaged" self which has been brought about through the early years of maturation, we will give particular attention to the formation of the self-concept in the child's developing personality. In some cases, the damage has been accidental and even incidental but too often the damage to the self-concept has been intentional and pernicious. A child's self-understanding, based on life situations and circumstances primarily but not exclusively since heredity must never be discounted, is brought about through a process of observation and emulation, of seeing and doing that which is observed in the life of the significant adults in the child's life. The assessment of the child's damaged self is evidenced psychopathologically and is both multi-tiered and multi-dimensional. Though childhood trauma may be singular in occurrence, that matrix of seeing and doing resulting in the damaged self is based on a complexity of contributing factors, both physical and social.

As has already been mentioned, the three fundamental components of the developing self-concept within a child as purported by Rogers and Maslow constitute the core of factors involved in affecting the healthy development of the personality of the child and, conversely, potential damage if occurring dysfunctionally. These components are self-image, self-esteem, and the ideal self. In each of the schools of thought being considered here, we will explore the significance of these components relative to the fundamental character of each school and thinker always with attention specifically to the prospects and character of damage to the self when maturation is dysfunctional or insidious. The first component of the self-concept is that of self-image, that is to say, the way an individual views himself/herself consisting of such features as one's physical characteristics, designated social role within the family and community matrix, and distinctive personality traits. The nature of one's self-image is that it commonly does not actually reflect reality but rather and merely the individual's own sense of whom one this of oneself to be, whether that is an inflated or diminished sense of self. We shall see in the following explorations of the various schools of personality theory how this inflated and diminished sense of self has been inculcated in the damaged child's personality.

Beyond one's self-image is that of one's self-esteem, viz., that value or emphasis individuals place upon how they think of themselves. This evaluative process includes not just one's own assessment of oneself but one's assessment of the views of others towards oneself. The complexity of one's self-esteem is linked to the range of characteristics assessed as either positive or negative such that one may have positive self-esteem in one matrix of behavior but a negative self-esteem in another. The nurturing of self-esteem is socially contextual and the family environment and parental oversight constitute crucial components in maximizing positive self-esteem in a child and minimizing the negative. Because a young child embraces a sense of self fostered by the affirmations of the parents combined with the inclination to immolate parental attitudes and behaviors, much damage may be done to the child's sense of self-esteem if parental responses to the maturing child are not positive.

Informing the individual's sense of self and the esteem or lack of it which results from the maturation process is that growing quest, even thirst, for what the individual imagines the possibilities are for that individual in an ideal world. Recognizing that the inevitability of a self-image fostered through the socio-cultural and physical environment of maturation is often contrasted to rather than complementary to what the child has come to envision as their ideal self, the pressure on personality development to mediate between one's self-image and one's ideal self can be tremendously intense leading not uncommonly to a psychopathology of the *self-concept* itself in the child. The damaged self, which results from a failure in childhood development to foster a positive interfacing between self-image and the ideal self (called congruence), is a manifestation of this failure (called incongruence) such that the prospects of self-actualization and a holistic and meaningful life are greatly diminished. What is sometimes called "cognitive dissonance," this break down between a positive self-image and a promising ideal self, impedes the prospects for a nurturing self-actualization of the child such that a contextual vortex is created wherein mental illness inevitably looms large on the child's maturation horizon.

CHAPTER ONE

THE DAMAGED SELF AND THE NATURE OF A PSYCHOLOGICAL INJURY

The development of the self-concept is composed of a balancing integration of self-image and self-esteem and these are directly developed and nurtured through the maturation process in childhood. In clinical cases of a diminished sense of self (demeaned self-image and/or self-esteem), there is evidence of a failure within the family matrix of nurturing the child's sense of self, whether that failure is due to a self-conscious disregard of the child or an inadvertent failure to assume parental oversight in the child's development. A diminished life is the result of this failure to foster a positive and healthy self-concept in childhood and it is the intention of this study to explore the psychopathology resulting from this failure in what is being called here the diminished self.

From the classical concept of *mental illness* to the now standardized use of the term *mental disorder* constitutes a movement in medical sophistication and the realization that the use of the medical model to describe behavioral disorders is less helpful in determining the etiology, diagnosis, and treatment of a mental condition. Mental Disorders as defined by the *Diagnostic and Statistical Manual of Mental Disorders* are behavioral patterns producing significant disturbances in personal functioning which over time persist and frequently result in relapses though occasionally only appearing as a single episode. Mental disorders are clearly evident in their impact upon how an individual acts, feels, perceives, and thinks within the social context of daily functioning. The care and treatment of individuals with diagnosed mental disorders has a long and troubled history of early abuses due to misunderstanding and the absence of medical sophistication or psychological training. However, since the coming of Freud and the neo-Freudians, the psychiatric care of children suffering from mental disorders has advanced to a high level of refinement. Mental disorders range from a full spectrum of depression, from mild to debilitating, to variously measurable intensity of schizophrenia. The classification of personality disorders has proven of particular benefit in the treatment of child psychopathology (which we will discuss later) and the movement away from a medical model of *illness* towards a psychological model of *disorder* related to the description of behavioral dysfunctions within children has created a very positive environment for the practice of child psychiatry as well as psychoanalytic approaches to childhood behavioral disorders.

This movement towards a psychological matrix of definitional parameters and classifications of mental disorders has not been easy owing to the medical model's resistance to a shifting of emphasis from physical illness to behavioral disorder but the result has been outstandingly helpful in the overall care and treatment of child psychopathology. The emphasis upon dysfunction which is labeled "disorder" and frequently behavioral rather than mental has also helped in de-stigmatizing mental distress within the child patient. Even the suspension of the term *patient* in deference to *client* has been seen in many circles as productive in the elevation of the acceptance of psychological treatment for behavioral dysfunctions recognizing, as is emphasized in the DSM—5 handbook produced by the American Psychiatric Association, that an emotional syndrome or behavioral pattern associated with distress, functional disability, and the resulting loss of personal independence constitutes a major concern within the health care professional community. The eventual refinement of the concept of mental disorder occurred in 2013 in the American Psychiatric Association's DSM-V which centered around the description of an emotional syndrome consisting of a clinically verifiable emotional disturbance in an individual's cognitive capacity or the ability to reasonably regulates one's emotional behavior involving psychogenic and biogenic processes. The earlier DSM-IV had pointed out the difficulty often in differentiating between *medical* and *mental* definitions including the complexities of such categorization of assessments as pathology, symptomology, deviance from normative behavioral range of conduct, and etiology of the disorder, whether biogenic or psychogenic.

The striking conundrum in clinical classification of pathological behavior is due to competing systems of identification based on the theoretical orientation of the clinician. Presently, there are two dominant systems of mental disorder classification, recognized prominently within psychiatry and psychotherapeutic practice, viz., *ICD-10 Chapter V: Mental and behavioral disorders* (since 1949 part of the International Classification of Diseases produced by the World Health Organization), and the *Diagnostic and Statistical Manual of Mental Disorders* (DSM) produced by the American Psychiatric Association (APA) since 1952. A distinct characteristic of classical and neo-Freudian psychoanalysis was the insistence of avoiding this labeling agenda of classification using pre-determined definitional parameters of behavioral matrices for identification of mental disorders. Abjuring the medical model of attempting to differentiate mental configurations using dichotomous symptoms descriptive of a complex matrix of behavioral characteristics, there is no recognition within the practice of psychoanalysis of the categories of *abnormal* versus *normal* behavior but rather the recognition of a behavioral spectrum upon which all individuals can be located. To use the commonly quoted words of the later neo-Freudian psychiatrist Harry Stack Sullivan, "we are all of us simply more human than otherwise."

While one school of thought within the medical and psychiatric community suggests that the classification of any given behavioral matrix is based upon and motivated by a value judgment which embraces the idea of normal versus abnormal, another equally viable school of thought argues that the classification and labeling agenda is both objective and scientific employing clinical data for evidence-based verification. There is a broad school of thought, called eclectic psychotherapy, which affirms the legitimacy of both of these opposing perspectives within clinical reason. The use of the term "mental disorder" rather than "mental illness" redirects the assessment and treatment away from portraying such behavioral activity on the part of the patient as a *disease* as understood within medical parlance so long as the behavior being assessed has been clinically exempted from a neurobiological basis and rather based upon a clinical interview. The resolution of this on-going dispute is not in sight as yet and the coming of Freudian psychoanalysis and subsequent neo-Freudians has contributed to this lively debate.

CHAPTER TWO

FREUD and Psychodynamic Psychoanalysis

Though Sigmund Freud, M.D., began in a cloud of professional suspicion, every professional today practicing in the cognate fields of counseling are beholden to him and his system of theory and analysis whether they will admit it or not. But to admit being beholden does not mean that one is bound to it. Gratitude has its place, however, and we will see in the following discussion the range of Freud's work as exemplified in his life, theoretical development, and analytical methodology. Whether one comes away from this discussion convinced or confused, for or against, it is our intention to make sure that upon leaving Freud and his system of psychoanalysis the reader has a clearer idea of what there is to believe or disbelieve about it in its own terms. One can only be critical of that which one fully and clearly understands. We aim here, then, for clarity of vision and then, and only then, will we have a right to say yes, no, or maybe to Freud and his followers.

To be fair to the development of any theory, and some might suggest this is particularly true of psychological theory, there is the need to understand the theorist. By this we mean, know from whence he came, who he was, what he did, and, as best we can, grasp his own self-understanding of his life and work. Let us be clear, the psychoanalytic understanding of child personality development and the etiology of mental disorders in childhood all begin with Freud. So let's take a look at, or if the case may be another look at, the life of Sigmund Freud, a 19th century physician from Vienna who changed forever our understanding of the unconscious and its profound impact upon our grasp of the maturation process from childhood to adulthood. If we are to understand the psychodynamic factors involved in the concept of the damaged self which occurs commonly in childhood, there is no better place to begin than with Freud and psychoanalysis.

Freud's father, Jakob Freud, was from a region in southeastern Europe consisting of a large minority of Jews called

Galicia. He was a wool merchant and following the 1867 Emancipation of the Jews in the Austrian Empire and his marriage and the birth of their first son, Sigmund, the Freuds moved first to Leipzig and then to Vienna where Sigmund Freud would live the next eighty years. Jakob had done what many ambitious Jews were doing, namely, he embraced a reasonable compromise between his Jewish culture and the business and secular culture around him. Though it has been suggested that he was secretly a closet Hassid, i.e., Jews who embraced a kind of mystical tradition based on the sacred book called the Kabbala, he was able to effect an integration into Austrian secular culture without relinquishing his Jewish faith. His mother, Amalia Nathanson, was from a distinguished and well-to-do Jewish family of Galicia. She was Jakob's second wife for he had two sons, approximately her own age, at the time of their marriage. Over the next ten years of marriage, Amalia gave birth to eight children, the first being Sigmund on May 6, 1856. She was acclaimed to have been very attractive, authoritarian, and a great admirer of her first-born son, Sigmund. Though born in Freiburg, Moravia (now in the Czech Republic), Freud at the age of four moved with his family to Vienna where he would live, except for the final fifteen months of his life living in London, for the next eighty years.

Without doubt, Freud was precocious, a mama's boy, and an excellent student in the schools of Vienna. It is said that his retentive visual memory and exceptional writing skills elevated him to the highest levels in school and, even though he was uncertain as to his career goals, he was early on predisposed to biology and was greatly influenced during his formative years by the evolutionary theory of Charles Darwin whose monumental work was published in 1859. In Vienna, Freud attended the *Leopoldstadter Kommunal-Realgymnasium*, a prominent high school, and Freud proved most outstanding, graduating the "Matura" in 1873 with honors. Eventually, Freud first considered studying law, which was now permitted to Jews, but finally entered medical school at the University of Vienna in 1873 which was under the direction of the famous Darwinist Professor Karl Claus. In no particular hurry, he completed his medical degree in eight years which allowed him an addition three years beyond the five-year minimum for medical degrees to expand his interests in philosophy and literature. From research in zoology and comparative anatomy during his medical school years, Freud shifted his interests and activities to microanatomy, becoming the lab assistant to the distinguished Viennese Professor Ernst Brucke who, though a positivist, influenced Freud considerably in the areas of physics and chemistry. A German physiologist, Professor Ernst Wilhelm von Brucke, in collaboration with Professor Hermann von Helmholtz, were proponents of the use of the concept of "psychodynamics" in the study of living organisms. In 1874, this concept was radical and revolutionary and Brucke and Helmholtz explicated the theory in the publication of their studies entitled, *Lectures on Physiology.* Any living organism, of special interest being the human person, is a dynamic system to which the laws of chemistry and physics apply. This, it should be pointed out, is believed to be the beginning of Freud's dynamic psychology of the mind and his concept of the unconscious.

During these crucial formative years, Freud was greatly influenced by a postdoctoral fellow, Dr. Joseph Breuer, who worked in Brucke's laboratory and shared with Freud details of various cases of hysteria including the now famous case of Anna O. Following a mandatory year in the military in 1879, Freud returned to work in Brucke's lab after finishing his medical exams during which time he translated a book by John Stuart Mill dealing with empiricism. Though very much disinclined to practice medicine, Freud had fallen in love with Martha Bernays, an attractive and strong-willed Jewish girl from a very distinguished Viennese family. In fact, Martha's grandfather was Isaac Bernays, chief rabbi in Hamburg. The road to financial solvency was through the practice of medicine and that was a requirement to gain permission to marry. So, Freud resigned himself to practice medicine and the specialization he chose was clinical neurology and due to his having distinguished himself as a teaching assistant at the medical school, he was taken on staff at the highly prestigious Viennese General Hospital (VGH). Having tried hypnosis in his private practice, he was dissatisfied with the results and turned to what he eventually came to call simply the "talking cure" in the treatment of mental disorders.

During the following few years at the VGH, he engaged in various research projects including work on the use and effects of cocaine as a stimulant, an aphrodisiac, and a cure for morphine addiction which was quite common at the time due to medical practices in service hospitals. Unfortunately, he came under increasing scrutiny and criticism due to his work in the area of addiction and a major paper he wrote on the use of cocaine in ophthalmological surgery fell on deaf ears at the local medical association meetings. He subsequently passed in his examination to become a *privatdozent* (private lecturer) at the University of Vienna in the field of neuropathology and following his official appointment was given a traveling grant to study with the famous psychologist and neurologist of Paris, Jean Martin Charcot. Freud always attributed this experience to his turning from traditional neurophysiology and towards the practice of medical psychotherapy.

Two major experiences served Freud's long-term interest in treating mental disorders. First, Charcot demonstrated how non-hysterical patients could be trained under hypnosis to exhibit hysterical symptoms such as paralysis and tremors, and second, Charcot demonstrated how physical symptoms of hysteria were derived from mental activity, thus, hysteria seemed clearly to be a "mental" disorder rather than merely a biogenic malfunction. Ironically, it was Charcot who first suggested to Freud the importance of sex by indicating that frequently sexual problems were related to mental disorder, particularly hysteria. Alas, whereas Freud went to Paris to become a neurologist, he returned as a fledgling psychiatrist!

Co-authoring with his old lab colleague, Dr. Josef Breuer, Freud drew more attention to himself with the publication of their 1895 highly acclaimed *Studies in Hysteria* which, according to historians of psychology, marks the actual beginning of psychoanalysis as a school of thought. Freud's chapter on psychotherapy established him as a major voice in this new field. Though deeply committed to his relationship with Breuer, Freud began a long and tedious journey away from his old colleague owing to Freud's heavy emphasis upon the essential role assigned to sex in the etiology of all neuroses. Breuer's tentative hesitation gave rise to a deepening gulf between them and finally resulted in a permanent break. This friendship was replaced by William Fliess, an ear, nose, and throat surgeon from Berlin who for the next several years proved to be Freud's closest confidant in the gradual development of the theories of psychoanalysis.

As is common knowledge, the fundamental bases of Freud's development of psychoanalytic theory grew out of his own self-analysis. Confidence in himself ran high and low but overall Freud continued to believe in himself and his ability to development therapeutic modalities which would facilitate his capacity to plumb the depths of his own psyche, particularly his unconscious through, initially, the interpretation of dreams. On the strength of his insights into mental functions gained from his practice as a psychiatrist, he gradually and unequivocally developed a psychosexual theory of personality development that would dominate psychoanalytic theory for the next hundred years. His confidence is reflected in a statement made in correspondence to his friend and colleague, William Fliess, when he wrote: "I cannot give you an idea of the intellectual beauty of the work."

Freud became convinced over a period of years of intense self-analysis that dreams are essentially disguised forms of infantile wishes and thought processes and the meanings of them can be discovered by means of the analytical modalities developed in psychoanalysis, particularly dream analysis. In 1900, he published what has been recognized by most practitioners as his most distinguished book, *The Interpretation of Dreams*. The publication of this book marked the end of his emotionally wrenching self-analysis and the beginning of his drive to establish psychoanalysis as the dominant school of psychotherapy. He was now free to move beyond his old confidants of bygone days, namely, Charcot, Breuer, Brucke, and Fliess. He would no longer look to them for counsel nor seek from them advice in his future work. Psychoanalysis was his creation and it was his place to establish it throughout the western world as the undisputed leading school of psychotherapy.

Needless to say, Freud was not revered nor loved by many of his professional colleagues. Freud was a Jew, a self-promoting Johnny-come-lately who proposed to plumb the depths of the human psyche using unorthodox methods and non-clinically tested and proven techniques boarding on the scandalous. That a self-respecting physician and psychiatrist would propose to foist off on the unsuspecting public hocus-pocus spells designed to interpret mentally disturbed patients' dreams was more than many could take and they let it be known through Vienna that Freud was to be watched. The criticisms were in print and on the tongues of many respected physicians and psychiatrists of the day and, therefore, Freud had his work cut out for himself and his new school of psychotherapy called psychoanalysis. His two books to-date didn't help much as they were hardly read until years after he had become a household name and respected internationally.

Yet, among the medical establishment there were brave and inquisitive physicians eager to learn more and to be engaged in this new adventure. Five key practitioners proved early on most helpful and though all but one eventually abandoned ship, while they were involved they proved most reassuring to Freud and his fledgling organization called the International Congress of Psychoanalysis held for the first time in 1908. The next year saw the launching of the journal which proved pivotal in the stabilizing of the movement. The five key figures were Karl Abraham of Germany, Carl Jung of Switzerland, Ernest Jones of Great Britain, and Alfred Adler and Otto Rank of Austria.

Psychoanalysis was destined to become the dominant psychotherapeutic treatment modality of mental disorders in America. To facilitate that process unwittingly, the president of Clark University in Massachusetts, an ambitious new institution seeking to make a name for itself, invited Freud, among others, to come to America to participate in the celebration of that University's twentieth anniversary. G. Stanley Hall, the President of the University, was America's leading psychologist at the time, a position shared with William James of Harvard, and Hall had been known to say of Freud and psychoanalysis that it was "a series of fads or crazes." Yet, invite Freud he did and come Freud did, giving five outstanding, though unprepared, lectures on psychoanalysis. Later, these essays were prepared for publication back in Vienna and went a long way in advancing the case for psychoanalysis in Europe and most especially in America.

However, as the professional organization of psychoanalysis began to grow by leaps and bounds, bringing on more and more young psychiatrists in Europe and certainly in America, the seasoned veterans of the early formative years of psychiatric practice began to resist and counter theoretical developments within psychoanalysis which were approved by Freud but not by the old guard. Alfred Adler broke with the orthodox school over issues related to the dominance of sex-based theorizing relative to child development, preferring to focus upon the human drive to mastery or what he chose to label *the will to power* whereas Carl Jung, who was designated the heir-apparent by Freud himself, moved with precision and strategy to establish his own school of thought, called Analytical Psychology. These were major blows to the professional organization and only with sustained focus upon the orthodox theories did Freud and his followers weather the storm of dissent without permanent damage. These other schools of thought will be discussed later.

In the midst of it all, Freud never stopped treating patients. For a physician who early and publicly proclaimed a distaste for the profession, Freud practiced nearly sixty years as a physician. During that time, he concentrated upon fine tuning his theories, exploring new territory, and developing new insights in mental illness. He published extensively and prolifically, both in book form and periodicals. Three major works beyond those first two already mentioned were *The Psychopathology of Everyday Life* (1901), *Introductory Lectures on Psycho-analysis* (1916-1917), and *New Introductory Lectures on Psycho-analysis* (1933). One never to be accused of not continuing to press forward with investigations, analyses, and theoretical explorations, Freud moved beyond just an interest in the individual patient to broader social issues of the day. Both social psychology and social philosophy became a sustained interest of his during his waning years of productivity and his now highly acclaimed classic, *Civilization and Its Discontents* represents him at his best. It is an application of psychoanalytic theory to the broad social issues of human behavior in society. This study of Freud's, written when he was in his closing years of life, offers a pessimistic view of the human condition. The best life has to offer, Freud suggests, is merely a compromise between the inevitable and the irreconcilable demands that dominate our existence. The year he published this now famous work, 1930, was the year the German government awarded him the Goethe Prize in appreciation for his contribution to psychology and to German literary culture. It is this book we have chosen to study more systematically later in this chapter.

The very personal and tragic side to Freud's life has to do with both the necessity of his leaving his home in Vienna and the physical struggles with his health. When Freud turned sixty-six years old, he was diagnosed with mouth cancer brought on, it was believed, by his addiction to cigars. Over the next nearly twenty years he underwent thirty operations including the removal of the entire roof of his mouth which was replaced by a metal prosthesis which he called "the monster." Yet, he continued to write and see patients through it all. In 1938, Vienna say the annexation of Austria to the German Reich by Adolph Hitler, bringing with it the oppression of the Jews without discrimination or regard for professional status in the community. With much insistence from his professional colleagues and friends who knew that both Einstein's physics and Freud's psychoanalysis were anathema to the Nazi, Freud with his wife and youngest daughter Anna fled to London where he died fifteen months later. Freud prevailed upon his personal physician and friend, Dr. Max Schur, to assist him in taking his own life. At this time, Freud wrote to Schur: "My dear Schur, you certainly remember our first talk. You promised me then not to forsake me when my time comes. Now it is nothing but torture and makes no sense anymore." Schur administered three doses of morphine over many hours that resulted in Freud's death on September 23, 1939. The pain of the final stages of Freud's cancer led him to this decision. Freud's body was cremated in England during a service attended by many Austrian refugees and he ashes were placed in the columbarium there at Golders Green Crematorium where his wife, Martha, was likewise buried in 1951 and later his daughter Anna as well. His four younger sisters, now in their old age, were murdered in the SS concentration camps of Germany. To those who rejected his theories, Freud is said to have responded to G. Stanley Hall: "They may abuse my doctrines by day, but I am sure they dream of them by night."

The impact Freud's thought has had upon Western culture in the last century is profound. Since the publishing of his *Die Traumdentung, 1900 (The Interpretation of Dreams,* 1955), Freud's thought has gained such widespread usage that it would be difficult to imagine a modern world devoid of his contributions to the understanding of the individual in society. If his studies of the human psyche have revolutionized our thoughts about and attitudes toward the unconscious, his writings on religion, society, and culture have shaken older images of human experiences and ushered in a new era of religious and social theorizing.

Not unaware of the profound shock his thought would have on modern times, Freud saw himself in a select line of great minds who have shaken the Western World. There have been three narcissistic shocks to Western consciousness, thought Freud. First was the Copernican or Cosmological shock which shook Western culture loose from its anthropogeocentric cosmology which located humanity and the earth at the center of the universe. This rude awakening brought trauma to Western thinkers who then had to learn how to live in a world where neither the human person nor the earth could claim centrality, but rather had been pre-empted by a heliocentric cosmology. The sun, a gaseous ball devoid of life, became the center.

The second and equally traumatic shock to the Western mind was dealt by Charles Darwin – the Biological Shock – which demonstrated the biological relatedness of all living things, humanity included. If Copernicus had challenged the status of humankind in the universe, Darwin had surely succeeded in establishing the dependence of humanity upon the earth and our kinship with all earth's creatures. The fact that we had persisted even after Copernicus in an anthropocentrism which over-valued the differences between us and animals as well as between various genetic groupings within the human family made even more difficult the acceptance of Darwin's revelation. To this very day, there are vocal if not large pockets of supposedly modern people who still decry the atheism erroneously assumed implicit in Darwin's biology which still lays claim to a primitive worldview nurtured by a creation-story literalism.

Last and most profound of the shocks to Western consciousness has been the Psychological Shock mercilessly dealt by Sigmund Freud. The shock was ushered in by a succession of scientific bomb-blasts: *The Interpretation of Dreams (1911), Totem and Taboo (1912), Beyond the Pleasure Principle (1920), The Future of an Illusion (1927), and Civilization and Its Discontents (1930).* By no means the whole bibliography of profound, challenging, and highly controversial studies, these works are, nevertheless, exemplary of the breadth of Freud's research and interests. His study of the origin and function of religion, published under the significantly descriptive title, *The Future of an Illusion,* is without question his most controversial and most widely read study outside the specific field of psychoanalysis. And yet, his *Civilization and Its Discontents (identified subsequently as simply CID)*, which reviews the arguments in the religion book, represents his most mature thoughts on human society and the individual's relation to it. David Bakan, in his provocative and highly controversial study on Freud, entitled, *Sigmund Freud and the Jewish Mystical Tradition (1969)*, has cogently argued that Freud was himself a most exemplary thinker in the Kabbalistic tradition of Jewish mysticism. Kabbalism was an esoteric tradition which chose for reasons of safety and privacy to speak of the human spiritual condition in terms of the dark mysteries and primitive symbolisms of sexuality. If Bakan is right in this bit of theorizing, then the following statement from Freud gains even more profound eminence in modern religious thought: "The tendency on the part of civilization to restrict sexual life is no less clear than its other tendency to expand the cultural unit." But let us look more closely at his work before we pass judgment on Freud's either apt or warped view of the human condition.

The emergence of the ego ("...there is nothing of which we are more certain than the feeling of our self, of our own ego"), says Freud, is "through a process of development..." The ego is developmentally the inevitable result of a confronting of the pristine libidinal impulses of the undifferentiated id with the external world of sheer actuality. The id, having its motivational impetus centered in the *pleasure-principle*, confronts the *reality-principle* as the individual infant begins to discover the unpleasantness of the otherness, separateness, and outsideness of the real world. There is a strong motivation on the part of the id-driven child to "separate from the ego everything that can become a source of what Freud has labeled *unpleasure,* to throw it outside and to create a pure pleasure-ego which is confronted by a strange and threatening 'outside' (CID:15." The id begins necessarily to develop a negotiating capability – the ego as executor of libidinal powers — whereby the desires of the id are pacified with substitute gratifications which are physically accessible and socially acceptable. "In this way," says Freud, "one makes the first step towards the introduction of the reality principle which is to dominate future development."

Freud is here explaining a scenario of ego-development

which will address the issue of the oceanic feeling, and thus the subject of religion. This executive function of the differentiated ego serves as the primary medium of negotiation between the pleasurable desires from within (the raw libido of the id) and the realities of the outside world (social restraints upon behavior). The more responsible the ego is to the reality-principle, the greater the experience of separateness from the external world – "Our present ego-feeling is, therefore, only a shrunken residue of a much more inclusive, indeed, an all-embracing feeling, which corresponded to a more intimate bond between the ego and the world about it (CID:15)." There, Freud concludes that to the extent that this earlier primary ego feeling of virtual undifferentiation of self and world in infancy has persisted alongside the narrower demarcated ego feeling of self-separation from the world in maturity, there is the likelihood that feelings of "limitlessness and of a bond with the universe," i.e., the oceanic feeling, will be present.

Freud contends that "...in mental life nothing which has once been formed can perish...(CID:16)," and, therefore, such feelings as these considered here are simply the residue of infantile experience. And though Freud is reluctant to connect the feeling of "oneness with the universe" with the origins of religion, he is "perfectly willing to acknowledge that the 'oceanic' feeling exists in many people, and (is) inclined to trace it back to an early phase of ego-feeling." In conclusion to this topic of oceanic feelings, Freud is wont to trace the origins of the oceanic feeling to "a first attempt at a religious consolation," which is to say, a feeling resulting from the developing ego's growing awareness of the external world. Furthermore, he is anxious to rearticulate his 1927 theory of religious origins, which says that "The derivation of religious needs from the infant's helplessness and the longing for the father aroused by it...(is) incontrovertible, especially since the feeling is not simply prolonged from childhood days, but is permanently sustained by fear of the superior power of Fate." Though this point will be considered in a later context, it must be noted here that for Freud, the energy output demonstrated by the ego's undying efforts to responsibly direct the otherwise unbridled powers of the id is the result of a deep feeling whose function is the "expression of a strong need."

The religious feeling, says Freud, is a source of energy because it is expressive of a powerful need, viz., the helpless infant's longing for a powerful father. In considering religion, Freud consistently was "concerned much less with the deepest sources of the religious feeling than with what the common man understands by his religion...(CID:2)." And yet, he was often so convincing in his critique of religion's object being nothing more than an "enormously exalted father" that it is difficult if not impossible to separate the "deepest" from the "common" in religion. Freud had no patience with the "great majority of mortals" who were, as infants, dependent on this projected father-image as a substitute for ego-development and personal maturity. "The whole thing is so patently infantile," complained Freud, a painful reality that most people, avoiding true maturity, opt for a "pitiful rearguard" attachment to childish fantasies of a loving Providence which, watching over us, will reward us eternally in heaven if we are good.

The question of "the purpose of human life," says Freud, bespeaks humanity's "presumptuousness." Religion alone can answer this question, for the whole "idea of life having a purpose stands and falls with the religious system (CID:23)." And though these metaphysical complexities lie outside Freud's investigation here, he chooses to get at the question by an inquiry into the nature of human behavior which demonstrates humanity's purpose and intention in life. And in answer to this question, "What do men show by their behavior to be the purpose and intention of life?", Freud answers simply, "They strive after happiness, they want to become happy and to remain so." That is, they seek the "absence of pain and unpleasure" while seeking the "experiencing of strong feelings of pleasure." Therefore, Freud concludes, the rhetoric of religion to the contrary notwithstanding, "what decides the purpose of life is simply the programme of the pleasure principle."

Happiness, i.e., the satisfaction of needs too seldom gratified, is difficult to realize and impossible to sustain. Society is ever ready to condemn violations of its laws, and unrestrained self-gratification, i.e., personal happiness, inevitably results in a clash of the individual's desires (pleasure principle) and society's rules (reality principle). Therefore, "unhappiness is much less difficult to experience" because the individual is threatened with suffering from three sides: from our own body due to its finitude, from the external world with all its rules, and from our relations with other people. Since happiness is hardly possible at all, and never for any significant duration, we have, necessarily, had to develop techniques for controlling the instincts which given free rein would inevitably bring catastrophe to the individual and to society.

Through the executive services of the ego, the libidinal forces are displaced (focused upon a secondary and socially acceptable object choice) and the instincts are systematically sublimated. In the movement from pleasure to reality, the individual adopts two kinds of "satisfaction...obtained from illusion...(which arise out of) the imagination (CID:27)." Both religion and the enjoyment of the arts are the result of sublimated instincts and displaced libido. Freud says: "A special importance attaches to the case in which this attempt to procure a certainty in happiness and a protection against suffering through a delusional remolding of reality is made by a considerable number of people in common. The religions of mankind must be classed among the mass-delusions of this kind. No one, needless to say, who shares a delusion ever recognized it as such" according to Freud. And, says Freud, those who define happiness in life as the pursuit and love of beauty fail to realize that aesthetic impulse is simply the result of an ungratified primary sexual motivation. The tensions experienced in the perpetual struggle between the desire for happiness (pleasure principle) and avoidance of pain (reality principle) often lead to neurosis and even psychosis. "Any attempt at rebellion (against society, i.e., reality) is seen (either) as psychosis," or "as a last technique of living, which will at least bring him substitutive satisfaction, (i.e.)...that of a flight into neurotic illness." Freud's concluding remark regarding the function of religion in this context is worth quoting: Religion restricts this play of choice and adaptation, since it imposes equally on everyone its own path to the requisition of happiness and protection from suffering. Its technique consists in depressing the value of life and distorting the picture of the real world in a delusional manner which presupposes an intimidation of the intelligence. At this price, by forcibly fixing them in a state of psychical infantilism and by drawing them into a mass-delusion, religion succeeds in sparing many people an individual neurosis. But hardly anything more. (CID:31-32). Why has humankind singularly, collectively, and consistently failed in our quest for happiness and the prevention of suffering? In attempting to answer this question, Freud says that a kind of "suspicion dawns on us" which says that maybe the answer lies in "a piece of our own psychical constitution." That is, the contention which "holds that what we call our civilization is largely responsible for our misery...(for) it is a certain fact that all the things with which we seek to protect ourselves against the threats that emanate from the sources of suffering are part of that very civilization." Can it be? Civilization serves both to protect us against nature and to adjust our mutual relations. Wherein lies the evil, then? Certainly, our civilization bore the culture from which came technical skills, fire and tool usage, writing and dwelling houses. And also, we invented gods to whom were attributed our own cultural ideals. Furthermore, beauty, cleanliness and order became "requirements for civilization." And of all characteristics of civilization esteemed and encouraged most highly are our higher mental activities, i.e., intellectual, scientific and artistic achievements, and "foremost among those ideas are the religious systems." The "motive force of all human activities," argues Freud, "is a striving towards the two confluent goals of utility and a yield of pleasure...(CID:41)."

The last and significantly problematic characteristic of civilization is the manner in which relationships of individuals to one another are regulated, i.e., family and state. "Human life in common," contends Freud, "is only make possible when a majority comes together which is stronger than any separate individual and which remains united against all separate individuals." Thus, a concept of the right or social good develops in opposition to individual brute force. "This replacement of the power of the individual by the power of a community constitutes the decisive step in civilization (CID:42)." The first requirement of this newly formed community is, therefore, justice – the assurance that the good of the many expressed in law will be honored over the desires of any single individual. "The liberty of the individual is no gift of civilization." And in this connection, Freud would have us see that there is a great "similarity between the process of civilization and the libidinal development of the individual." As sublimation functions in the individual for the development of a strong ego and creative capacity to deal with the principle of reality, so likewise, "sublimation of instinct is an especially conspicuous feature of cultural development; it is what makes it possible for higher psychical activities, scientific, artistic or ideological, to play such an important part in civilized life."

As we move closer to Freud's perception of the nature of the individual in society – our stumbling futile attempts to construct a viable meaning to life – we are confronted by an indispensable dialectic between life and death, especially as Freud had earlier developed the idea in his book, *Beyond the Pleasure Principle (1920)*. He explains its development: There still remained in me a kind of conviction...that the instincts could not all be of the same kind...Starting from speculations on the beginning of life and from biological parallels, I drew the conclusion that, besides the instinct to preserve living substance and to join it into ever larger units, there must exist another, contrary instinct seeking to dissolve those units and to bring them back to their primordial, inorganic state. That is to say, as well as Eros there was an instinct of death (CID:66). Within every society, as within every individual, there are two conflicting instincts. The life instinct is at the service of society so long as society is devoid of aggression, for aggression is a stark manifestation of the Death instinct. Aggression, says Freud, "is an original, self-subsisting instinctual disposition of man...(and it) constitutes the greatest impediment to civilization." Eros and Death share "world-dominion" and explain the movement of civilization back and forth upon the scale of creativity and destruction. This eternal and unexplainable struggle is essentially what life is all about, and the evolution of civilization is simply described "as the struggle for life of the human species." There is only futility in attempting to explain the meaning of life beyond this simple reality – the meaning of life is the struggle of *life against death*. "And it is this battle of the giants," concludes Freud, "that our nurse-maids try to appease with their lullabies about Heaven (CID:69)."

It is the super-ego which constitutes the source of the human feelings of guilt. The super-ego evolves in consort with the development of the ego. As the ego gains relative control over the id, it does so by means of taking to itself the moral expectations of society, as society in turn, through the agency of parents, impresses its values upon the child. The super-ego is the projection of society's self-image into such an exalted state as to elicit devotion and adoration. But as the ego becomes educated to the reality principle, as a balancing source to the id's pleasure principle, the super-ego is being socially reinforced in the adoption of an ideal principle. As the ego's sense of reality confronts the super-ego's sense of the social ideal, tension results within the individual. The super-ego serves as the conscience which testifies against the ego's reluctance to support the ideals of society. "The tension between the harsh super-ego and the ego that is subjected to it," says Freud, "is called by us the sense of guilt; it expresses itself as a need for punishment (CID:70)." The stronger the ego, the weaker the super-ego, and vice versa. Society's moral expectations are mediated through the child's parents and give rise to a conscience educated to certain idealistic expectations. "Civilization, therefore," says Freud, "obtains mastery over the individual's dangerous desire for aggression by weakening and disarming it and by setting up an agency within him to watch over it..."

Guilt, which is really a social anxiety though frequently misnamed "bad conscience," often results from a "fear of loss of love" on the one hand and a "fear of punishment" on the other. But fundamentally, our sense of guilt springs from the Oedipus complex "which was acquired at the killing of the father by the brothers banded together" as classically illustrated in Freud's scenario of the development of primeval human community in his *Totem and Taboo* (1912). And thus, what began in relation to the father is completed in relation to the group. Freud reasons:

If civilization is a necessary course of development from the family to humanity as a whole, then – as a result of the inborn conflict arising from ambivalence, of the eternal struggle between the trends of love and death – there is inextricably bound up with it an increase of the sense of guilt, which will perhaps reach heights that the individual finds hard to tolerate. It was Freud's intention from the beginning "to represent the sense of guilt as the most important problem in the development of civilization and to show that the price we pay for our advance in civilization is a loss of happiness through the heightening of the sense of guilt (CID:81)."

Quick to make a qualitative distinction between a *sense of guilt* and a *consciousness of guilt*, Freud argues that guilt plays its greatest role in the human experience when operating in the unconscious. And when functioning here, "...the sense of guilt is at bottom nothing else but a topographical variety of anxiety; in its later phases it coincides completely with *fear of the super-ego*." To the extent that guilt remains unobserved in the dark chambers of the unconscious, we are condemned to writhe in our own dissatisfaction – a sort of *malaise* produced by civilization itself. "Religions," says Freud, "have never overlooked the part played in civilization by a sense of guilt." The sense of guilt, the harshness of the superego, the severity of the conscience – all are demonstrative of a need for punishment. This need, says Freud, "is an instinctive (manifestation on the part of the ego) which has become masochistic under the influence of a sadistic super-ego..." Religion, as an illusion produced out of the imaginations of sublimated instincts, functions as a social neurosis which protects us from the stark realities of life devoid of any ultimate transcendent meaning. Mature individuals must eventually rid themselves of illusion and imagination and learn to face squarely and without guilt the meaninglessness of life.

Unless we begin with Freud, we cannot proceed with any degree of insightfulness regarding the rise of modern-day psychotherapeutic practice. That there are a myriad of psychotherapeutic modalities employed daily in hospitals, clinics, counseling centers, and residential treatment facilities goes without saying. But that the proliferation of these various and sometimes competing modalities of treatment is the outgrowth of Freud is indisputable. We have chosen in this study to focus upon eight schools of thought and we have continued to insist that given their originality they all owe homage, even if ever so grudgingly given, to the birth of psychoanalysis.

As has been shown, Sigmund Freud has established himself as the instigator of one of the three Cosmic Shocks to western culture. Whereas Copernicus shocked the intellectual world by demolishing the notion that man is the center of the universe (the Cosmological Shock) and Darwin with his discovering of the emergent evolution of life on this plant (the Biological Shock), Freud presented to the modern world an insightful discovery of the nature and role of the unconscious in our daily lives (the Psychological Shock). Modern science and the understanding of humanity will never be the same due to these three great discoveries. And so, without dissent, we must begin with Freud who, during his forty years of psychoanalytic practice, developed the first comprehensive theory of personality, developed a thoroughgoing method of treating mental illness, and produced an extensive body of clinical literature based upon his theories and methods of treatment.

Briefly, there are four areas of Freud's work which have the greatest impact upon counseling practice today, and they are (1) levels of consciousness -- conscious, preconscious, unconscious, (2) psychosexual development, (3) the structure of personality, and (4) psychoanalytic therapy. These four major categories of his work which have an immediacy and relevance to the practice of counseling in the modern setting and clearly their relevance to the psychoanalytic treatment of children and the damaged self is profoundly relevant to this inquiry.

In Freud's fascination with and desire to describe the functioning of the human mind, he set out to develop a map of how the human mind worked. He was intrigued with the possibility, even the necessity, of delving into the inner workings of the human mind to understand the relationship between the function of the mind and human behavior and he came to believe that much of what goes on in human behavior is cued by the human mind in ways unknown to and not understood by the conscious person. He was, essentially, committed to a *psycho- cartography* of human behavior, a "mapping of mental functions." In this process, he believed he had discovered that the human mind consists of three levels of function --the conscious, the preconscious, and the unconscious. To understand the nature of human behavior, the therapist must understand the interrelationship of these three levels, how they affect each other, and how to accept their content for closer scrutiny, for only by doing so can the therapist understand the "why" of behavior.

The conscious level of the human mind includes everything that the individual is aware of at any given moment. This, of course, includes thoughts, perceptions, feelings, memories, etc., but really constitutes only a small part of mental functioning. Freud believed that a "selective screening process" functioned to permit only certain information to be at any given moment immediately available to the mind and he was interested in why this screening process was necessary and what it excluded from immediate awareness of the conscious person.

The preconscious (or what is now more commonly called "subconscious") dimension of the human mind consists, said Freud, of all that which is available to memory but not to immediate awareness. It requires an intentional reflection but is free from the "screening" process of the unconscious. Freud believed that the subconscious functioning of the human mind constituted a sort of link between conscious and unconscious. Most if not all of what is in the subconscious domain of mental function is available, upon demand, by the conscious functioning of the individual but, when that information is no longer needed in the immediacy of living, falls back into the subconscious compartment of the human mind.

It is to the unconscious reservoir of the human mind that Freud was most attracted because it is here, he believed, that much of what affects human behavior resides yet subject to the screening function of the conscious mind. Though certainly not the first western thinker to ponder the unconscious mind, Freud was decidedly different in his queries from the 17th and 18th century philosophers who speculated about the complex functioning of the human mind because Freud brought both a medical and an empirical commitment and insight into his investigations. The unconscious was, for Freud, not merely a "hypothetical abstraction" to be pondered and wondered at, but rather was an empirically functioning part of the human mind. To understand the unconscious functioning of the human mind would provide real insight into human behavior, especially and particularly mental illness.

As a physician and psychiatrist, Freud was determined to plumb the depths of that compartment of the human mind which, while radically affecting human behavior, seemed ever to elude consciousness and the human will's capacity to control it. Because unconscious components of the human mind are inaccessible to the conscious mind, given the conscious mind's intent upon protecting itself from the materials found in the unconscious compartments of the mind, it was Freud's belief that a psychologically-driven archaeology of the mind would release this screened information which affects human behavior. By releasing or exposing this materials, the patient suffering from mental illness caused by this protected material (later called repressed material) could commence a journey towards mental health. The screening and protecting mechanisms of the conscious mind for this unconscious materials include dreams and fantasies and it was here that Freud set about to do his work and, eventually, to develop what he called "psychoanalysis."

Within the context of this mapping and tracing of mental functions, Freud believed that the human personality was comprised of three fundamental structures which worked in consort with the three levels of consciousness. These three personality constructs he called the *id,* the *ego*, and the *superego*. Believing that these personality constructs were essentially "hypothetical" as are the three constructs of consciousness, due to the insufficiently of microanatomy to locate them within the central nervous system, he nevertheless insisted upon their reality and their primary functioning within the human mind and the human personality. Whereas the id functions within the domain of the unconscious, the ego is primarily located in the preconscious or subconscious and conscious portions of mental function. The superego is superimposed over the domain of the ego with capabilities of affecting the functions even of the unconscious domain of mental processes.

The id, Freud believed, was the repository of all instinctual functions of the human animal and is governed by the *pleasure principle* which we have discussed earlier. It is essentially uninhibited and irrational and functions strictly under the energy of animal drives, particularly sexuality and aggression, and is the cause of tension within the person owing to a confliction of instinct and control. To understand the relationship between the driving energy of the id and the mandated social comportment and propriety of the ego would go a long way in identifying the causes of human stress and resulting mental illness. The maturation process of the human animal, then, is directly related to the process of mediating between instinct and social order, between the demands of the id and behavior deemed appropriate by the ego.

The ego, then, is that part of the personality which seems to pacify the irrational desires of the instinctual id while guiding behavior to appropriately moderated forms of acceptable behavior. The stronger the ego, the more controlled the person is in terms of social expectations of propriety; the weaker the ego, the less control and, thus, the greater the danger of violating the rules of society. It is the ego which is responsible for the protection and survival of the individual for the id is only interested in immediate gratification without regard to safety or propriety. Whereas the id is governed by the pleasure principle, the ego is governed by the reality principle. Primary process governs the id because instincts are dominant; secondary process governs the ego because reason and logic take the upper hand. Finally, we can say that the ego is the *executive branch* of the human personality and the center of intellect and propriety.

While the ego is the executive branch of the personality, moderating the demands of the id while honoring the propriety of the ego, it is to the superego that the personality must go for guidance regarding appropriate behavior. The ego is moderator but not the instigator of the individual's sense of values, norms, and attitudes. These fall to the domain of the superego. If the superego is extremely restrictive and controlling by providing only a short rope for existential decision-making, then the ego is repressed in its capacity to be creative. A repressed ego results in a warped and dysfunctional personality due to the lack of creative spontaneity for the ego to manage the id. The superego is a force operating outside the ego, introduced in the maturation process of the human individual. It is the mother, the parents, the community, society at large and the world of religion which constitute the source of the superego. With the coming of issues related to good and bad, right and wrong, we see the emergence of the superego. Balancing the irrational demands of the id with the social demands of the superego is the responsibility of the ego and the ego develops in direct relationship to the capacity to manage the tensions produced by this balancing function. Herein lies the fertile ground for mental illness brought on by the damaging of the self-concept in childhood personality development.

The superego consists of two countervailing forces -- the conscience and the ego-ideal. The conscience is concerned with compliance to parental and social demands about right and wrong, good and bad, behavior. Whereas the conscience has to do with guilt-inducing non-compliance, the ego-ideal is derived from approved behavior of parents and society. The aim is for self-control to replace parental control, but whereas the id is controlled by instincts and is based on the pleasure principle, the superego is controlled by socially approved behavior and is based on the reality principle as negotiated by the ego. The trouble comes when the superego presses beyond the reality principle to perfectionist goals beyond the capacity of the ego to respond. Much psychiatric fall out from religious fanaticism is located in this complexity of interactive struggles between id, ego, and superego.

Complimenting Freud's concept of the three levels of mental functioning -- conscious, subconscious, unconscious -- is his notion of the four-stage sexual development of the human personality - oral, anal, phallic, and genital. It is quite evident that these stages are named for the specific regions of the body from which sexual energy is discharged. Each stage is identified, then, with what Freud called a primary erogenous zone. The term *psychosexual* emphasizes quite clearly his agenda in exploring these developmental stages and their functions in the development of human personality and, of course, their relationship to mental illness. Freud is emphatic about the nature and function of these development stages of human personality and paid a dear price throughout his career for his insistence upon their utility in analysis.

The *oral stage* characterizes the first year of life when the infant is fixated on oral gratification and its relationship to feeding. Though an important erogenous zone throughout life, the mouth is primary during the first year of life and sucking and tactile sensitivity around the lips is fundamental to the infant's development and ends at the time of weaning. Freud believed that in cases where either there was excessive or insufficient amounts of stimulation there is likely to emerge an oral-passive personality in adulthood. Such a personality is characterized by having an optimistic view of the world, having established trusting dependent relationship with others, and one who expects others to "mother" him. This person's psychological adjustment is characterized by gullibility, passivity, and immaturity.

The *anal stage* comes during the second and third year of life and involves a shifting of the child's attention from the mouth to the anal region of the body, particularly retention and expulsion of feces and urine. The bowels and bladder become a major focus of attention in children of this age and depending upon the parental guidance in this area, the child is destined to a sound personality development or one severely warped by mismanagement. Freud believed that many cases of mental illness derived specifically from this stage in personality development. He was convinced that the way in which parents carry out toilet training has specific effects on later personality development and claimed that all later forms of self-control and mastery issues have their origin in the anal stage of development.

The *phallic stage* comes during the fourth year of development when the libidinal interests of the child shifts erogenous zones from the anus to the sex organs. Psychosexual development during this stage includes genital manipulation for pleasure, masturbation, and a growing verbal interest in matters related to birth and babies and similar topics usually posed to the parent. It is during this stage that Freud's now famous concept of the Oedipus complex emerges. The classic concept in Freudian psychoanalysis is used to indicate the situation where the child of either sex develops feelings of love and/or hostility for the parent. In the simple male Oedipus complex, the boy has incestuous feelings of love for the mother and hostility toward the father. The simple female Oedipus complex exists when the girl feels hostility for the mother and sexual love for the father. Psychoanalysts generally agree that adult males who fixate at the phallic stage are usually brash, vain, boastful, and ambitious. Phallic types strive to be successful and attempt at all times to assert their masculinity and virility. In the case of women, Freud believed that the phallic fixation results in traits of flirtatiousness, seductiveness, and promiscuity even though the individual may appear naïve and innocent in sexual relationships. He further believed that the primary source of subsequent neurotic patterns of behavior related to impotency and frigidity derive from this stage of personality development.

The *genital stage* comes with the onset of adolescence and puberty. Following what Freud called the latency period of relative calm, the pubescent child experiences an increased awareness of and interest in the opposite sex. Due to biochemical and physiological changes in the body, the child is now subjected to an influx of drives and desires heretofore unknown or unacknowledged. Freud believed that most children at this point go through a homosexual stage during which time the child, girl or boy, fixates on a same-sex friend or acquaintance. Eventually, the shift to the opposite sex usually occurs with the onslaught of crushes and puppy love. Freud believed that for an adult to attain the ideal genital development, that person must relinquish the passivity of early childhood days when love, security, physical comfort, etc., were freely available and must learn to work, postpone gratification, become responsible, and above all, assume a more active role in dealing with life's problems.

Though we have explored in detail Freud's personal life and his work, looked at a major text of his, and here have reviewed a few of his monumental contributions to psychoanalytic theory, we should not leave until we have explored briefly the therapeutic practice of psychoanalysis as employed by Freud. As with all schools of psychotherapy being considered here, the theoretical foundations have been built for the purpose of psychotherapy rather than merely an exercise in theory building. Freud was intent upon constructing a psychodynamic psychotherapy utilizing his conceptual insights into the nature of the human mind as it relates to mental illness and mental health.

Psychoanalytic psychotherapy has been developed for the purpose of addressing virtually all forms of mental illness. From was not reluctant to draw from a variety of social and behavioral sciences such as sociology and anthropology as well as both philosophy and religion in the development of his system. It was Freud's clinical experience of working with neurotic patients which generated his fundamental insights into mental illness and which led to the development of this monumental school of thought. It was upon the clinical experience he had as a practicing psychiatrist that he relied in the testing of his hypotheses. "The teachings of psychoanalysis," Freud said, "are based on an incalculable number of observations and experiences, and no one who has not repeated those observations upon himself and upon others is in a position to arrive at an independent judgment of it." Though the further refinement and sophistication of psychoanalytic theory and application to the treatment of damaged children will not occur until the coming of the monumental work of Anna Freud, Karen Horney, and Melanie Klein, the initial insights into the maturation process of child personality began with Freud and all subsequent work is the result of the fundamental foundation of psychoanalysis.

SELECTED PRIMARY SOURCES OF SIGMUND FREUD

(1895). Studies on Hysteria (with Josef Breuer). (*Studien uber Hysterie*)

(1900). The Interpretation of Dreams. (*Die Traumdeutung*).

(1901). The Psychopathology of Everyday Life (*Zur Psychopathologie des Alltagslebens*)

(1905). Three Essays on the Theory of Sexuality (*Drei Abhandlungen zur Sexualtheorie*)

(1905). *Jokes and their Relation to the Unconscious (Der Witz und seine Beziehung zum Unbewußten)*

(1913). Totem and Taboo (*Totem und Tabu*)

(1914). On Narcissism (*Zur Einführung des Narzißmus*)

(1920). Beyond the Pleasure Principle (*Jenseits des Lustprinzips*)

(1923). The Ego and the Id (*Das Ich und das Es*)

(1927). The Future of an Illusion (*Die Zukunft einer Illusion*)

(1930). Civilization and Its Discontents (*Das Unbehagen in der Kultur*)

(1939). Moses and Monotheism (*Der Mann Moses und die monotheistische Religion*)

(1940). *An Outline of Psycho-Analysis (Abriß der Psychoanalyse)*

CHAPTER THREE

SULLIVAN and Interpersonal Psychiatry

In some circles, Harry Stack Sullivan is considered the "father of modern psychiatry," but, of course, this is prior to the emergence of the psychiatrist as "meds monitor"! Today, unlike his day, psychiatry has been disastrously reduced to monitoring medication without the slightest effort to offer therapeutic counseling which has, by and large, been left to either the social worker or the pastoral counselor. Psychiatry can no longer function as the therapeutic dispenser it was from Freud to Sullivan because the insurance companies and the HMOs have precluded the affordability of such functions. Psychiatrists must dispense and monitor the psychopharmacological industry's involvement with clients and patients, leaving what counseling even occurs other professionals, namely, social workers and pastoral counselors. Of course, it is the patient and client who suffer, but such is the fee-driven market system operative in American society today. Sullivan constitutes a profoundly helpful insight into the nature of the damaged self and injured life experience affecting personality development in the child by virtue of his own personal life story. He spoke often and freely about the nature of his own personality development calling attention to his childhood for illustrative materials when recounting factors related to the development of mental disorders in adulthood traceable to the child's life situation. We will consider his life in some detail thereby pointing to its relevance in our consideration of the self-concept, self-esteem, self-image, and the ideal self.

Herbert "Harry" Stack Sullivan was born on the 21st of February, 1892, in a small farming village called Norwick in New

York State. The only surviving child of a poor Irish family, his childhood was lonely and uneventful exacerbated by the fact that his family were the only Catholics in an all-Protestant town. His father, Timothy Sullivan, was quiet and distant and his mother, Ella Stack Sullivan, with whom he was close, was sickly and of a complaining nature. Two sons died in infancy before Harry's birth and, needless to say, this bore heavily upon his mother. She was unhappy in marriage, having chosen a mate well below her family's station in life, as she thought of it romantically back in Ireland, and she was not disinclined to verbalize her disappointment in marriage and with her life to her only son and companion. When Harry was three, his mother disappeared for about eighteen months, probably for a mental hospital stay, during which time he was cared for by his maternal grandmother whose Gaelic accent was often indecipherable to the child. When his grandmother died in 1903, a maiden aunt came to share the duties of motherhood so, in a sense, he had three mothers to raise him. As a child with only one friend, a little boy named Clarence Bellinger up the road who, interestingly enough, also became a psychiatrist, Harry invented several imaginary playmates but remained essentially an outsider during his school years. It is said that his Irish brogue was strong and his high marks set him apart from his peers at school. Brilliant and taciturn, "Harry" was an outstanding student and was groomed, not for farm work, but for university. He graduated, at the top of his high school class, earlier than most of his peers.

At sixteen, he was off to Cornell University to which he had won a scholarship from the State of New York, but, for various speculative reasons offered up by friends and relations in his home town, Harry did not graduate with a major in physics as he had planned but failed out his second semester. For two years, he disappeared and often referred to his hospitalization during this time for a mental breakdown. However, in 1911, he entered medical school and completed his studies in 1915 but did not receive his diploma until he was able to pay his outstanding tuition debt in 1917. He graduated without a sterling academic record from the Chicago College of Medicine and Surgery, a legitimate but somewhat disreputable institution not unlike many at the time in all large cities. He always spoke disparagingly of the quality of medical education he received. Because of his poor training and virtually nothing in psychiatry, he was not exposed to the major theoretical systems in psychiatry and psychology of the day. This later proved to be an advantage in the development of his own school of thought.

During these trying years of effort to establish himself, he worked with schizophrenic patients at various hospitals, demonstrating a notable capacity to bring some success in dealing with schizophrenics using what he was already calling "interpersonal therapy." This approach he was developing involved the training of staff to enact safe, corrective interpersonal interactions with the patients, arguing as he did that the institutional environment was artificial and counterproductive to personality development. He subsequently served as a staff physician in the U.S. Army but two years later, during which time his fortunes were neither sterling nor well documented, he landed a position at the St. Elizabeth's Hospital in Washington, D.C, where, without any previous training in psychiatry what so ever, he was most fortunate in working with the notable Dr. William Alanson White, an early and successful psychiatrist trained in the Freudian school of psychoanalysis. Additionally, clinical research at Sheppard and Enoch Pratt Hospital consumed a portion of his life and passion from 1923 to 1930 as did a brief appointment in the University of Maryland's School of Medicine. He quickly established a reputation for successfully treating patients with schizophrenia and began to write and publish his research findings.

During what he called his "Baltimore period" of theoretical development, he was engaged in extensive clinical experience and reach with schizophrenics. It was here that he began to think about interpersonal relations as a key ingredient in the therapeutic treatment of the mentally ill. In attempting to decipher the non-sensical speech of the schizophrenic, he realized that their illness was a means of coping with anxiety generated from a social or interpersonal environment rather than of biogenic origins. (After his death, DNA research has shown that Chromosome 11 is absent in 89% of the cases of schizophrenia.)

By 1931, he was sufficient well-established and known to be asked to participate, indeed, even lead an initiative which led to the creation of the Washington School of Psychiatry. At this time, he moved to New York where he developed a large and lucrative private psychotherapeutic practice and, interestingly enough, underwent 300 hours of psychoanalysis from Dr. Clara Thompson, a well-established Freudian therapist. In later years, he was both a professor and head of the department of psychiatry at the Georgetown University Medical School and subsequently served as the president of the William Alanson White Psychiatric Foundation. Part of his role was to serve as editor of a newly created and soon to be considered internationally distinguished journal, *Psychiatry*, commenced in 1938, while simultaneously serving as chairman of the council of Fellows of the Washington School of Psychiatry. During this very productive years, he became a colleague and friend of Edward Sapir, a cultural anthropologist, and Harold Lasswell, a political scientist, both from the University of Chicago. Of special relevance to his theory-building enterprise of international relations was his friendship with George Herbert Mead, Robert Ezra Park, and W. I. Thomas, all international distinguished sociologists at the University of Chicago. Other major figures with whom he came in contact and with whom he established personal friendships including such professionally distinguished persons as Karen Horney, Erich Fromm, Frieda Fromm-Reichmann, and of special mention is Adolf Meyer. These experiences greatly broadened Sullivan's grasp of the behavioral and social sciences which eventually had a profound effect upon his theory of personality.

On the 14th of January, 1949, he died of a persistent cardiovascular disease while visiting Paris, having been attending an international conference, the World Federation for Mental Health which he help found, in Amsterdam where his life's work was being discussed in some depth, both positively and negatively. He was buried in Arlington National Cemetery, having had a well-respected term of service in the U.S. Army as a practicing psychiatrist during and following the 2nd World War.

Sullivan never married though he did adopt a young man who was considered by all his friends as his "son," and, though considered anti-Catholic and non-religious by his friends and colleagues, his will called for a Catholic burial which he received. One distinguishing characteristic of his interpersonal psychotherapy was his desire, not always realized, to stay away from professional nomenclature when speaking of human relations. "I think," he wrote, "we should try to pick a word in common usage in talking about living and clarify just what we mean by that word, rather than to set about diligently creating new words by carpentry of Greek and Sanskrit roots." In spite of his desire and intent, his system itself produced a plethora of neologisms which require a glossary to wade through them.

In 1939, the William Alanson White Foundation decided that a series of lectures should be given to honor the memory of White, a colleague of Sullivan's, who had died in 1937, and, of course, Sullivan was chosen to give the first series. He actually gave five lectures to small groups in an auditorium in a building owned by the Department of the Interior in Washington, DC. In these lectures, Sullivan made his first public attempt to present both a comprehensive and well-thought-out explanation of his concept of personality development including psychiatric disorders and treatment. In February of 1940, they were all published in the journal, *Psychiatry*, at the insistence of Sullivan's friends and colleagues, but against his best judgment. He was not pleased with his performance but finally consented and they appeared. Not surprisingly, they attracted much attention within the psychiatric and social science communities and in the following years many mental health and social science professional workers wrote to secure copies of this issue of the periodical.

Finally, in 1947, much to the chagrin of Sullivan who believed his presentation of his thoughts was "grossly inadequate," a new printing of these lectures came out again in *Psychiatry*. This issue was in hardback and carried the somewhat dubious title of *Conceptions of Modern Psychiatry*. This was actually his only book, at least in his lifetime, to see the light of day though several subsequent volumes of his lectures and essays, all touted to be Sullivan's books, finally appeared. This one, however, sold 13,000 copies over the next several years and the William Alanson White Foundation gained considerable attention because of them. Under the same title, this book was published four years after the death of Sullivan and it still sells well. Sullivan, however, denounced many of the premature conceptual developments in the work and discounted its value.

Nevertheless, it is a pivotal work for our consideration and a few remarks are justified before we move to the driving concepts and theories of Sullivan's notions of personality. "Psychiatry," he wrote, "is the study of processes that involve or go on between people. The field of psychiatry is the field of interpersonal relations, under any and all circumstances in which these relations exist." This is the thesis set forth by Sullivan in his book. It is the first place where he expressed the central ideas of his theory of personality particularly as relates to the damaged self of the child. Through his development of the theory, he made not only a vital contribution in the treatment of mental disorder -- in particular, schizophrenia -- but he opened an entirely new approach to the study of human personality. In the view of many analysts, he made the most original contribution to psychiatry since Freud. Rollo May has gone on record as saying, "As Freud was the prophet for the Victorian age of sexual suppression, Sullivan is the prophet for our schizoid age -- our age of unrelated ness, in which, beneath all the chatter of radio and newspapers and all the multitudes of 'contact,' people are often strangers to each other." Sullivan's book, *Conceptions of Modern Psychiatry* consists of reprints of the first William Alanson White Memorial Lectures, delivered by Sullivan in 1939, as has already been mentioned. They are profound and open a whole new world of interpretation of the nature of personality and the practice of psychiatry as an interpersonal relations science.

In this work, he created a new viewpoint which is known today as the "interpersonal theory of psychiatry." Sullivan's fundamental emphasis related to a theory of personality which is a "relatively enduring pattern of recurrent interpersonal situations which characterize a human life." Radically shifting from the psychoanalytic focus on the unconscious, Sullivan brought to his clinical research and practice a behavioral and social science perspective which had not been considered a significant component of personality theory until he did it himself. He argued that the concept of "personality" is itself a hypothetical entity which cannot be isolated from interpersonal situations and, indeed, interpersonal behavior is all that is observable about personality. The rest, he suggests, is strictly metaphorical speculation and creative imagery. It is futile and fruitless to speak of a person's personality outside the social interactive matrix of the living person. Not discounting the significance of heredity and the maturation process affected by the physical environment, the real thing that determines the nature of a human person is social interaction with others. Of this, Sullivan was very insistent and unrelenting.

Never before had such an attempt been made to merge psychiatry and social psychology. His theory of personality is the product of such a merger and it is greatly enriched by his acquaintance with and utilization of the social sciences. He writes: "The general science of psychiatry seems to me to cover much the same field as that which is studied by social psychology, because scientific psychiatry has to be defined as the study of interpersonal relations, and this in the end calls for the use of the kind of conceptual framework that we now call *field theory*. From such a standpoint, personality is taken to be hypothetical. That which can be studied is the pattern of processes which characterize the interaction of personalities in particular recurrent situations or fields which include the observer." This attitude about the place and relevance of the "observer" in the clinical situation became a benchmark of Sullivan's innovative approach to the therapeutic encounter. He was, of course, influenced by the science philosopher, Heisenberg, on this point particularly.

Modern psychiatry as defined and practiced by Sullivan consists of a study of personality characteristics which can be directly observed in the context of interpersonal relationships. Systems of psychiatry based on statements about what is going on in the patient's mind are therefore similar to a system of thought which is built on axioms such as "All events are controlled by Divine Providence." The truth or falseness of this statement cannot be established by things that reasonably well-educated people can see, hear, and feel. Much human experience can be cited to support such a statement, and much human experience can be cited to nullify it, but it is so set up that it must always remain a matter of faith. For Sullivan, a "personality characteristic" is defined as a thing which people can see, hear, and feel in their relationships with other individuals. This is the most fundamental working hypothesis in his personality theory.

Though Sullivan is only willing to allow personality to be purely hypothetical apart from the actually observable reality of social interaction, he does assert that it is a dynamic center of various processes which occur in a series of interpersonal fields. This "dynamism" is a key concept in his overall personality theory.

He give significant place to these processes by identifying and naming them as he constructs a platform of their characteristics. These processes, then, are *dynamisms, personifications*, the *self-system*, and *cognitive processes*. Let's explore each briefly here as they constitute the backbone of his major work, *Conceptions of Modern Psychiatry*.

The smallest unit of study in interpersonal relationships is what he calls "dynamism." It constituted an energy transference which meant any unit of behavior, either actual act or mental experience. They become habitual ways of acting which involve the physical body of the person, such as the mouth, hands, arms, legs, etc. These dynamisms can then be broken down into a plethora of subsets, such as the fear dynamism, intimate dynamism, etc. The dynamisms which are distinctively human in character are those which characterize one's interpersonal relations and function primarily to satisfy some basic needs of the individual. Three major dynamisms are malevolence, lust, and intimacy. Malevolence is the driving dynamism that one is living among one's own personal enemies and, if this negative dynamism emerges early in a child's life, he may find it difficult ever in adulthood to reach a fully trusting relationship with another person. Sullivan expressed it poignantly: "Once upon a time everything was love, but that was before I had to deal with people." Lust is another driving dynamism of the individual. Lust for Sullivan consists of the complex urges, feelings, and interpersonal actions which have genital sexual activity as their distant or immediate goal. Lust begins in early adolescence.

Sullivan rejected the Freudian concept of sexuality and suggested that it was more or less inconsequential in childhood and early adolescence, but lust constitutes a major driving force in later adolescence. Intimacy for Sullivan is potentially a profoundly positive dynamism. It occurs when the well-being of another person is as important to an individual as his own well-being. It does not occur in parent-child relationships and does not involve lust or sexual behavior and, says he, occurs only between members of the same sex. Lust becomes, then, a contaminant of intimacy for lust seeks to serve itself rather than the other person.

Personifications consist of an image that an individual has of himself or of some other person. It is a complex of feelings, attitudes, and conceptions that grows out of experience with need-satisfaction and anxiety and, for example, Sullivan speaks often of the "good-mother," "bad-mother," and "overprotective mother" as examples. When these personifications are shared by a large social grouping, they become stereotypes such as "all Irishman are drunks," "all Catholics lie," etc., and these stereotypes are held by social groups without experience of their reality but of a shared personification of imagined peoples' behavior.

The self-system is another dynamism which is crucial to personality structure. It functions as a security measure to protect the individual from anxiety. In order to avoid or minimize actual or potential anxiety, the person adopts various types of protective measures and supervisory controls over his behavior. These security measures form the self-system which sanctions certain forms of behavior, such as the "good-me" self, and forbids other forms of behavior, such as the "bad-me" self.

Sullivan's unique contribution to the role of cognition in personality theory has to do with his development of a threefold classification of experiences, for, says he, experiences occur in three different modes -- *protaxic, parataxic, and syntaxic.* These experiential modes merit a brief description of each in order to appreciate their relevance to Sullivan's interpersonal relations description of psychiatry. Sometimes called "types of experience" and sometimes called "types of cognition," this tripartite foundation of personality is worthy of close attention.

The simplest and most fundamental mode of experiencing reality at the beginning of life is what Sullivan chose to call the *prototaxic* mode. It consists of essentially a flowing of sensations, feelings, and images without any necessary connection between them, a kind of "stream of consciousness," if you will. Sullivan himself describes it this way: "It may be regarded as the discrete series of momentary states of the sensitive organism." It occurs, of course, during the earliest months of infancy and must precede the others as a preparation form them. The *parataxic* mode of thinking, Sullivan explains, consists of seeing causal relationships between events that occur at about the same time but which are not logically related. Getting the connection wrong is what this mode of experience is all about. It is magical thinking, says he, for there is no logical connection between two events experienced by the child in which the child assumes there is. It is essentially the "elementary externalization of causality." In childhood it occurs regularly when the child assumes that something he has done is the cause of something that is quite decidedly unrelated but he thinks it is. In adulthood, the residuals of parataxis modes of experiencing occur in such things as the presumed relationship between "praying hard" and "getting well."

Finally, the third and most advanced mode of experience is called *syntaxic* and it corresponds to logical, analytical thought. Syntaxic experience of reality thus presupposes the ability to understand physical and spatial causality, and the ability to predict causes from knowledge of their effects. The meaning of words and the use of numbers constitutes the most poignant examples of the function of syntaxic experience and when the child learns the meaning of specific words and their uses and the nature of numbers and how they work, the child has reached this level of experiential sophistication needed in the development of interpersonal relationships.

Harry Stack Sullivan's distinguishing contribution to contemporary psychiatry was his heavy emphasis upon the social factors which contribute to the development of human personality. Though schooled in Freudian psychoanalysis, he was not a Freudian in the sense that he differed from Freud in viewing the significance of the parent-child relationship as being an early quest for security rather than, as in Freudian psychoanalysis, primarily sexual in origin and nature.

Drawing from his own personal life's story, Sullivan saw this child-mother relationship as central, not the sexual drive of libidinal instincts. Sullivan, on the other hand, was intent upon integrating the multiple disciplines of the behavioral and social sciences into the work of psychiatry such that sociology and social psychology in the tradition of George Herbert Mead and Charles Horton Cooley proved most helpful in Sullivan's eventual development of what became known as interpersonal psychiatry, later interpersonal psychotherapy. He was not averse to reaching across disciplinary lines for theory and method, from evolution to communications, from learning theory to social organization. It was "interpersonal relations" which, he believed, constituted the fundamental ingredient in the personality structure.

Sullivan was averse to that form of psychiatry and clinical

psychotherapy which dealt with mental illness through the study of institutionally-isolated patients. He had extensive experience in working with the mentally ill, particularly with schizophrenics, and he felt that those institutionally committed constituted a weak source of clinical insight. Personality characteristics, for instance, he felt were determined by the interpersonal relationships between therapists and patients and that the institutional environment was artificial and counterproductive. Sullivan contended that personality develops according to people's perception of how others view them. "Others," in Sullivan thought, included personifications, like the government, as well as imaginary and idealized figures like Jesus or Moses or even movie stars. He believed, based upon his own clinical encounters with severely mentally ill patients, that cultural forces were largely responsible for their psychological condition. He contended that a healthy personality is the result of healthy relationships and that most of what goes in our society as mental illness is neither biogenic nor psychogenic but rather "sociogenic." Sullivan refused to employ the concept of "personality" as a unique, individual, and unchanging entity as so often was the case with traditionalists. He much preferred to define personality as a manifestation of the interaction between individuals, namely, interpersonal relations.

Sullivan's clinical work in a variety of settings over several years of medical assignments led him to firmly believe in the impact interpersonal relationships have upon personality development. He noted that individuals tend to carry distorted views and unrealistic expectations of others into their relationships. His solution was to become, as a clinical psychotherapist, a "participant observer" in dealing with his clients, taking a more active therapeutic stance than the traditional psychoanalytic "blank screen" approach popular at the time and particularly with the Freudian school of psychoanalysis. By focusing upon what he called "interpersonal behavior," he would observe the client's reaction to the therapist and the therapeutic environment. He believe that emotional well-being could be achieved by making an individual "aware" of their dysfunctional interpersonal patterns of interaction and thereby grow into a healthy self-awareness of their interactive behavior.

Before we consider Sullivan's now paradigmatic stages of personality development, we should say something about his concept of human nature and, it has been suggested by him many times, it can be summed up in the expression, "everyone is much more simply human than otherwise." Having made this his standard operational modality, he utilized it throughout his career and summed up its meaning this way: "In other words, the differences between any two instances of human personality from the lowest grade imbecile to the highest-grade genius -- are much less striking than the difference between the least-gifted human being and a member of the nearest other biological genus."   Sullivan was outspoken on this point.

Denying that there were any really operative instincts left in the human person, and thus separating himself profoundly from Freud and the classical school of psychoanalysis, Sullivan contended that it is the social environment in which we mature that determines the effectiveness of our maturation. Interpersonal relationships are the essence of human development. We are only human in so far as we develop within the context of other people. We need to learn to compete, cooperate, and compromise with other children as we mature in order to maintain mental health. "Personal individuality is an illusion." We exist only in relationship to other people.   When we mature within a healthy social environment, this positive progression of interpersonal events leads to an integrated personality, an adult who is capable of establishing satisfying interpersonal relations and who is able to both give and receive love. This is the essence of the human personality.

Sullivan's elaborate and well-developed description of the stages of human development were reminiscent of Freud's elaborate system. But whereas Freud built his developmental scheme around the central core of childhood sexuality, Sullivan built his around the fundamental core of interpersonal relationships. There are seven developmental stages in his schema and we will just mention them briefly here before concluding with remarks about his therapeutic method. Infancy is from the beginning to about eighteen months and the first expressions of the "self system" appear when the infant encounters and relates to the "good me", "bad me" feeding experience in relationship to his mother. Childhood commences with the acquisition of language and goes through the preschool years. Syntaxic experience develops and the child encounters and deals with the reality and necessity of living with others as peers and authority figures. The juvenile person corresponds to the grade school years to about age eleven and here interpersonal relations includes competition, cooperation, and comprise as developmental necessities. Preadolescence is short, eleven to thirteen more or less, and here intimacy emerges in relationship to same-sex peers and chums and marks the first real instance of what Sullivan calls "genuine human relations." Early adolescence commences the heterosexual years of stress and physical development and the intimacy dynamic is matched with lust and lasts through the beginning of the high school years when late adolescence produces the profound demands of complex interpersonal relationships and particularly heterosexual ones which are inevitably fraught with anxiety. Adulthood is arrived at with the composite of strengths and weaknesses in the personality which have developed through the interpersonal experiences of the maturing process.

Sullivan's psychotherapeutic methodology was quite unique to his own understanding of the function and nature of interpersonal relationships. Sullivan firmly believed, based upon his extensive clinical experience, that mental disorders derive from interpersonal failures and, therefore, therapeutic procedures must be based upon a genuine effort to improve the patient's relationship skills in dealing with others. In keeping with his overall worldview, interpersonal relationships constitute the core of psychotherapeutic treatment. In this situation, it is imperative that the therapist understand that his role is primarily that of a "participant observer," for, despite all protestations to the contrary from traditionalists, the therapist becomes necessarily part of an interpersonal, face-to-face relationship with the patient. This process actually creates the opportunity for the patient to establish a syntaxic communication with another person, namely, the therapist himself.

Because of the emphasis upon the therapeutic role being that of an "observer," the therapist is exempt from becoming "involved" with the patient but, as with the Freudian tradition, the therapist must establish a relationship based upon his role as an expert in relationships, instead of as a friend, chum, or colleague. Unlike the work of Carl Rogers, Sullivan is insistent that the therapist "not" become a friend of the patient, thereby destroying the "observational" character of the therapist's relationship to the patient. Sullivan had three primary objectives in the therapeutic situation. First, he intends to help the patient improve foresight, discover difficulties in interpersonal relations, and restore the ability to participate in consensually validated experiences. This occurs when three questions are addressed: "(1) How can I best put into words what I wish to say to the patient? (2) What is the general pattern of communication between us, and (3) What precisely is the patient saying to me?" Are these simplistic? Certainly not!

The therapeutic interview is divided into four stages: (1) formal inception, (2) reconnaissance, (3) detailed inquiry, and (4) termination. Let's explicate just briefly the character of each stage. At the first meeting, the psychiatrist promotes confidence in the patient by demonstrating interpersonal skills and permit's the patient to express the reasons for seeking therapy in the first place. The therapist, then, formulates tentative hypotheses regarding the declared cause for seeking treatment, and then decides on a possible course of action.

During reconnaissance, there is a general personal and social history established between the patient and the therapist attempts to determine by the patient came to develop a particular personality type. Here, the therapist asks specific questions about the patient's age, birth order, mother, father, education, occupational history, marriage, children, etc. Open ended questions are asked to invite the patient to feel free to express his emotional state at the time. Then, the detailed inquiry attempts to improve upon his understanding of the patient and the patient's understanding of his own situation, particularly articulating why he has sought therapy. The fourth and final stage of the interview is termination, or, in some cases, interruption. Of course, this means that the interview has come to an end. Quite commonly, the therapist gives the client "homework," something to do or some memory to recall for the next session. After each such session, the therapist makes copious notes about the session, what progress has been made and what issues have arisen that need addressing in the next session. For Sullivan, the therapeutic ingredient in this process is the face-to-face relationship between psychiatrist and patient, which permit's the patient to reduce anxiety and to communicate with others on the syntaxic level.

Whereas Freud was initially focused upon a medical model of mental health and the treatment of emotional disorders, only later moving away from the medical model in preference for the psychodynamic approach to personality development, Sullivan focused his attention as a psychiatrist specifically upon the acute mental illness of schizophrenia. His emphasis was upon his notion that mental illness is primary suggestive of "problems in living" and that "we are all simply more human than otherwise." By so doing, he abandoned the medical model of his training in medical school and embraced a broader behavioral model wherein the tracing of the child's development from early infancy onward constituted the matrix within which the seeds of mental illness could be located. This inclusion of behavioral science understanding of human development constituted a major advancement in the treatment of mental disorders and Sullivan's concept of interpersonal psychotherapy paved the way for further sophistication in research methodology investing how, why, and when the child's self-concept is damaged and his life's prospects diminished.

SELECTED PRIMARY SOURCES OF HARRY STACK SULLIVAN

(1953). *Conceptions of Modern Psychiatry: The First William Alanson White Memorial Lectures*, NY: W. W. Norton & Co.

(1965). *Personal Psychopathology*, NY: W. W. Norton & Co.

(1953). *The Interpersonal Theory of Psychiatry*, NY: W. W. Norton & Co.

(1954). *The Psychiatric Interview*, NY: W. W. Norton & Co.

(1956). *Clinical Studies in Psychiatry*, NY: W. W. Norton & Co.

(1962). *Schizophrenia as a Human Process*, NY: W. W. Norton & Co.

(1964). *The Fusion of Psychiatry and Social Science*, NY: W. W. Norton & Co.

CHAPTER FOUR

ROGERS and Unconditional Positive Regard

Throughout his career, Carl Rogers made much of what he called the "good life" in which he used a term for that experience, namely, the "fully functioning person." The good life, for Rogers, is not a static state of experience, but a process, a direction, a way of living and comporting oneself through all of life's trials and tribulations. The good life "is a process of movement in a direction which the human organism selects when it is inwardly free to move in any direction. The general qualities of this selected direction appear to have a certain universality," Rogers contends, and "the person who is psychologically free moves in the direction of becoming a more fully functioning person." There are five major personality traits of such individuals and we will recite them briefly here. (1) Openness to experience (wherein the individual is not temperamentally closed to new situations, encounters, opportunities, challenges), (2) Existential living (wherein the individual is ready and willing to face whatever may come his way with hope, courage, and fortitude), (3) Organismic trusting (wherein the individual has confidence in his ability to make sound decisions and to act upon them with assurance of their wisdom), (4) Experiential freedom (wherein the individual embraces the possibilities of life without false or shallow constraints superimposed by family and society but with a willingness to explore possibilities for living), and (5) Creativity (wherein the individual is fully at liberty to venture into new realms of experiential living and expressiveness of life's possibilities). "The good life," Rogers expounds, "involves a wider range, a greater richness, than the constricted living in which most of us find ourselves. To be a part of this process means that one is involved in the frequently frightening and frequently satisfying experience of a more sensitive living, with greater range, greater variety, greater richness."

Roger's person-to-person therapeutic method is a reflection of his whole image of man in general and more specifically of the therapist as a facilitator of personal growth of the client towards self-actualization. Believing individuals are innately inclined to personal fulfillment, Rogers is ever optimistic about the healing process. His phenomenological theory has produced a great deal of research dealing with self-concept and his methodology has been widely adopted by various schools of psychotherapy, and not least with the ranks of pastoral counselors who have benefited the most and utilized his method extensively in their training and practice. Without question, Rogers and his followers have set a high standard of excellence in theory and practice.

The fourth of six children, Carl Ransom Rogers was born on the 8th of January, 1902, in Oak Park, Illinois. His father, Walter Alexander Rogers, was a civil engineer and his mother, Julia Cushing Rogers, a devout Christian woman and traditional housewife. His father held both a degree in engineering and some advanced graduate training as well, all from the University of Wisconsin, and his mother had completed two years of college before she married Walter. In his closing years of life, Carl described his parents as "down to earth individuals" but "rather anti-intellectual, with some of the contempt of the practical person toward the long-haired egg-head." Carl was the fourth child and third son but nearly six years later he had two more brothers, Walter and John, who were born in 1907 and 1908 respectively. His oldest brother Lester and his sister Margaret were nearly nine and seven years his senior and he found himself closest emotionally to his younger two brothers. Because Carl was both obviously a gifted child and could read before entering public school, he began in the second grade, and one of his classmates was Ernest Hemingway as well as the children of Frank Lloyd Wright. At the age of twelve years old and owing to the financial success of his father's career, the family relocated to a farm about an hour west of Chicago and for the remainder of Carl's adolescent years, they lived there.

Life was hard for a city boy moved abruptly to the country where farm chores were difficult and demanding, carried out within the strict spirit of an aggressive Protestant ethos and worldview. He believed that his parents were masters of the art of subtle control for he wrote, "I do not remember ever being given a direct command on an important subject, yet such was the unity of our family that it was understood by all that we did not dance, play cards, attend movies, smoke, drink, or show any sexual interest." Little encouragement was given for free time, day dreaming, and child's play and, in the face of such a restricted life, Rogers became somewhat introverted, isolated from his fantasy world, independent of spirit, however, and quite decidedly self-disciplined.

Rogers often spoke of his boyhood in less than glowing term for, says he, they were years of structured, strict, and uncompromising religious and ethical standards dominated by devotion to a fundamentalist kind of faith. "I think the attitudes toward persons outside our large family," he wrote, "can be summed up schematically in this way: Other persons behave in dubious ways which we do not approve in our family. Many of them play cards, go to movies, smoke, drink, and engage in other activities -- some unmentionable. So the best thing to do is to be tolerant of them, since they may not know better, and to keep away from any close communication with them and live your life within the family." This uppity condescension characterized the family and, unfortunately, too often characterized his own behavior. In speaking of his high school years, he wrote: "I made no lasting associations or friendships. I was a good student and never had any difficulty with the work. Neither did I have problems in getting along with the other students so far as I can recall. It is simply that I knew them only in a very surface fashion and felt decidedly different and alone, but this was compensated for by the fact that my brother and I went together much of this time and there was always the family at home."

It was to the University of Wisconsin, in 1924, that Rogers was sent to pursue a mixed bag of interests. Both his parents and three of his siblings had attended the University of Wisconsin and al alternative school was never seriously contemplated. Beginning, typically, as an agriculture major with youthful plans of becoming a successful farmer, he drifted towards history, then religion for what he thought would be the ministry, and then, eventually and finally, he took up a serious and sustained interest in clinical psychology. Of course, the University of Wisconsin was just the right place to be to study clinical psychology for it was becoming rather quickly the leading center in the mid-west for that discipline. He always professed to believing that the discovery of psychology constituted the fundamental turning point in his life.

This turning point came during his third year at the University when he was chosen to go to Peking for the "World Student Christian Federation Conference" for the purpose of "evangelizing the world for Christ in this generation!" He wrote later, "I consider this a time when I achieved my psychological independence. In major ways I for the first time emancipated myself from the religious thinking of my parents, and realized that I could not go along with them." He recounts a particularly insightful moment while on board ship returning from the Peking evangelism trip. One evening, aboard ship, a traveling companion, Dr. Henry Sharman, a student of the sayings of Jesus, made some provocative remarks. "It struck me in my cabin," Rogers later wrote, "that Jesus was a man like other men -- not divine! As this idea formed and took root, it became obvious to me that I could never in any emotional sense return home." The major result of this trip to Peking and this new insight into his own faith-based self-understanding was that he developed a duodenal ulcer. "Something of the gently suppressive family atmosphere," he mused, "is perhaps indicated by the fact that three of six children in our family developed ulcers at some period in their lives. I had the dubious distinction of acquiring mine at the earliest age."

Having earned his B.A. in history from the University of Wisconsin in 1924 , Rogers had only taken one course in psychology and that by correspondence. In 1924, he married Helen Elliot, a childhood sweetheart, and they soon thereafter moved to New York City where he pursued a master's degree from Columbia University while simultaneously attending the Union Theological Seminary, a bastion of liberalism in the 1920s and 1930s. He and Helen eventually had two children, a boy and a girl. At the seminary, he took a course on the ministry, the nature of the career, its demands and expectations, and during this time he decided, against his parents' wishes and expectations, to transfer to psychology at the Teachers College of Columbia University in 1926 and where, in 1927, he won a fellowship to work in the Institute of Child Guidance. At the Institute he gained an elementary knowledge of Freudian psychoanalysis, but was not much influenced by it as his later theoretical work demonstrated. At the Institute he also attended a lecture by Alfred Adler who shocked

Rogers and the other staff members with his contention that an elaborate case history was unnecessary for psychotherapy.

Rogers subsequently took both a masters in psychology in 1928 and a doctorate in psychotherapy in 1931 from Columbia University. He was enthralled with clinical work and had already commenced his lifelong career in this field at the Rochester Society for the Prevention of Cruelty to Children. There, he studied Otto Rank's theory and therapy techniques and that experience drove him to believe that he himself could develop operational theories and techniques unique to his own insights and experience. For the next ten years, Rogers applied himself to psychological services for delinquent and underprivileged children.

At the age of thirty-eight, Rogers received an appointment as "full professor of psychology" at Ohio State University. Despite his fondness for teaching, he might have turned down the offer if his wife, Helen, had not urged him to accept and if the University had not agreed to start him at the top, with the academic rank of full professor. He often told his younger students and colleagues that the only way to enter the academy was to do so as full professor. Anything less was not acceptable as it required too much work in areas of no particular interest to the young professor but necessary in order for him to prove himself worthy of the appointment. A major breakthrough in his own self-understanding occurred quite surprisingly in response to a lecture he was invited to give to the Psi Chi chapter at the University of Minnesota. The lecture, entitled, "Newer Concepts in Psychotherapy," raised such furor and controversy that it occurred to him that he was saying something quite new and provocative. This lecture became the backbone of the second chapter in his new blockbuster book, *Client-Centered Therapy,* published in 1942.

From 1940 to 1945, he taught psychology and, in 1942, he published his first of several major books. This one, entitled, *Counseling and Psychotherapy: Newer Concepts in Practice,* was the first of its kind in the profession of psychological counseling where the psychologist's clinical results based upon the recording and transcript of the client's therapy sessions were used for analysis in print. He set a precedent and the profession burst upon the scene with therapy-session based clinical reports and analyses like it had never done before. His publishing became prolific in the journals as a result of this new method of presenting psychological data.

After five years of teaching at Ohio State, Rogers took a one-year appointment in 1944 in New York as Director of Counseling Services for the United Service Organization. Rogers was subsequently offered a post at the Counseling Centre of the University of Chicago where he served from 1945 to 1957 and where he wrote, in 1951, the most important book of his career, entitled, *Client-Centered Therapy: Its Current Practice, Implications, and Theory*. The groundbreaking nature of this book's fundamental theories about counseling would change the face of that profession forever and would catapult Rogers into international acclaim. That same year and thanks to the notoriety of the book, he was appointed head of the Counseling Center at the University of Chicago. At the time, the famous Dr. C. George Boeree made this following assessment: "Rogers' theory is particularly simple -- elegant even! The entire theory is built on a single 'force of life' he calls the actualizing tendency. It can be defined as the built-in motivation present in every life-form to develop its potentials to the fullest extent possible. We're not just talking about survival: Rogers believes that all creatures strive to make the very best of their existence. If they fail to do so, it is not for a lack of desire." It was within this professional setting of dealing with children and the difficulties involved in the maturation process within the troubled child when the concept of the damaged self and the injured life of the development child personality gained much of his attention.

Though his six years at the University were outstandingly successful, he left in 1957 to take up a joint post at the University of Wisconsin as both Professor of Psychology and Professor of Psychiatry. He stayed, however, only two years for he found that he was becoming disillusioned with the therapeutic and diagnostic techniques of the establishment at the time particularly in the psycho-pharmacologically-driven department of psychiatry as well as with the overall pedagogical philosophy of the graduate program generally. So, in 1959, he joined the Western Behavioral Sciences Institute in La Jolla, California. In 1961, he wrote what has become his most internationally recognized published, *On Becoming a Person*. During the years 1962-1963, he was a Fellow at the Center for Advanced Study in the Behavioral Sciences at Stanford University. He concentration was on group social relations, and by

1968, he had a handful of colleagues who chose to separate from the Institute and found their own, known as the Center for the Studies of the Person, based in La Jolla as well. A summary report indicated that, "...subsequently, throughout the 1960s and 1970s, Rogers spearheaded the development of personal-growth groups, and his influence spread to working with couples and families; and his idea were also applied to administration, minority groups, interracial and intercultural groups, and international relationships." At the Center, he continued to provide therapy for select individuals and couples, and was prolific in his research and writing. In 1987, having broken his hip, he died in surgery on the 4th of February.

Rogers early on avoided the development of a theory of personality but eventually, from peer pressure, he worked on his theory of personality which became a core of all of his writings. First expressed in sketchy form in his 147 Presidential address at the American Psychological Association, he further developed it in his great classic, *Client-Center Therapy* in 1951 and eventually fully developed in his greatest work of all, *On Becoming a Person.* Nevertheless, he was always insistent that the theory should remain tentative. It is with this thought that one must approach any discussion of Rogerian personality theory.

Carl Rogers was honored the world over and towards the end of his life was nominated for the Nobel Peace Prize for his work with national inter-group conflict in South Africa and Northern Ireland. He had received countless honorary degrees from distinguished institutions such as the University of Santa Clara, Gonzaga University, the University of Cincinnati, and Northwestern University as well as a D.Ph. From the University of Hamburg in Germany and the Doctor of Science degree from the University of Leiden. As early as 1944, he was president of the American Association for Applied Psychology and two years later assumed the presidency of the American Psychological Association. In 1956, he became the first president of the American Academy of Psychotherapists and in 1964 was selected Humanist of the Year by the American Humanist Association. We can close this biographical sketch with the citation given to Rogers by the American Psychological Association when, in 1972, they awarded him the coveted Distinguished Professional Contribution Award. It reads:

"His commitment to the whole person has been an example

which has guided and challenged the practice of psychology in the schools, in industry, and throughout the community. By devising, practicing, evaluating, and teaching a method of psychotherapy and counseling which reaches to the very roots of human potentiality and individuality, he has caused all psychotherapists to re-examine their procedures in a new light. Innovator in personality research, pioneer in the encounter movement, and a respected gadfly of organized psychology, he has made a lasting impression on the profession of psychology."

Some psychotherapists have established their reputation on the basis of one major book. Others wrote numerous books to establish themselves. Rogers, though he wrote much and often, established himself on the basis of two major works, namely, *Client-Centered Therapy* (1950) and *On Becoming a Person* (1961). Roger's first and overriding characteristic in the writing of his first major book was to emphasize the warmth and acceptance of the counseling relationship between the counselor and the client or patient. His first major book was meant to emphasize the new rationale of his approach, namely, "The client, as the term has acquired its meaning, is one who comes actively and voluntarily to gain help on a problem, but without any notion of surrendering his own responsibility for the situation."

From non-directive counseling to client-centered counseling to, finally, person-to-person therapy, Rogers' thought continued to grow and expand. Yet, his initial entry into the cauldron of psychotherapeutic theorizing in his first book (1950) to his major opus of 1961 finally culminating in his late work all bespeak a capacity to grow through learning in the clinical environment. He gradually came to realize that the relationship between therapist and client is the most important aspect underlying personality change. Herein lay his interest and this is where he concentrated the bulk of his entire career.

Rogers brought to the psychotherapeutic table a new way of seeing the counselor's role in relationship to the client. He suggested that the emphasis shift should be from an objectified standoffish posture to rather an "empathic" approach in understanding the client's world, and then to seek to "communicate" that understanding directly to the client. In mirroring back to the client the feelings the counselor picks up on in the interview encounter, the counselor simultaneously transmitted the desire to perceive the world as the client perceived it, thus, the role of "non-directivity" in the dyadic relationship. Rogers insisted that the counselor's role was to achieve an "internal frame-of-reference" with the client. "It is the counselor's aim," says Rogers, "to perceive as sensitively and accurately as possible all of the perceptual field as it is being experienced by the client ... and having thus perceived this internal frame of reference of the other as completely as possible, to indicate to the client the extent to which he is seeming through the client's eyes."

In this new approach to psychotherapy, Rogers emphasized four important principles. First, the new therapy "relies much more heavily on the individual drive toward growth, health, and adjustment. Therapy is not a matter of doing something to the individual, or of inducing him to do something about himself. It is instead a matter of freeing him for normal growth and development." Second, "this new therapy places greater stress upon the emotional elements, the feelings aspects of the situation, than upon the intellectual aspects." Third, "this new therapy places grater stress upon the immediate situation than upon the individual's past." And, fourth, this new approach "lays great stress upon the therapeutic relationship itself as a growth experience."

Here the individual learns to understand himself to make significant independent choices, to relate himself successfully to another person in a more adult fashion. Rogers firmly believed that individuals by and large had it within themselves to solve their own problems. The task, then, of the therapist in Rogers' view was to establish the conditions which would allow individuals to attain this insight for themselves. "Attainment of insight" was, therefore, one of the key goals of nondirective therapy. On the other hand, the counselor's chief task was to reach the "clarification of feelings" through rephrasing the emotional content of the client's statements such that the client gained a new insight into his own stated condition. "Effective counseling," says Rogers, "consists of a definitively structured, permissive relationship which allows the client to gain an understanding of himself to a degree which enables him to take positive steps in the light of his new orientation."

The three major elements characterizing Rogers' personality theory and new modality of psychotherapy were (1) the necessity for the counselor to provide a warm and permissive relationship for the client, (2) the necessity for the counselor to assume the internal frame of reference of the client and to communicate empathic understanding of the client's world, and (3) finally, to reach a mutual expression of feelings between the client and the counselor thereby realizing the full potential of the client-centered theory of personality and psychotherapeutic treatment.

Rogers identified six conditions of client-counselor relationships which, if met, would constitute the basis for a successful therapy. He believed he had already proven clinically that a theoretical rationale for personality change in therapy was possible which implied that constructive alterations in personality could occur regardless of the specific verbal techniques employed by the counselor. He recited these six conditions to reinforce his theory. First, two persons are in psychological contact such that each of them is fully aware that the other's presence makes a difference. Second, the client is in a state of incongruence in relationship with the counselor due to a "discrepancy" between the client's self-image and his existential experience in the counseling environment. Third, the therapist is, on the other hand, congruent (which means integrated) in the relationship due to the pre-set definition of his role in the situation. Fourth, the therapist experiences unconditional positive regard for the client as this is crucial in order to establish a report in the counseling milieu. Fifth, the therapist experiences an empathic understanding of the client's internal frame of reference and endeavors to communicate this experience to the client such that the encounter proves therapeutically successful in direct correlation to the therapist's capacity to emote empathy. And, sixth and finally, the communication to the client of the therapist's empathic understanding and unconditional positive regard must be minimally achieved or, otherwise, no helpful therapeutic result will occur.

Rogers was a conspicuous member of the Third Force, the humanistic psychological school which set itself alongside but *vis a vis* both psychoanalysis and behaviorism. His understanding of human nature was, of course, central to his position as a leader in the Third Force movement. He speaks of the driving force in his work which is "the continuing clinical experience with individuals who perceive themselves, or are perceived by others to be, in need of personal help." Since 1928, for a period of nearly thirty years (he wrote in 1958), Rogers reported that "I have spent probably an average of 15 to 20 hours per week, except during vacation periods, in endeavoring to understand and be of therapeutic help to these individuals. From these hours, and from my relationships with these people, I have drawn most of whatever insight I possess into the meaning of therapy, the dynamics of interpersonal relationships, and the structure and function of personality." Rogers firmly believed that at the core, every human being is fundamentally good, being essentially purposive, forward-moving, constructive, realistic, and trustworthy. Because of this essential goodness of the human person, every individual given the right opportunity for growth, love, and affirmation will blossom forth in his own innate potential, optimum personal development and effectiveness. Rogers' increasingly sophisticated understanding of the damaged self and the resulting injured life of the troubled child gained increasing international attention and respect as he continued to research and write.

Christianity, he argued, has nurtured a core belief in the innate evil of the human person, an inclination to evil and sin. Furthermore, he is unabashed in arguing that this demented notion of human nature has been influenced, even trumped, by Freud and the psychoanalytic school of psychotherapy. If permitted to run free from the scrutiny and domination of the ego and the superego, the human personality's id and unconscious would manifest itself, according to Freud and Christians, in incest, homicide, thievery, rape, and other horrendous acts of self-destructive behavior. People do engage in such behavior and this occurs when they have been stifled, been misdirected, or their personality development has been suppressed from its natural inclinations. When, however, people are able to function as "fully human beings," when they are free to experience and express themselves, they show a positive and rational approach to life which elicits trust and nurtures harmony in interpersonal relationships.

Rogers protested against those cynical and jaded psychotherapists who thought him to be naïve and simplistic: "I do not have a Pollyanna view of human nature," he argued. "I am quite aware that out of defensiveness and inner fear individuals can and do behave in ways which are incredibly cruel, horribly destructive, immature, regressive, anti-social, and harmful. Yet, one of the most refreshing and invigorating parts of my experience is to work with such individuals and to discover the strongly positive directional tendencies which exist in them, as in all of us, at the deepest levels." This driving force in human nature towards the good and self-fulfillment he calls the "actualizing tendency," and he believes it is latent in every human being. He defines it as "the inherent tendency of the organism (the personality) to develop all its capacities in ways which serve to maintain or enhance the person." Therefore, says he, the fundamental principle guiding every person's life is the drive to actualize, maintain, or enhance themselves, indeed, to become the best that their inherited natures will permit them to be. This is, essentially, the sole motivating principle in Roger's theory of personality and the humanistic intent of psychotherapy.

To be sure, there are certain definitive characteristics which establish this actualizing tendency. Let us explore them momentarily here. Of course, and to begin with, says Rogers, there is a "biological factor" which is operative here, namely, this tendency is an inborn characteristic necessary to maintain the individual but also for the enhancement of the individual by providing a mechanism for the development and differentiation of the body's functions, growth, and development. But, of more importance than even this is the motivating force which the actualizing tendency provides for in increased autonomy and self-reliance in pursuit of the individual's full potential in life. Furthermore, the actualizing tendency is not merely for the reduction of tension in the stresses of one's physical or biological life, contrary to Freud's insistence on the prominence of instincts. Rather, the individual is motivated, says Rogers, by a growth process in which potentialities and capacities are brought to realization. This actualizing tendency, then, says he, "is the essence of life itself."

The actualizing tendency, explains Rogers, serves as a criterion against which all of one's life experiences are evaluated and, particularly, when individuals engage in what he calls the "organism-valuing process." This process involves the individual's overt effort in maintaining and enhancing the sought after and valued positive behaviors and experiences in life for they produce within the individual a strong feeling of satisfaction in the realization of one's full potential. This "process" is a mechanism for the evaluation, the weighing, the determining whether or not an experience is affirmative or negative to self-fulfillment. And, the most critical aspect of this actualizing tendency, says Rogers, is the individual's drive toward self-actualization, what he has called the "self-actualizing tendency." This particular tendency, then, is what gives a forward thrust to life, to the individual who must encounter and incorporate life's complexities, self-sufficiency, and maturity. "Self-actualization," then, is the process of becoming a more adequate person. The prospects for reaching this level of maturation, Rogers emphasized, are directly linked to the dangers of the self being damaged in the maturation process. Parenting skills or their lack constitute the matrix within which this development occurs.

Rogers counted himself among the phenomenologists of the day who were practicing humanistic psychology as members of the Third Force. The Third Force was never a formal body but consisted of humanistic psychologists who pushed their worldview as a viable alternative to Freud and Skinner, to psychoanalysis and behaviorism, in both theory and practice. Phenomenological psychology contends that the psychological reality of the individual's world is exclusively a function of the way in which the world is perceived by that individual. The truth doesn't really matter because it can never really be identified. What really matters to the individual is what that person thinks is true, sees to be true, acts in relationship to what he sees and thinks to be the truth. Phenomenological psychology argues that what is real to an individual, that is, what reality is thought, understood, or felt to be, is that which exists within that person's "internal frame of reference." It is this frame of reference which is important in the psychotherapeutic relationship. Rogers was insistent upon this point, namely, that every individual interprets his world and that interpretation is what the therapist must come to grips with. The only way to "understand" an individual's behavior and attitude is to come to an understanding of this internal frame of reference. It is the "subjective reality" of the client's perceived world which is important, not the objective truth.

Needless to say, Rogers' identification with the phenomenological approach to personality theory is based upon his strong conviction that the complexity of human behavior can only be understood within the context of the "whole person." His emphasis upon the "holistic view of personality," namely, that the person reacts as an integrated organism and that his unity cannot be derived from mere behaviorism, is at the core of his therapy. It is the "self" which constitutes the focus of his analysis for it is the fundamental center of human personality. His theory of personality development is based upon this conviction. "The self, or self-concept," says Rogers, "is defined as an organized, consistent, conceptual gestalt composed of perceptions of the characteristics of the 'I' or 'me' to others and to various aspects of life, together with the values attached to these perceptions. It is a gestalt which is available to awareness though not necessarily in awareness." The "self-concept" is comprised of (1) what the individual thinks he is, (2) what he thinks he ought to be, and (3) and the "ideal self" or what he thinks he would like to be. This tripartite composition of the self constitutes the core of Rogers' personality theory.

Rogers does not believe that the self as such manages and monitors the individual's behavior but rather it "symbolizes" the individual's conscious experiences of the world -- who he thinks he is, who he thinks he ought to be, and who he thinks he wants to be. He discounts, not possibly the reality of unconscious data, but its irrelevance to the individual's self-concept and its viability in the therapeutic situation for it is the individual's own self-understanding, as he explains it, describes it, characterizes it, that is important therapeutically. Phenomenology trumps unconscious data as the basis for psychological therapy, says Rogers, for the structure of the self is formed through the individual's interaction with the familial, social, and cultural environment. The "content of one's self-concept," argued Rogers, is fundamentally a social product and not the result of the bombardment of the psyche with unconscious and repressed data. At this juncture, there is a profound brake in Rogerian psychotherapy from that of Freudian psychoanalysis with the former focusing upon the interpersonal relationship involved in the maturation process between child and parent and the latter emphasis upon the unconscious.

Therefore, there are identifiable components needed for the development of a healthy self-concept and when they are absent or twisted from experience, the individual suffers. First, Rogers suggests that every person has a basic desire for warmth, respect, admiration, love, and acceptance from people important in his life. He calls this the "need for positive regard." Whether innate or socially learned, this drive is strong from the earliest days of childhood. A person as infant, child, adolescent, or adult, he believes will do almost anything to meet this innate need for "positive regard." There is a reciprocal component to this drive as well, namely, in the giving of this positive regard, one receives it in turn. The reciprocity of positive regard is a strong re-enforcer of social relationships. The self, says Rogers, is profoundly influenced by this need and rather than suggest that individuals are driven to satisfy the demands and expectations of their "self-concept," he argues that people are driven to satisfy their need for positive regard, both to give it and to receive it. Where there is a conflict between what the individual wants in service to his "self" and what he recognizes as in service to his "need" for regard, Rogers call this "incongruence." "This, as we see it, is the basic estrangement in man. He has not been true to himself, to his own natural organism valuing of experience, but for the sake of preserving the positive regard of others has now come to falsify some of the values he experiences and to perceive them only in terms based upon their value to others." The conflict internally, that is, "incongruency," is the result of the individual choosing to service his need for positive regard at the expense of serving his own self's perceived personal needs. The conflict often leads to psychological stress, tension, and mental illness. "Yet," Rogers continues, "this has not been a conscious choice, but a natural -- and tragic -- development in infancy. The path of development toward psychological maturity is the undoing of this estrangement in man's functioning. The achievement of a self which is congruent with experience, and the restoration of a unified organism valuing process as the regulator of behavior." Too often, it is the "people pleaser" who emerges from this incongruity, the individual who is so driven to please the other person that he forgets to please himself in the process.

Within the context of self-concept development in every individual from childhood is the presence of "conditional positive regard," namely, that situation in the family and society in which the individual is the recipient of positive regard only so long as that individual conforms to the expectations of the positive regard provider. In other words, positive regard is contingent upon compliance with outside expectations of family and society members. "I will love you so long as," or "only if" situations constitute conditional positive regard. This situation, Rogers believes, are detrimental to the child becoming a fully functioning and self-actualized individual. The child, and eventually the adult, "relinquishes" ownership of his own needs and desires in order to conform to the "conditions" laid out by the parent, the family, and society for the giving of positive regard. The individual runs the serious risk of "losing himself" to himself in the process of conforming to the conditions established by others for the giving of positive regard. The "condition of worth" is compliance with the expectations of others, regardless of one's own sense of what is valued. This was painfully true in Rogers' own personal life as a child raised in an extremely restrictive religious home environment. Illustrating the meaningfulness of understanding the life of the therapist, Rogers calls attention to his own experience of maturation and its relevance to the dangers of the diminished life experiences of a restricted childhood.

To counter act the mental health dangers of "conditional positive regard," Rogers developed the concept of "unconditional positive regard" and this concept characterizes all of his psychotherapeutic practice and theorizing. In light of his own childhood experience, Rogers developed this concept as a counterpoise to the detrimental character of the conditions of worth operative in conditional positive regard. He believed strongly that it is possible to give and receive positive regard without attaching it to behavioral compliance. Positive regard can be given to individuals in situations where the behavior of the other individual is not necessarily to the liking of the positive-regard-giving individual. This requires every individual to be accepted and respected for who and what they are, without conditions of ifs, ands, or buts. Such unconditional positive regard is most evident in a mother's love of a misbehaving child. Parental love is not, then, given to the child when and only when the child "conforms" to the parents' behavioral expectations but love, positive regard, is given "unconditionally." Rogers was quick to criticize the Christian saying from Jesus, "You are my friends if you do what so ever I tell you." This is conditional worth and not love.

Rogers believes that children raised in the unconditional positive regard family environment, "then no conditions of worth would develop, self-regard would be unconditional, the needs for positive regard and self-regard would never be at variance with organism evaluation, and the individual would continue to be psychological adjusted, and would be fully functioning. This chain of events is hypothetically possible, and hence important theoretically, though it does not appear to occur in actuality." Discipline is not absent from the family environment, but the circumstances under which it is used and understood by child and parent are radically different which disassociated from self-worth. The creation of an unconditional love "atmosphere" provides the mechanism for a positive use of discipline wherein the child can grow into a fully functioning and potentially self-actualized person with a deep and unchallenged sense of self-worth.

Growing out of Rogers' understanding of the nature of the experience of "incongruity" were the experiences of "threat," "anxiety," and "defense." These three very common experiences are all interrelated and are manifested in the presence of the individual's awareness or lack of awareness an incongruous situation. Every individual strives for what Rogers' calls "consistency" in behavior, attempting at all times to keep an even keel in interpersonal relationships based upon the individual's self-concept. Where there is incongruity between the individual's self-concept and the social situation making demands upon him inconsistent with his idea of himself, that individual feels a "threat." The threat in Rogers' theory occurs when a person recognizes an incongruity between his self-concept and its condition of worth corollary and the experience which precipitates the incongruity. This "threatening" situation is not always self-evidently conscious but the individual feels "anxious" by the encounter. Whenever this experience of incongruity exists in the individual's encounter where self-concept and outside experience are at odds, the individual feels a sense of vulnerability and often personality disorganization. Anxiety is, then, an emotional response to a threat to the individual's self-concept such that there is real danger of a debilitating discrepancy between the person and the situation.

When this situation arises, namely, a perceived conflict between self-concept and objective situation, the individual attempts to protect himself by the use of a defense mechanism. The process of defense, explains Rogers, is the behavioral response of the individual to the threat. The goal is for the reestablishment and maintenance of the self-concept. "This goal," Rogers continues, "is achieved by the perceptual distortion of the experience in awareness, in such a way as to reduce the incongruity between the experience and the structure of the self, or by the denial of any experience, thus denying any threat to the self." The production of defenses, then, is the individual's primary method of protecting himself, his self-concept, and his self-worth.

These defense mechanisms are of two kinds, says Rogers. There is the "perceptual distortion" and the "denial." The first occurs when an incongruent experience is allowed into an individual's perception but only in a form that makes it consistent with that individual's self-image and not something alien to his own experience. Thus, when an experience occurs challenging the individual but not outside the sphere of possibility, that individual employs a defense mechanism to explain the "distortion" in the experience rather than denying its reality. This occurs when someone is caught in theft when that individual is awareness that even though he is not habitually a thief it can, does, and might happen that he takes something that is really not his. This often occurs with employees of a company who help themselves to various items, aware that it is theft, but explaining to their own satisfaction that it is acceptable behavior. This, Rogers calls, "rationalization." Perceptual distortion produces rationalization thereby allowing an individual to maintain his self-concept without any or much jeopardy. However, in the case of "denial" as a defense mechanism, the individual attempts to protect his self-concept by simply denying that the situation of incongruity has occurred. When this defense mechanism, much more so than the previous one, is permitted to reign in a person's life, there is grave potential for the development of mental illness.

The juxtaposition of Rogerian psychology and that of Freud and Skinner is most profoundly realized in their differences over the nature of the human person. The Third Force of humanistic psychology was intentionally launched to counter the negativity and pessimism of both Freud's determinism and Skinner's behaviorism. Eight distinguishing ideologies are counterpoised in these schools of thought with Rogers and the phenomenological humanists on the one hand and the psychoanalysts and behaviorists on the other. First is that of freedom versus determinism, with Rogers strongly for the former and Freud and Skinner quite conspicuously on the side of the latter. Freedom, for Rogers, is an indispensable characteristics of human nature and without it the fully functioning individual has no chance of self-actualization. Again, rationality versus irrationality characterizes the radical distinction between these schools of thought. For Rogers, the human person is essentially a rational being, controlling and directing his own life when given the opportunity and, with help, can correct misdirection in one's life in a way that Freud and Skinner could never conceive nor would they allow. Holism, for Rogers, is the contra to behaviorism's "elementalism," by which is meant the behaviorist's happy dissecting of the human personality into elemental parts for analysis whereas with the humanists the person is treated and respected as an entity in its entirety.

A further distinction has to do with the difference between "constitutionalism" and "environmentalism," with the former on the side of the humanists who know that individuals are constituted of an innate tendency to self-actualization whereas the behaviorists would have us rely upon the organic and instinctual situation of the individual as determinate in behavior. Whereas Skinner and Freud would emphasize the "objectivity" of the human person's behavioral modalities of being without reference to the individual's own self-understanding, Rogers would have us know that the human person is essentially a "subjective" being with thought processes and behavioral modalities employed at his own initiative and to his own desired ends. Again, Rogers would have us know that the human person is "proactive" rather than "reactive" to life's situations and that the positive view of the human person is one in which every individual has the ability and is encouraged to assume responsibility for his actions rather than rely helplessly upon his instinctual urges and unconscious cuing for behavioral responses.

We are a proactive being rather than a mere reactive animal say the humanists of the Third Force. Because human beings are pontificated toward self-actualization, every individual is "heterostatic" rather than "homeostatic," that is to say, every person is in a mode of action, moving towards greater fulfillment, greater self-actualization, rather than bound and gagged by the instinctual and unconscious variables operative in his life but outside his control. Man is moving forward, not staked to his mere animal confines. And, finally, Roger would emphasize "knowability" whereas the behaviorists would claim "unknowability" as our life situation and destiny. Because of his embracing of the phenomenological school of psychology, Roger believed that man cannot use scientific knowledge to better understand who and what we are without a much greater reliance upon our own capacity at self-understanding. We are not merely the objective subject of scientific enquiry, but we are the subjective focus of interpersonal self-understanding. Science can help, but it must serve rather than dominate our enquiry.

Early on in our discussion, we called attention to the "evolution" of Rogerian psychotherapeutic methods of treatment, moving from a non-directive to client-centered to finally person-to-person centered focus. In this context, Rogers has identified six conditions necessary for the therapeutic relationship to be beneficial. In closing, we will itemize these and comment briefly. (1) Two persons are in psychological contact (wherein two individuals, one self-defined as therapist and the other as client, meet together to address a personal issue of the client); (2) The client is in a state of incongruence, being vulnerable or anxious (wherein the situation presumes an interactive relationship of the two individuals addressing the incongruent feelings of the client), (3) The therapist is congruent or integrated in the relationship (by which is meant that this individual is aware of his role, his situation, and his responsibility in relationship to the client), (4) The therapist experiences unconditional positive regard for the client (such that the client does not raise defenses and is rather openly convergent with the therapist about his situation of anxiety), (5) The therapist experiences an empathic understanding of the client's internal frame of reference and endeavors to communicate this experience to the client (such that the client is enabled to better see and assess the situation which has arisen in his life which has produced the incongruence), and (6) The communication to the client of the therapist's empathic understanding and unconditional positive regard is to a minimal degree achieved (thereby setting the client on the road to recovering or discovering a sense of self-worth and fulfillment).

Having previously explored the interpersonal psychotherapy of Harry Stack Sullivan, it is clear now that by combining Sullivan's emphasis upon the interpersonal dynamic operative within the maturation process of the child's personality development, Rogers becomes profoundly insightful through the development of his client-centered emphasis in therapy. By combining Sullivan's interpersonal theory of development with Rogers' client-centered orientation, a substantive address to the nature of the damaged self and the resulting diminished life becomes clearly evident in the maturation process of the child where the life situation is restrictive, negative, and limited.

CARL ROGERS' PRIMARY SOURCES

Clinical Treatment of the Problem Child, (1939).

Counseling and Psychotherapy: Newer Concepts in Practice, (1942).

Client-centered Therapy: Its Current Practice, Implications and Theory. London: Constable, (1951).

"A Theory of Therapy, Personality and Interpersonal Relationships as Developed in the Client-centered Framework." In (ed.) S. Koch, *Psychology: A Study of a Science. Vol. 3: Formulations of the Person and the Social Context.* New York: McGraw Hill, (1959).

On Becoming a Person: A Therapist's View of Psychotherapy. London: Constable, (1961).

Freedom to Learn: A View of What Education Might Become. (1st ed.) Columbus, Ohio: Charles Merrill, (1969).

On Encounter Groups. New York: Harper and Row, (1970).

On Personal Power: Inner Strength and Its Revolutionary Impact, (1977).

A Way of Being. Boston: Houghton Mifflin, (1980).

CHAPTER FIVE

MASLOW and Self-Actualization in Personality Development

Few psychologists of his day questioned but what Maslow was creative and astoundingly original in his thoughts, insights, and manner of presentation. Before Maslow, psychology and psychotherapy seemed to be dominated by the mentally ill and all theorizing focused upon the "cure" for those individuals. Not discounting the need to address the complex issues of mental illness, Maslow and the humanistic orientation of the Third Force movement turned its attention to human potential, to mental health and its nurture and development. Humanistic psychology gave rise to several different therapies, all guided by the idea that people possess the inner resources for growth and health and that the point of therapy is to help remove obstacles to individual's achieving this. Erik Erikson and Carl Rogers become major bearers of this new way of thinking about psychotherapy.

Humanistic psychology was a term coined by a group of psychologists in the 1960s who joined Maslow's movement towards an alternative psychotherapeutic orientation to that of Skinner and the behaviorists and Freud and the psychoanalysts. It was a movement, not a school of thought. Calling themselves the Third Force, humanistic psychologists shared a wide range of views and certain fundamental conceptions about the nature of the human person and personality development. Embracing the existential philosophy of "life is what you make it" found in Kierkegaard and Sartre, these psychologists found the fundamental tenets of existentialism to be at the core of their own thought and work, particularly the concept of "becoming." A person is never static; he or she is always in the process of becoming something different. Thus, it is the individual's personal responsibility as a free being to realize his own potentialities. Only by actualizing these potentials intrinsic to the human person can a truly authentic life emerge.

Requiring more than biological needs and sexual and aggressive instincts, the human person must build upon these needs towards a higher self-understanding. The process of becoming, of self-actualization, is, they contended, inherent to human nature itself and to stifle that or demean that character is to diminish humanity itself thereby destroying the person.

Abraham Harold Maslow was born in Brooklyn, New York, on the first of April, 1908, the first of seven children to parents who were uneducated Jews from Russia. Pushed hard to succeed by ambitious but misguided parents, he took solace in books from his loneliness and shyness perpetrated somewhat by an extremely aggressive and, as he later said, a schizophrenic mother. "With my childhood," Maslow wrote late in life, "it's a wonder I'm not psychotic. I was a little Jewish boy in the non-Jewish neighborhood. It was a little like being the first Negro enrolled in the al-white school. I was isolated and unhappy. I grew up in libraries and among books, without friends." During the summers, he worked for his family's barrel manufacturing company with his three brothers who still own the company. Because he was intellectually gifted, he did find some happiness and a sense of fulfillment during his four years at the Brooklyn Borough High School where he distinguished himself academically.

The study of law, his father's ambition for him, lasted only a few weeks at the City College of New York and he then transferred to Cornell for a few courses but returned to CCNY yet failed to complete his degree course. Later in life, he explained that he felt that law dealt too much with evil people and was not sufficiently concerned with the good, and it was the good, the wholesome, the fulfilling experience of a meaningful life that captured his imagination. At the time, Maslow married his high school sweetheart who was also his first cousin and, as he put it, his first and last love, Bertha Goodman, a local girl from a good Jewish family and they eventually had two daughters, the experience of which Maslow said changed the direction of his life forever. "Life didn't really start for me," he says, "until I got married and went to Wisconsin." They were married on Christmas Day, 1928, when Maslow was 20 and his bride 19.

Fascinated with the prospects of studying with some of the greatest scholars of the day, Maslow applied to and was accepted at the University of Wisconsin where he earned his B.A. in 1930, his M.A. in 1931, and his Ph.D. in 1934, all in psychology, enjoying the privilege of working with the then famous Professor Harry Harlow. It was his early involvement in the study of behaviorism, from which he later departed with a loud flourish of protestation, and the opportunity of working with Harlow, that he considered the two driving forces in his academic pursuit of a life's goal as research scholar and teacher. A whirlwind of study, research, writing, and teaching, he had taken Wisconsin by storm and after completing his studies, though somewhat disappointed that he wasn't able, after all, to study with the renowned scholars he went to Wisconsin to study with. "I was off to Wisconsin to change the world. But off to Wisconsin because of a lying catalog. I went there to study with Koffka, the psychologist; Dreisch, the biologist; and Meiklejohn, the philosopher. When I showed upon campus, they weren't there. They had just been visiting professors, but the school put them in the catalog anyway!"

After serving on the Wisconsin faculty as Assistant Instructor in Psychology (1930-1934) and Teaching Fellow in Psychology (1934-1935), Maslow was back to New York in a flash upon graduating with his doctorate specifically to work with E. L. Thorndike as his research assistant at Teacher's College, Columbia University, where he became interested specifically in research on human sexuality. At Columbia, he served as a Carnegie Fellow from 1935-1937. His Ph.D. dissertation was an observational study of sexual and dominance characteristics of monkeys! But this study introduced him to a whole new world of research. A full-time teaching post was offered him at Brooklyn College and it was during these years, he reflected in older life that provided him the unparalleled opportunity to meet and work with such people as Adler, Fromm, Horney, and several distinguished Gestalt and Freudian psychologists. Adler, at this time, was holding seminars in his home in New York on Friday nights and Maslow was invited to participate. He always expressed his gratitude for the invitation and the experience. Not inconsequently, he also went through psychoanalysis during this time in Brooklyn. Also, and a world expanding experience it was for him, he served as plant manager of the Maslow Cooperage Corporation, the family factory owned and operated by his three brothers.

He was particularly influenced by two mentors of his during these years, the anthropologist Ruth Benedict and the Freudian psychologist Max Wertheimer. Unlike Freud, Jung, and Adler, Maslow was disinclined to focus his attention and research upon the mentally ill, preferring to study why and how people are mentally healthy, happy, and fulfilled. Eventually, he would develop a whole psychodynamic schema of theoretical constructs and conceptual framework called the hierarchy of needs. Maslow saw needs arranged in a sort of ladder, leading from basic to more advanced levels in the maturation of human fulfillment. It was becoming a father that seems to have transformed him into a real force in humanistic psychology. "Our first baby changed me as a psychologist," he wrote, "It made the behaviorism I had been so enthusiastic about look so foolish I could not stomach it anymore ... I'd say that anyone who had a baby couldn't be a behaviorist." His two baby daughters made a profound effect upon him for two reasons. First, because they had such different temperaments, he was forced to assume that many basic personality characteristics were inherited. Second, the birth of his first daughter influenced him to relinquish his belief in behaviorism. He later wrote: "I looked at this tiny, mysterious thing (his first child), and felt so stupid. I was stunned by the mystery and sense of not really being in control. I felt small and weak and feeble before all of this." Maslow reflected upon this early experience of vulnerability and often traced his fledging interest in what would become a passionate desire to grasp the nature of the injury done to children during their maturation process wherein the self becomes damaged owing to psychosocial and family situational circumstances.

Without doubt, it was World War II and the aftermath that changed Maslow forever. It was the defining moment in a research psychologist's life when he turned from behaviorism to humanism and launched a whole new way of thinking about human personality. For him, war epitomized the prejudice, hatred, and baseness of humankind. The experience of witnessing a Victory Day parade, he explains, changed him for good. "As I watched," he recorded years later, "the tears began to run down my face. I felt we didn't understand -- not Hitler, nor the Germans, nor Stalin, nor the communists. We didn't understand any of them. I felt that if we could understand, then we could make progress. I had a vision of a peace table, with people sitting around it, talking about human nature and hatred and war and peace and brotherhood ... that moment changed my whole life and determined what I have done since.   Since that moment in 1941, I've devoted myself to developing a theory of human nature that could be tested by experiment and research." As we have seen, there was a paradigm shift in Maslow's search to understand the maturation process of the child's personality away from a behaviorist perspective and more substantively towards a humanistic awareness.

From 1951 to 1969, he enjoyed the privilege of teaching at Brandeis University near Boston and for several of those years was department chairman and it was during these fruitful years that he met Kurt Goldstein who planted the seed of an idea in Maslow which gave rise to his now internationally acclaimed concept of "self-actualization." Maslow eventually became the head of what became known as the Third Force in psychology, the humanistic school *vis a vis* Freudian psychology and behaviorism. He ended his teaching carrier by moving to California to become the first Resident Fellow of the W. P. Laughlin Charitable Foundation in Menlo Park. Here he had complete freedom to pursue his interests in the philosophy of democratic politics and ethics but it was here he died on the 8th of June, 1970, at the age of sixty-two.

Maslow was affiliated, albeit tangentially more often than not, with many professional societies. He served on the Society for the Psychological Study of Social Issues Council and was elected president of the Massachusetts State Psychological Association. He presided over the Division of Personality and Social Psychology of the American Psychological Association and was elected president of the APA in 1967. He was the founding editor of both the *Journal of Humanistic Psychology* and the *Journal of Transpersonal Psychology.*

Not a prolific writer but one who was able to put his major contributions into a coherent presentation, Maslow established himself as a major figure in American psychology and personality theory with his book, *Towards a Psychology of Being.*   "If we wish to help humans to become more fully human," Maslow wrote, "we must realize not only that they try to realize themselves, but that they are also reluctant or afraid or unable to do so. Only by fully appreciating this dialectic between sickness and health can we help to tip the balance in favor of health." In his book, there is a constant optimistic thrust toward a future based on the intrinsic values of humanity. Maslow states that "This inner nature, as much as we know of it so far, seems not to be intrinsically evil, but rather either neutral or positively 'good.' What we call evil behavior appears most often to be a secondary reaction to frustration of that intrinsic nature." He demonstrates that human beings can be loving, noble, and creative, and are capable of pursuing the highest values and aspirations.

Maslow had become disenchanted with classical psychoanalysis and contemporary behaviorism alike for some of the same reasons, primarily because of their intrinsic negativity about the human person and his potential. The first chapter in Maslow's classic is characteristically entitled, "Toward a Psychology of Health." Throughout his career, it was mental health, not illness, which fascinated him, that stirred within him the desire to know more and more about what it means to be human and to grasp the potential of humanity. From within the matrix of this optimism about humanity and our desire to realize our potential grew Maslow's now highly acclaimed fundamental contributions to humanistic psychology, namely, the "hierarchy of human needs" and "self-actualization." Then, as we shall see later, his third insight had to do with the emergence of humanistic psychology and what he chose to call the "Third Force."

"There is now emerging over the horizon," he wrote as his opening remarks in this classic text, "a new conception of human sickness and of human health, a psychology that I find so thrilling and so full of wonderful possibilities that I yield to the temptation to present it publicly even before it is checked and confirmed, and before it can be called reliable scientific knowledge." He would not be stopped. The basic assumptions implicit in this new way of thinking about mental health were these: (1) every person has an essential biologically based inner nature, (2) each person's inner nature is in part unique to himself and in part species-linked, (3) this inner nature can be scientifically studies, (4) this inner nature is not intrinsically evil but rather neutral or good, (5) because of this the inner nature should be nurtured and brought out into the light of day, (6) and if this inner core of our fundamental human nature is suppressed or stifled, we get ill, (7) this inner human nature, not like instincts, is frail and in need of much care and attention, (8) and even when suppressed, it endures within the core of human personality, and (9) the nurturing, the fostering, the supporting of these inner drives and characteristics inevitably bring mental health.

Toward a Psychology of Being is built upon the humanistic psychology of Maslow's Third Force and constitutes the cornerstone of his work. To read this book is to learn of the breadth and depth of the Third Force and to know Maslow at the very core of his professional enthusiasm. Its influence continues even today to spread not just throughout the psychotherapeutic community but through the general public, through the humanities, social theory, and pastoral counseling. Its enduring popularity rests with its address to the important questions of the day regarding mental health and the nurture of human potential. Its address to human nature and psychological well-being is a breath of fresh air after the depressing, if not oppressive, nature of classical psychoanalysis and individual psychology which are both built upon the presumption of a "dark closet" needing a good cleaning. Not so with Maslow for his aim is to promote, maintain, and restore mental and emotional health. "Capacities clamor to be used," he wrote, and "cease their clamor only when they are well used ... Not only is it fun to use our capacities, but it is necessary for growth. The unused skill or capacity or organ can become a disease center or else atrophy or disappear, thus diminishing the person."

In his developing work in personality formation, Maslow has put forth a great deal of thought and effort into producing a needs-based framework of human motivation based upon his clinical experiences with humans rather than open the behaviorism of Skinner and followers which was fundamentally based upon animal behavior. He was, of course, at odds with Adler, Jung, and Freud as relates to their pessimistic assessment of the human situation for he was both optimistic about human nature and enthusiastic about the development of ways and means of nurturing and fostering human potential and the fulfillment of human aspirations. Form his theory of motivation, many in the fields of management and leadership find Maslow's theory of motivation provocative and stimulating.

The basis of Maslow's theory is that human beings are motivated by unsatisfied needs, and that certain lower factors need to be satisfied before higher needs can be met. We will discuss these in more detail in the "concepts and theories" section but for now let it be said that according to Maslow, there are "general types of needs" such as physiological, survival, safety, love, and esteem, which must be satisfied before an individual can act unselfishly. These he called "deficiency needs" and as long as the human person is being motivated by these drives, we are moving towards growth, toward what he came to call "self-actualization." Satisfying needs, then, according to Maslow, is healthy, necessary, beneficial to the individual, whereas the stifling of this drive to satisfy the fundamental needs leads to mental illness. As a leading founder of the humanistic perspective in psychotherapy, Maslow both introduced and advanced the concept of needs assessment relative to the child personality development wherein damage to the self-esteem and self-concept of the child becomes profoundly vulnerable to the absence of such needs inevitably leading to a diminishment of self-actualization within the child.

Maslow understood human needs to be hierarchical in the sense that one builds upon another like the steps of a ladder or like a staircase. The most basic and almost primordial or instinctual needs, he suggests, are air, water, food, and sex. Above those, which must be met in order to progress up the hierarchy, are safety needs such as security and stability and those are followed by more psychologically charged social needs including the need to belong, for love and acceptance. At the upper echelons of the needs ladder are the self-actualizing needs by which Maslow meant the need to fulfill oneself, to realize one's own potential. In order to progress up these stair steps to fulfillment, each level must be realized. There is no "skipping" of the various needs recited here, says Maslow, otherwise, the stifling at one level precludes full realization at the next level. Not everyone is destined to progress; some never do and thus mental illness is forever a reality. Few reach the highest echelon of self-actualization and Maslow would have us understand that these are not static levels but fluid and fluctuating with time and life circumstances.

The goal, of course, is to reach the highest realms of human potential and that, Maslow calls "self-actualization." The fundamental features of this level of personal growth includes such things as focusing upon the problems outside oneself, others' problems and issues rather than one's own. Also, having a genuine sense of what is true versus the false and phony are features of this level. Being spontaneous and creative while honoring, not mindlessly conforming to social conventions, all bespeak the self-actualized person. Maslow enjoyed identifying such individuals within society, particularly within his own social circles. He often used Ruth Benedict as the quintessential example of the truly self-actualized person.

In *Toward a Psychology of Being*, Maslow ventured into the swift and changing waters of "peak experience" as a way of addressing those moments in some people's lives, though not everyone, when the most provocative and stimulating experiences of inner ecstasy occur. These "peak experiences" are, according to Maslow, those profound moments of love, understanding, happiness, rapture, or insight, when a person feels "more whole, alive, self-sufficient and yet a part of the world, more aware of truth, justice, harmony, goodness, and so on." These peak experiences are reserved for the few self-actualized people in society.

Few would argue that Maslow's lasting contribution to psychotherapy and personality theory are his three fundamental concepts of (1) the Third Force, (2) the hierarchy of needs, and (3) self-actualization. All of his other contributions are subsumed within these three insights. Let us look at each of these more closely in our discussion of the fundamental contributions Maslow has made to psychotherapy.

Maslow's theory of personality represents an alternative to the two major shaping forces of contemporary psychology evidenced in both behaviorism and in Freudian psychoanalysis. This alternative personality theory construct and treatment modality led Maslow and his compatriots to think of what they were developing as a third way of treating mental health and mental illness. Thus, it became known and first called "The Third Force" by Maslow himself. This humanistic psychology was decidedly developed intentionally as a third and alternative way from behaviorism and psychoanalysis, both perceived to be pessimistic about human nature and rather inclined to think of the human personality as in some way fundamentally flawed by instinctual motivations at the expense of personal health and wholeness.

Maslow's emphasis and that of the Third Force movement was on mental health and ways of fostering that process of fulfillment evidently desired by all human beings. Toward the end of his life, Maslow pointed out that he did not intend to distance himself and his movement from behaviorism and psychoanalysis for each of those schools of thought had a contribution to make in the understanding of mental illness. He felt, rather, that he had embodied the best of both of these viewpoints and had gone beyond them to a psychology of transcendence. Near the end of his life, Maslow became increasing hopeful about fostering this commitment of the profession to a focus upon mental health and wholeness. He envisioned a psychological Utopia in which healthy, self-actualized people would live and work in harmony. Naturally and inevitably, a substantial address to factors leading to the damaged self of the child incurring injury to the self-concept occupied a major part of Maslow's research and writing interest.

The Third Force held certain insights to be endemic to the movement and to their understanding of human potentiality. (1) The individual is an integrated whole and must not be chopped up into component parts but studied, nurtured, and guided as a single entity. (2) The Third Force held to the belief that animal research was essentially a waste of time for human psychologists. Self-reflective awareness and a sense of hope towards the future make the human person unique in the animal kingdom and must be studied in terms of these realities. (3) Man's inner nature is essentially good, not evil, and, therefore, the psychotherapeutic agenda is to nurture the inner self of every individual. (4) The human person's own unique potential is to be cherished above all else. This is often perceived to be the most significant concept in humanistic psychology. (5) The emphasis upon psychological health was the reigning principle guiding the development of humanistic psychology and was the guiding principle of the Third Force. Maslow ranted against the notion that the human person is fundamentally demented by instinctual drives. He said that the two other schools of psychological thought did an injustice to the healthy human being's functioning, modes of living, and life's goals. Freud's obsession with the study of neurotic and psychotic individuals came under particular criticism from the Third Force.

Now let us turn again and more closely look at the nature of Maslow's "Hierarchy of Needs." The fundamental idea behind Maslow's hierarchy of needs is that our lowest level of needs must be satisfied or relatively so prior to moving higher up the scale. We are motivated proportionate to the level of needs we have fulfilled and our motivation comes from their fulfillment. Each level has its own integrity and no movement upwards can occur until there is a reasonable satisfaction of the lower-level needs. Those who fail to satisfy the lower-level needs are doomed to failure in their aspirations for better things and, says Maslow, mental illness awaits those who try it.

We will here explore the major needs categories developed by Maslow when proposing the "hierarchy." They are (1) Physiological Needs, (2) Safety Needs, (3) Love and Belongingness Needs, (4) Esteem Needs, and (5) Self-Actualization Needs. Later in their development and with insights gained from the Third Force, Maslow added Aesthetic Needs, Cognitive Needs, and Neurotic Needs to fulfill his attempt at comprehensiveness.

The most fundamental of human needs are the physiological needs without which there is no life. They include food, water, oxygen, maintenance of body temperature, etc. They are essentially the basic needs of all living things. These physiological needs differ from the higher human needs in two important ways. First, they are the only needs that can be completely satisfied or even overly satisfied. Too much food, for example, is always a possibility. A second characteristic peculiar to these physiological needs is their recurring nature. One is recurrently hungry know matter how satisfied one is at any given moment of eating. Hunger reoccurs.

When once these most basically fundamental needs are being met, one then is motivated to seek safety and its cognates, such as physical security, stability, dependency, protection, and freedom from such threatening forces as illness, fear, anxiety, danger, and chaos. The need for law, order, and structure are also safety needs, explains Maslow. Though these are likewise on the lower end of the spectrum with physiological needs, they are indispensable for the further development of the human person. In modern societies, these are routinely met but for children, who are more often than adults conspicuously motivated by these needs, protection from the threats of darkness, animals, strangers, and punishments are most common and motivate the child to seek their removal from their daily lives. Neurotic adults, also, feel relatively unsafe most of the time. These individuals spend much more time and energy than do healthy individuals in seeking to satisfy their needs for safety and reassurance about the world. These individuals, says Maslow, suffer from what he calls "basic anxiety" which comes with the failure to meet the safety needs of the individual. He and his colleagues went on to demonstrate clinically that the etiology or origin of much adult mental illness is traceable to a diminishment of the child's sense of self.

If physiological and safety needs are commonly and regularly met in modern society, the need for love and belonging has a somewhat different story to tell. Here we find that most of us find ourselves spending a disproportionate amount of time addressing this need for love and belonging. Within the needs complex is the need for friendship, the wish for a mate and family, the need to belong to a group, a neighborhood, a political body, or even a nationality. Sexual relations, human contact, and social interaction are all components of this driving need for love. Without love, Maslow explains, a child cannot grow to psychological health. Adults, however, sometimes become proficient at disguising their need for love just as they may also be adept at hiding the fact that their safety is threatened. Adults who have failed to receive love or have failed to develop the capacity to give love often find themselves engaging in self-defeating behavior. They frequently take own such characteristics as cynicism, coldness, aloofness, calloused disregard for interpersonal interaction, all as a protective mechanism, denying themselves the opportunities for securing love thereby. Others go to the opposite extreme and become so outspokenly needy and solicitous as to drive others away, losing the very thing they seek and need.

Contrary to the Beatles' song, "Love is all we need," Maslow says not so. Beyond love and belonging and when those needs are being effectively met, the human person reaches higher up the ladder to what is called the "esteem needs" of human experience. With the strength and assurance of the basic needs having been met and with love and belonging well in hand, the human person seeks more, seeks the respect of others as well as self-respect, confidence, competence, and the esteem of others. The esteem needs function, says Maslow, on two levels. The first is reputation, which is the person's perception of the prestige, recognition, or fame he has achieved in the eyes of other people, and second is self-esteem, defined as the person's own feeling of worth and confidence. Esteem needs, then, are bidirectional. One needs the esteem of others and one needs to have esteem for oneself. You really can't have one without the other and maintain mental health. Self-worth must, however, precede esteem of others. When one has self-confidence, self-esteem, and self-worth, one can then begin to develop a sense of reciprocal esteem from the social environment. It cannot, however, work the other way around. Without self-esteem, one cannot experience the esteem of others. When this does occur, mental illness is most commonly the result.

The final and highest level of the hierarchy of needs is that of self-actualization. But it doesn't automatically follow for most people in the world. To have reached the level of esteem needs, most people have arrived at their functional level of behavior and do quite well at it throughout their lives. Only a few can even aspire to another higher, but for those who do, there is a great sense of personal fulfillment, what Maslow calls "self-actualization" which occurs. Only those who embrace what Maslow has called the "B-Values" can make the final step to self-actualization. Those who hold in high respect, says Maslow, such values as truth, beauty, and justice are potentially likely to reach the fullest level of human personal development. We will consider this final step separately and more fully below.

Maslow went on to suggest that there are three more levels of needs beyond self-actualization! As surprising as that might appear, he felt that the aesthetic needs of individuals come after, not before, self-actualization. Not every person and not every culture is particularly susceptible to the aesthetic needs of human development. But there are individuals who are themselves fulfilled by this need, namely, the need for beauty an aesthetically pleasing experiences. From the artistic displays of Paleolithic man, the human person and the human community has been aware of and appreciative of this need for beauty. Preferences for beauty over ugliness, order or chaos, structure over disarray has characterized the human community from earliest times.

A complimentary balance to the aesthetic needs beyond self-actualization is that of one's cognitive needs. There is that intrinsic curiosity of the human animal, the human person has a desire to know, to understand, to grasp the meaning and purpose and direction of things. This is a fundamental human drive and has characterized the human animal from Paleolithic times. When these needs, the cognitive needs, are stifled, all other needs are potentially threatened because without knowledge, with information, without understanding life becomes problematic! Self-actualization, says Maslow, depends on utilizing fully one's cognitive potentials, though self-actualizing people need not have outstanding inherent intellectual powers. They do, however, need to know and understand what is going on in the world around them. Knowledge brings with it the desire to know more, to theorize, to test hypotheses, or to find out how something works just for the satisfaction of knowing. This is a human compulsion.

Maslow was no superficial optimist and was fully cognizant of the potential for mental illness within any person. When needs are not met, psychological stagnation and pathology often are the result. It is the deprived child, the one who needs and seeks but fails to find love and affirmation whose life's situation eventuates to a damaged self-image and the downward spiral of a diminished life of psychological injury. Maslow introduced the concept of "neurotic needs" to refer to behavior which is not productive, nurturing, or beneficial to human personality. These neurotic needs perpetuate an unhealthy style of life and have no value in the striving for self-actualization. Usually reactive rather than active, they serve as compensation for unsatisfied basic needs. In the absence of safety, for example, a person may have a strong desire to hoard money or property and this motivator is worthless and even destructive to mental health. This, says Maslow, is the indicator of a neurotic need, namely, it fails to contribute to mental health. "Giving a neurotic power seeker all the power he wants does not make him less neurotic, nor is it possible to satiate his neurotic need for power. However much he is fed he still remains hungry (because he's really looking for something else). It makes little difference for ultimate health whether a neurotic needs to be gratified or frustrated." In therapy, the counselor will seek to determine what need is not being met and assist the client in addressing that issue, thereby reducing or displacing the neurotic need caused by the unfulfilled legitimate need of self-actualization.

Finally, and in concluding our discussion of Maslow, we must address his major contribution to personality theory called "self-actualization." The development of this concept came about due to Maslow's concentration on mental health rather than mental illness. Adopting the term "self-actualization" from Kurt Goldstein at Columbia University, Maslow went on to develop it into a fully operational concept and focal point of his personality theory. Self-actualization is the highest level of human motivation characterized by full development of all one's capacities.

It is the rare individual, says Maslow, who reaches this level of needs fulfillment in their personality development. First, the individual seeking self-actualization must not be neurotic nor have any psychopathic personality disorders. Furthermore, the individual must have the "full use and exploitation of talents, capacities, potentialities, etc." These individuals, rare though they be, are the embodiment of all needs fulfillment. They have the capacity to deal with delayed or denied needs for they have a fully understanding of themselves, their capacity to abstain, to do without, to postpone needs gratification without panic or feelings of deprivation. Maslow summed up a thoroughgoing description of just who these individuals really are. "They listen to their own voices," Maslow explains, "they take responsibility; they are honest, and they work hard. They find out who they are and what they are, not only in terms of their mission in life, but also in terms of the way their feet hurt when they wear such and such a pair of shoes and whether they do or do not like eggplant or stay up all night if they drink too much beer. All this is what the real self means. They find their own biological natures, their congenital natures, which are irreversible or difficult to change.'

In another major work, *Motivation and Personality,* in 1970 and in response to a continual plea for a recitation of the scope of characteristics of the self-actualized person, Maslow listed fifteen quality which characterize this category of person. Let us list them here and in most instances they appear self-explanatory. (1) More efficient perception of reality (they really see things as they are and not as one would like them to be), (2) Acceptance of self, others, and nature (they are realistic in their assessment of themselves, those around them, and the world outside themselves), (3) Spontaneity, simplicity, and naturalness (they are not phonies in their life and work and are eager to respond to situations as they arise), (4) problem-centered (they are quick to recognize problems outside themselves and equally ready to address them), (5) The need for privacy (they are pleased to have social interaction but equally happy to be alone within themselves without having the experience of loneliness), (6) autonomy (they are not demanding of others or the environment around themselves but enjoy the freedom of personal self-satisfaction), (7) Continued freshness of appreciation (they are those people who are forever able to see the new and different with appreciation and a valuing of each moment and each experience for its own merits), (8) The peak experience (These are the ones who have both the capacity and the reality of entering into a fundamentally ecstatic experience of life through love, art, music, beauty, the challenge of living, etc., with a sense of purpose. Transcendent experiences are not alien to them nor are they frightened by them but rather enjoy the opportunity of living through them to their fruition.), (9) *Gemeinschaftsgefühl* or social feeling and interest (An Adlerian term which characterizes the self-actualized person in his capacity to commit to the whole community with passion and care and selflessness), (10) Interpersonal relations (they have the gift of focusing upon relationships which nurture and enrich each participant), (11) The democratic character structure (they embody the sense of fair play, what is right for each and every one, how to make it happen, and how to foster it in others), (12) Creativeness (they experience the joy of creating things, not just writing poetry or music nor simply doing crafts but a thoroughgoing sense of happiness with their own ability to create something new and different which reflects their own interests and values and passion without the need of praise from others for having created it), (13) Philosophical sense of humor (the thoroughgoing capacity to see the humor in life and in interpersonal relationships without cynicism or rancor), (14) Discrimination between means and ends (they have a healthy capacity to determine what is important to be done and how best it might be accomplished without there being the gross contradictions of means and ends issues about what is of value and worthy of effort), (15) Resistance to enculturation (these are the people who can rise above an existential situation and thereby gain a broader, more complete picture of life's situations and, therefore, are not victimized by their own cultural or situational myopia).

A closing word about the actual psychotherapeutic approach of Maslow seems to be a fitting closing statement for all of his work grew out of clinical practice and was designed to serve clinical training to those who joined the Third Force in psychology. Maslow realized that those who need psychotherapy are normally those least likely to seek it out for they have not met their own needs for fulfillment and, thus, seeking help is not in their purview of options to solve their life's problems. Most individuals who come to therapy have difficulty satisfying love and belongingness needs, says Maslow, and therefore psychotherapy is largely an interpersonal process for these individuals, when and if they choose to seek help. Through a nurturing experience with the therapist, the client may gain satisfaction of their need for love and a sense of belonging and thereby gain confidence and a sense of self-worth. This experience gives the client the capacity to establish healthy relationships outside the clinical environment. To bring this about, the therapist himself must be mentally healthy, a situation which does not always exist and, in fact, many times individuals are attracted to clinical psychotherapeutic practice owing to their mental instability. "The aim of Maslovian therapy," explains Jess Feist, a leading figure in contemporary Third Force psychotherapy, "is to free the person from dependency on others so that the natural impulse towards growth and self-actualization ca become active." He goes on to point out that psychotherapists, because they are just people, do not have the capacity to operate in a value-free clinical environment. Yet, they mission is to foster the sense within each client of their own quest for wholeness by pointing out ways and nurturing efforts on the part of the client to reach a sense of needs satisfaction, of fulfillment, of eventually self-actualization.

SELECTED PRIMARY SOURCES OF ABRAHAM MASLOW

A Theory of Human Motivation (originally published in *Psychological Review*, 1943, Vol. 50 #4, pp. 370-396).

Motivation and Personality (1st edition: 1954)

Religions, Values and Peak-experiences, Columbus, Ohio: Ohio State University Press, 1964.

Eupsychian Management, 1965; republished as *Maslow on Management*, 1998

The Psychology of Science: A Reconnaissance, New York: Harper & Row, 1966; Chapel Hill: Maurice Bassett, 2002.

Toward a Psychology of Being, (2nd edition, 1968)

The Farther Reaches of Human Nature, 1971

CHAPTER SIX

COOLEY and the Looking-Glass Self

The essential task of the social sciences according to Charles Horton Cooley is to attempt to understand the organic nature of society as it evolves through the individual's perceptions of others and of self. If we are to understand society, we must concentrate its attention upon the mental activities of the individuals who make up society. "The imaginations people have of one another," explained Cooley, "are the solid facts of society ... Society is a relation among personal ideas." "Self and society," wrote Cooley, "are twin-born." This emphasis on the organic link and the indissoluble connection between self and society is the theme most common in Cooley's writings and remains even today the key contribution he made to modern social psychology and sociology. Cooley constitutes a direct line of theory development from Herbert Spencer through William Graham Sumner and George Herbert Mead to his own development as a social scientist. He was decidedly and appreciatively reliant upon and indebted to the social psychology which emerged from Mead's extension of Sumner's elaborated expansion of Spencer's concept of social evolution.

Charles Horton Cooley (August 17, 1864 – May 8, 1929) was born in Ann Arbor, Michigan, immediately adjacent to the University of Michigan campus where he was destined to spend the entirety of his life as child, student, and faculty member. With New England roots back to 1640, Cooley's people came via New York to Michigan in search of a better life than they had back East as a farmer. From editor to realtor to lawyer, his father advanced the family's social standing considerably during his life, gaining a faculty appointment in the school of law at the University of Michigan four years before Charles was born, and in 1864, his father was appointed Supreme Court Justice where he remained for the duration of his life.

Born the fourth child of a judge into very comfortable living and circumstances, Charles could hardly expect to rise to the prominence of his distinguished father and, thus, reverted to introversion and reclusiveness, a lifestyle he maintained throughout his own life, suffering from various illnesses and ailments, many considered by doctor and family as psychosomatic. He once wrote to his mother: "I should like as an experiment to get off somewhere where Father was never heard of and see whether anybody would care about me for my own sake." With a speech impediment and few playmates, Cooley drifted into an enduring habit of daydreaming himself into greatness which, alas, nearly eluded him. Owing to illness and European travel and a sideline venture into draftsmanship, Cooley took seven years to complete his degree at Michigan in engineering, a subject of little real interest to him but the minor courses in philosophy and economics did appeal to him.

The reading of Darwin, Spencer, and the German scholar Albert Schaffle led Cooley to return to the University of Michigan for graduate work in political economy and sociology, reminiscent of the abiding interests of Spencer, Sumner and Mead. His pioneering thesis on a theory of transportation in the field of human ecology merited a Ph.D. from the University in 1894. Having published some significant early papers and having read a key paper on transportation theory at a national convention of political economists, Cooley was offered and took an assistant professorship at the University of Michigan two years prior to actually receiving his Ph.D.

The uninterrupted concentration on his academic life and work was greatly facilitated by his marriage in 1890 to Elsie Jones, the daughter of a professor of medicine at the University of Michigan. Sheltering him from the outside world and nurturing his contemplative life of study, Mrs. Cooley, however, was herself an outgoing and dynamic personality and quite capable of protecting him from outside intrusions. Three children, two girls and a boy, were born to the Cooleys, and they lived a quiet university-style life adjacent to, but disconnected from, the University campus as much as was necessary in order for them to maintain their independence. Cooley, with a cooperative wife and children, used the family environment as a laboratory of insights into personality development and social relations. Owing to his work ethic and strong scholarly productivity in the academic journals and professional associations as well as in view of his great popularity among University students, Cooley advanced rapidly to full professor by 1907. The brightest of the bright students were the ones most attracted to Cooley and he responded generously to their enthusiasm.

The massive productivity required of academic professionals today was not required of professors during his creative years so when he did produce a major book or publish a paper or read a scholarly essay at a national convention, it was evidence of his best and most thoughtful work. His first major book, published in 1902, was *Human Nature and the Social Order,* followed in 1909 by *Social Organization.* In 1918, his third major work, *Social Process,* along with a journal he kept throughout his life, entitled *Life and the Student* (1927), constituted the sum total of his scholarly output save papers read at conventions and articles published in the best journals of the day. A posthumous volume, *Sociological Theory and Social Research*, published in 1930 due to the efforts of his graduate students, proved the culmination of his scholarly output. In spite of his reclusiveness, he did participate in the creation of the American Sociological Society in 1905, becoming its president in 1918. His sense of personal fulfillment and personal happiness was linked to his growing international reputation and the popularity of his several books contributed to this self-confidence. Finally, towards the late middle of his professional life, it was thought by his many friends and colleagues that Cooley reached a satisfactory level of contentment accompanied by the gradual waning of his insecurities and presumed illnesses. Though a recluse and distant emotionally from his colleagues at the University of Michigan, Cooley thoroughly enjoyed the pleasure and privacy of his own family – wife and three children – and they built a cabin on Crystal Lake in Northern Michigan as a getaway summer holiday home. This he enjoyed immensely, writing in his journal – "I am glad of life here," he wrote, "glad of the air, the food, and the lake, glad of the work of my hands, glad of my family, glad that I can probably come here every summer, glad of my books, my thoughts, my hopes." Late in 1928 Cooley's health began to fail, and the following March his trouble was diagnosed as cancer. He died on May 7, 1929, at age 65.

We have noted the historic shift for which Cooley is credited in redirecting attention away from large-scale social institutions to more substantive considerations of the nature of the individual, especially conceived of as "mind," within society's institutions. The major social institutions for Cooley were language, the family, industry, education, religion, and the law. To the extent that these institutions constitute the "facts of society" available for sociological study, they are defined and established products of the public mind. They are, says Cooley, the outcome of organization and crystallization of thought around the forms of customs, symbols, beliefs, and lasting sentiments. As we can see plainly here, Cooley did not attribute to a real need as an abstraction called society but rather located those fundamental human needs specifically within individuals who create society. Therefore, institutions are mental creations of individuals and are sustained by human habits of mind almost always held unconsciously by virtue of simple familiarity. As Cooley has pointed out, when society's institutions are understood primarily as mental creations, the individual is thus not merely an "effect" of the social structure, but is a creator and sustainer of it as well.

Primarily, Cooley concentrated his analytical skills upon the development of his fundamental dictum -- "The imaginations people have of one another are the solid facts of society." In his first book, *Human Nature and the Social Order,* he focused upon a theory of the social self, i.e., the meaning of the "I" as observed in daily thought and speech. This primal idea of "I" refers not so much to one's body as to one's "feelings." This mental picture of oneself is what Cooley came to be called the "looking-glass self." Having been greatly influenced by William James' definition of psychology as the study of states of consciousness, Cooley adopts this definition and expands it by establishing the sociality of selfhood as it relates to the thoughts of others. This is the point in his development as a social psychologist when he began exploring what would eventually constitute a foundational construct in understanding the emergence of the self-concept in the child and inevitably the prospects for either a healthy personality or a damaged self-image and diminished life prospects.

The social self is an empirical self, verified by observation. It is not an *a priori* Cartesian assumption nor a metaphysical abstraction. It is a product of social interaction, emerging from one's perception of one's self as reflected in the perceptions of others. It is, just as with social institutions, a quality of mental habit.

In a word, it is generated in and verified by the mind -- one's own mind and the minds of others. The concept of mind as employed by Cooley is rather specific. A favorite expression of Cooley, and one which best portrayed his enduring sensitivity to the reciprocal relationship of self and society, was "self and society are twin-born." For Cooley, to be aware of oneself was to be aware of society -- thus, social consciousness and self-consciousness are inseparable. Self-image can only emerge with a reference group. And these "consciousnesses of society and self," says Cooley, are located in the mind, i.e., human imagination. Unlike the natural sciences, all data of the social sciences are located in the human mind, in man's imaginative propensities. As Cooley observed: "The imaginations which people have of one another are the solid facts of society, and that to observe and interpret these must be a chief aim of sociology." He was insistent upon the recognition and acknowledgment of the relevance of life's contextualization of the maturation process for the healthy development of the self within the child wherein the social matrix of siblings, family, and community hold sway.

For Cooley, the best way of talking about man's imaginative propensities, i.e., the mind, was by paying attention to the emergence of the "self." As an individual develops a sense of "I" he also develops simultaneously an awareness of and sensitivity to others as "you," "he/she," and "they." Through interaction with other selves, the self emerges. The self is neither individual nor social primarily or firstly, but rather is a creation of dialectics between the individual and his social environment. An individual's awareness of himself is a reflection of his perception of other's ideas of who he is, a process of one mind responding to other minds. As we have already noted, this phenomenon Cooley called the "looking-glass self."

In a real sense, for Cooley, social interaction with its concomitants of self and society, is a genuine "meeting of the minds." The concept of the "looking-glass self," which probably constitutes the single most important and enduring contribution of Cooley to sociology and social psychology, is composed of three principal dimensions: (1) How we imagine our appearance to others; (2) How we imagine other's judgment of that appearance; and (3) Our personal feeling about that judgment. When a child reaches the age of reflective self-awareness, an evolutionary progression in the early months and years, he becomes increasingly aware of others' recognition and evaluation of him. From the first human encounter with his mother, then his father, and then siblings and more and larger groups of people, his social arena develops. As he perceives others' estimations of his appearance, his "self" develops accordingly. Not only is he aware of or able to imagine how he appears to others, he becomes also conscious of others' judgment and evaluation of his appearance. The result of this dual mental image, that is, of how he appears to and is evaluated by others, is a responsive feeling on his part to this evaluation -- of pride or mortification or self-doubt, etc. It is within this matrix of development that the prospects for a damaging of the self can occur owing to a failure of the parents to foster a positive self-image and the nurturance of a strong self-esteem. Failure to do so results inevitably in a diminished life of a depleted self-concept commonly resulting in mental illness in adulthood.

The logical extension of this "looking-glass self" concept as descriptive of fundamental human social relationships is Cooley's idea of the "primary group," which constitutes the fundamental meaning of all social organizations. The primary group is the seedbed of society and is indispensable in the forming of social nature, i.e., man's ideals, the experience of love and need for freedom and justice. The primary group is characterized by intimacy, face-to-face interaction, emotional warmth, and cooperation. Through the coincidental development of self-consciousness and social consciousness there is similarly the emergence of a sense of "I-me" and "us-we." This sense of we-feeling fosters a strong identification of the self with group-life, for example, children's play groups, family, etc. Of course, all social interaction does not occur within a close-knit primary group, and, therefore, Cooley characterized the "secondary group" as essentially and necessarily impersonal, contractual, formal, and rational, e.g., professional associations, corporations, bureaucracies, governments, etc.

The primary group -- the most important ones being the family, the play group of children, and the neighborhood -- is the universal breeding ground for the emergence of cooperation and fellowship. "In these primary groups," explains Cooley, "human nature comes into existence. Man does not have it at birth; he cannot acquire it except through fellowship, and it decays in isolation." The group forces the individual to give up individualistic interests in favor of group concerns and nurtures in-group feelings of sympathy and affection. Fundamentally, these groups are harmonious and affectionate, but competition, self-assertion, and passionate contentions also emerge. "These passions," Cooley suggests, "are socialized by sympathy, and come, or tend to come, under the discipline of a common spirit. The individual will be ambitious, but the chief object of his ambition will be some desired place in the thought of the others." It is here that the emergence of mental disorders frequently appear for the etiology of mental illness is traceable to the child's earliest experience of positive nurture or negative diminishment of a sense of self-worth.

Cooley's social thought centered upon a confidence in human progress of an ever-widening expansion of human sympathy -- a movement beginning in the primary groups of family and neighborhood and moving outwards to encompass the community, the state, and the world. Not only was he an optimist and romantic idealist, he was thoroughly humanitarian, arguing cogently that the sociologist must display a sympathetic concern in his portrayal of the human predicament.

As with Max Weber, but independently of him, Cooley argued that the study of social life must be concerned with the "meanings" which individuals attribute to their actions and circumstances. Sociology, quite necessarily, then, must go beyond the mere study of behavior. The sociology of the rabbit hutch must necessarily be strictly a behavioral description. But the sociology of human life can and must rise above simple behavioral data to a higher place of analysis since it can effectively probe beneath the surface behavior into the subjective meanings of human actions. "Although our knowledge of people is behaviorist," observes Cooley, "it has no penetration, no distinctively human insight, unless it is sympathetic also."

When sociology and social psychology rule out the efficacy of a close examination and sympathetic analysis of "motivation" in human behavior, they are deprived of a valuable, even an indispensable, tool for human understanding. Cooley simply points out that the difference between our knowledge of a dog and our knowledge of individuals is our ability to have a "sympathetic understanding" of the individual's motivations. "Knowledge requires both observation and interpretation, neither being more scientific than the other. And each branch of science must be worked out in its own way, which is mainly to be found in the actual search for truth rather than a priori methodology" explains Cooley.

Similar to Weber's "verstehen" and Sorokin's "logico-meaningful" methodology, Cooley used the concept of "sympathetic introspection" as his methodological label. Sympathetic introspection is the process of putting oneself in touch with various other persons, attempting to imagine how the world appears to them, and then recollecting and describing as closely as subjectively possible, but, Cooley argues, since human behavior, unlike instinctual animal behavior, is fundamentally subjective, the method fits the data under investigation. The looking-glass self and the primary group, then, are not only the object of analysis, they are also the tools used in the analysis. "In general," explains Cooley, "the insights of sociology are imaginative reconstructions of life whose truth depends upon the competence of the mind that makes them embrace the chief factors of the process studied and are produced or anticipate their operation."

The case study approach to sociological phenomenon interested Cooley far more than the use of statistics of which, of course, he was not opposed but was by and large disappointed in the positivistic behaviorism which early on began to make its presence known in the field. Cooley preferred an empirical approach based on observation. His first book, *A Theory of Transportation,* was published in 1894, and that book's orientation, probably influenced by a deference to his father's wishes, was essentially in the field of economic theory. This field of interest, the confluence of transportation routes and the emergence of new towns, could not hold his interest in the face of his real passion, namely, that of the interplay between individuals and social processes. His 1902 book, however, allowed him to apply his broader interests under the title of *Human Nature and the Social Order.* Paralleling Mead's exploration into the symbolic nature of the self's emergence through social interaction, Cooley elaborated and expanded upon this notion with his now classic concept of the "looking-glass self," developed most fully in his subsequent treatment of social organization.

Cooley's significant contribution to sociological method complimented his work in social theory for, though independent of Weber yet very much reflective of Weberian sociological method, he argued that the study of human actions and behavior must be focused upon the meanings those actions have attributed to them by the human actors. Human behavior only has meaning as determined by the humans engaged in those behavioral actions. Thus, he argued, the study of mere behavior is inadequate to understand and interpret the meaning of human behavior. Beyond the actually observable behavior itself, the analysis of social behavior can and must reach deeper into the subjective meanings attributed to behaviors in order to grasp the significance of human actions. If the social and behavioral sciences disallow the pursuit of the "motivational structure of human action," they deprive themselves of the essence and core of human behavior.

In this context, Cooley made a crucial distinction between what he called "spatial knowledge" and "material knowledge." The latter type of knowledge is based on human-to-human interaction, communication based on the capacity to understand the process of thought and the sentiment implied in the sharing of ideas between people, between what he called their "states of mind." Both visualized and imagined behavior is possible between people, an experience which is precluded in relationship with other animals, what he calls "spatial knowledge." The distinction between human knowledge and knowledge between that of humans and animals is rooted in the human capacity to sympathize with the motives of others which produces a behavioral matrix. We can observe animal behavior but we have the uncanny ability to "understand" and "sympathize" with human behavior. Sharing of these sentiments wherein individuals can identify with the motivational factors influencing behavior allows for genuine understanding.

Though Cooley was criticized by his colleagues within both the fields of sociology and social psychology, suggesting he was actually too empathetic to be objective in his analysis, nevertheless, he is unquestionably a key figure in the gradual development of research methods which contributed to the elevation of both disciplines to a level of respectability previously not enjoyed.

Cooley shared with Weber the firm belief that the study of the human social world must necessarily focus upon methods designed to probe and analyze the "subjective meanings of human actors," meanings attributed to their actions, their choice of behaviors, and this analytical capacity must be built upon the capacity of the scientist to both understand and sympathize with the human person.

Cooley's open reliance upon and acknowledgment of his debt to Freud and psychoanalytic theory constituted a first in the early development of social psychology. Cooley's work in primary groups such as family, play groups, and work groups in which, with Freud, he emphasized the role these groups play in the development of the individual's sense of morality, of sentimentality, and of ideology constituted a major stepping stone into the furtherance of social psychology's role in both sociological analysis and psychoanalytic theory building. The individual's attachment to the morals, ethics, sentiments and ideas of the small group are carried over into the full spectrum of social behavior within the individual's communal matrix. This tendency is so prevalent that individuals tend to create primary groups, i.e., sub-sets, within the broader matrices of large social organizations. Society itself, explains Cooley, is the product of this process of constantly enlarging social experience and in fostering variation in relationships. The development of these complex social forms tends to create formal institutions and even social class systems based on the core of primary groupings.

Cooley's further extension of this idea of evolution from primary groups to social institutions was evidenced in his third major work, *Social Process* (1918), which emphasized the non-rational and tentative nature of social organizations and, interestingly enough, the significant role of social competition. Up to this point, sociologists had spent little time dealing with competition and the conflict which develops from this form of human behavior. Drawing from his belief in the central importance of the primary group and its key values of love, ambition, and loyalty, Cooley proposed that much of social conflict emerged from within the matrix of these key primary group values producing within the social institutions generated by these primary groups such values as impersonal ideologies such as progress and, he courageously suggested, even Protestantism. Societal efforts to manage its stability -- political and economic as well as social -- find that the balancing of primary and institutional values constitutes the focus of their struggle.

Three fundamental theories Cooley developed to deal with the emergence of human society. The interplay between the subjective mental processes of individuals and the emergence of social processes of interaction was a balancing of the one-to-the-many, of individuals to societies, in which neither the person nor society could exist and thrive without the other. Furthermore, the dynamics of social interaction must necessarily allow for, indeed, even account for states of chaos in the world as "natural phenomenon" which by their very existence creates an opportunity for society to develop "adaptive innovation" techniques to account for and respond to such natural occurrences. Finally, there is the indispensable necessity of providing society with the capacity to maintain and perpetuate an "informed moral control" over such natural occurrences which offer a framework for confidence in dealing with such phenomenon in the future. These three constructs addressing the human dilemmas of daily life, namely, the interplay between the individual and the social group, the dynamics of interpretive control over chaos in the world, and a moral code which can stand the test of time, Cooley believed were necessary for society's survival.

No one concept or theory can or should characterize a major thinker in any field of research and study. Freud is not synonymous with the "id" nor is Maslow with the "hierarchy of needs" or even Einstein with "relativity." Yet, there are key concepts associated with great thinkers which highlight their creativity. Such is the case with Cooley's "looking-glass self." Cooley believed that neither the individual nor society can be thought of as a concept within itself, defined and functioning within its own exclusive parameters. Rather, both terms can only take on reality when used in consort with the other, namely, individuals only exist within the context of society and society can only exist in the presence of individuals. This matrix Cooley chose to call a "mental-social complex" and the term most descriptive of this complex interplay between individual and society he called the "looking-glass self." An eventual refinement of this concept he called "empathic introspection" in which an individual imagines how he appears to others and, by extension, Cooley suggested this imaginative function has macro-sociological implications as well.

Developed in his 1902 book, *Human Nature and the Social Order,"* Cooley suggested that this looking-glass self-consisted of three elements, viz., (1) the imagination of our appearance to the other person, (2) the imagination of one's judgment or assessment of that appearance, and (3) and a responding sense of personal worth or feeling, whether positive or negative. Fully aware of his debt to Herbert Spencer's notion of the interplay between society and the individual, Cooley expanded this idea based on his conviction that the individual and society are linked and inseparable phenomena. Because of this intrinsic interdependence, individuals cannot have a sense of self in the absence of a social matrix of interaction in society. "The social origin of his life comes by the pathway of intercourse with other persons" is the simple way Cooley describes this relationship. There is no self-identity for the individual in the absence of a social network within which self-emergences. Harry Stack Sullivan has shown us how the absence of this interpersonal relationship leads to mental illness. Durkheim was, at the same time as Cooley, suggesting in his own study of suicide that there is, however, a danger of "over identity" with the social matrix at the expense of self-identity. This debate as to emphasis and over emphasis is still going on within sociological theory today. For our purposes, the relevance of Cooley's emphasis upon the dynamic interaction between the individual and the social matrix within which maturation occurs is crucial to our understanding of the dangers of things going wrong in this process such that the self is damaged and life's prospects are diminished.

Fully aware that he was expanding the nature and application of William James' idea of self to also incorporate the capacity of the individual for self-reflection on his own personal behavior within the matrix of society, Cooley was eager to emphasize, in keeping with the expanding school of social psychology, that other people's assessment of the individual results in changes within the self-image of the individual himself. Using the analogy of biological evolution employed by Herbert Spencer, Cooley was insistent upon the continuous interrelationship of social processes and that the interplay between the individual and the social matrix was crucial to both personality development and social stability and cohesion.

Openly sensitive to the Marxian contention that the individual is defined by the work he does, Cooley pointed out that "Our life is all one human whole, and if we are to have any real knowledge of it we must see it as such. If we cut it up it dies in the process." This statement could have as easily been made by Sullivan who summed up his own assessment of the human condition with this aphorism: "We are all of us simply more human than otherwise."

While openly drawing from Spencer, Darwin, and Freud, Cooley chose to concentrate his analytical skills and theories on the interplay between the individual and society, leaving considerations of the environment to others, including to George Herbert Mead. As with all social theorists, personal history clearly played a role in Cooley's theoretical development for when he emphasized the point that the self grows within the context of social relations, he could not help but refer implicitly to the complex and unfulfilling relationship he had with his father. Similar to Marx's emphasis upon personal identity with one's work within the social matrix of personal development, Cooley emphasized the central importance of human interaction for such development with Sullivan later showing us how failure in interpersonal relationships leads to a diminishment of personality growth and constitutes the origins of much mental illness in society. As we have already seen, Cooley drew freely from the work of William James and found himself in a philosophical tussle with Descartes over the Cartesian notion of the disconnectedness between the knowing and thinking subject of the individual and the external social and physical world. The social world, for Cooley, constituted an integral and inseparable component of the individual's own mind and sense of self. Cooley sought to remove the conceptual block which Descartes had set up between the individual and society, between the subjective and the objective experience of social being. Cooley was keen to emphasize their inseparable nature when he said, "A separate individual is an abstraction unknown to experience, and so likewise is society when regarded as something apart from individuals." Cooley was adamant in his contention that the individual's self-notion or self-image grows out of and evolves naturally within the social matrix of interpersonal relationships. "There is no sense of 'I'," he explained, "without its correlative sense of you, or he, or they."

When speaking of society specifically, Cooley was keen to

emphasize its holistic nature, not something easily separated out from human experience, dissected into various component parts for individualized analysis. Society, according to Cooley, "is an interweaving and interworking of mental selves." Society as a concept and as an experience occurs by virtue of the internalization of the idea of society within the individual's own mind, his psyche. It becomes a reality in the process of integration with human experience, human interaction, human reflectivity merging these experiences within the social matrix of society.

Cooley's insistence upon the individual and society constituting a single holistic organism of interaction was promoted within the context of his severe criticism of American society's overemphasis upon individuality at the expense of social cohesion. He suggested that the belief in the primacy of the individual versus society is so strong that Americans (and he included the English as well) have difficulty imagining a social cohesiveness wherein the individual is experienced as a central part of society without dominating social values in the process. Society is an organic whole such that, says Cooley, "our life is all one human whole, and if we are to have any real knowledge of it we must see it as such. If we cut it up it dies in the process."

Within this context, George Herbert Mead, Cooley's friend and colleague, was to critique Cooley's overemphasis upon what was thought of as the "mentalistic view of the formation of the self," fearing a drift into a kind of depth psychology outside the purview of sound sociological theory and practice. Nevertheless, Cooley was given ample credit along with James, Freud, and Durkheim for dislodging the Cartesian bifurcation of mind and world once and for all among social and behavioral scientists. Cooley's developed notion of the relationship between the individual and society, the self and others, constitutes such a convincingly holistic approach to human development that sociologists and psychologists alike can focus upon the emergence of personality within the matrix of self and society, of mind and social reality. And, given the nature of this holistic approach to man and society, it is understandable that Cooley would value as healthy and productive the presence of conflicts within society. Conflicts are a normal product of a healthy give and take between the individual and the social structure, between the primary group and the social institutions of a democratic society. Democracy, for Cooley, is a healthy mode of governance seeking a moral cohesiveness and ethical unity through the employment of social forces implicit in public opinion rather than in institutional suppression and governmental oppression. Democracy is the natural expression of a healthy configuration of self and society, of individual and social groupings, all tending towards a positive and constructive cohesiveness of collegiality.

SELECTED PRIMARY SOURCES OF CHARLES HORTON COOLEY

1891: *The Social Significance of Street Railways,* Publications of the American Economic Association 6, 71-73.

1894: *Competition and Organization,* Publications of the Michigan Political Science Association 1, 33-45.

1894: *The Theory of Transportation,* Baltimore: Publications of the American Economic Association 9.

1896: *Nature versus Nurture' in the Making of Social Careers,* Proceedings of the 23rd Conference of Charities and Corrections: 399-405.

1897: *Genius, Fame and the Comparison of Races,* Philadelphia: Annals of the American Academy of Political and Social Science 9, 1-42.

1897: *The Process of Social Change,* Political Science Quarterly 12, 63-81.

1899: *Personal Competition: Its Place in the Social Order and the Effect upon Individuals; with Some Considerations on Success,* Economic Studies 4.

1902: *Human Nature and the Social Order,* New York: Charles Scribner's Sons, revised 1922.

1902: *The Decrease of Rural Population in the Southern Peninsula of Michigan,* Publications of the Michigan Political Science Association 4, 28-37.

1904: *Discussion of Franklin H. Giddings', A Theory of Social Causation,* Publications of the American Economic Association, Third Series, 5, 426-431.

1907: *Social Consciousness*, Publications of the American Sociological Society 1, 97-109.

1907: *Social Consciousness*, American Journal of Sociology 12, 675-687 Previously published as above.

1908: *A Study of the Early Use of Self-Words by a Child*, Psychological Review 15, 339-357.

1909: *Social Organization: a Study of the Larger Mind*, New York: Charles Scribner's Sons.

1909: *Builder of Democracy*, Survey, 210-213.

1912: *Discussion of Simon Patten's The Background of Economic Theories*, Publications of the American Sociological Society 7, 132 .

1912: *Valuation as a Social Process*, Psychological Bulletin 9, Also published as part of Social Process .

1913: *The Institutional Character of Pecuniary Valuation*, American Journal of Sociology 18, 543-555. Also published as part of Social Process .

1913: *The Sphere of Pecuniary Valuation*, American Journal of Sociology 19, 188-203. Also published as part of *Social Process* .

1913: *The Progress of Pecuniary Valuation*, Quarterly Journal of Economics 30, 1-21. Also published as part of *Social Process* .

1916: *Builder of Democracy*, Survey 36, 116.

1917: *Social Control in International Relations*, Publications of the American Sociological Society 12, 207-216.

1918: *Social Process*, New York: Charles Scribner's Sons .

1918: *A Primary Culture for Democracy*, Publications of the American Sociological Society 13, 1-10.

1918: *Political Economy and Social Process, Journal of Political Economy 25*, 366-374.

1920: *Reflections Upon the Sociology of Herbert Spencer*, American Journal of Sociology 26, 129-145.

1924: *Now and Then*, Journal of Applied Sociology 8, 259-262.

1926: *The Roots of Social Knowledge*, American Journal of Sociology 32, 59-79.

1926: *Heredity or Environment*, Journal of Applied Sociology 10, 303-307 .

1927: *Life and the Student*, New York: Charles Scribner's Sons

1928: *Case Study of Small Institutions as a Method of Research*, Publications of the American Sociological Society 22, 123-132.

1928: *Sumner and Methodology*, Sociology and Social Research 12, 303-306.

1929: *The Life-Study Method as Applied to Rural Social Research*, Publications of the American Sociological Society 23, 248-254.

1930: *The Development of Sociology at Michigan.* pp. 3–14 in *Sociological Theory and Research, being Selected papers of Charles Horton Cooley*, edited by Robert Cooley Angell, New York: Henry Holt .

1930: *Sociological Theory and Social Research*, New York: Henry Holt .

1933: *Introductory Sociology*, with Robert C Angell and Lowell J Carr, New York: Charles Scribner's Sons.

CHAPTER SEVEN

MEAD and the Social Self

George Herbert Mead was an influential leader in philosophical pragmatism and sociological social psychology and, following his death, his students edited four volumes from his social psychology lectures at the University of Chicago with his additional notes and selected but unpublished papers under the general editorship of Arthur E. Murphy, Charles W. Morris, and Merritt H. Moore. These four volumes, if nothing else of his prolific writings of over 100 scholarly articles had never seen the light of day, would have assured Mead's place in sociological history. Spaced posthumously over an eight-year period every two years, they were *The Philosophy of the Present (1932), Mind, Self, and Society (1934), Movements of Thought in the Nineteenth Century (1936)*, and *The Philosophy of the Act (1938)*. Mead always contended that the human mind, the self, perception, and linguistic symbolization could only be understood within the context of society and social interaction. His emphasis upon sociological processes and concerns within the context of psychological phenomena drew heavily from his colleague, Charles Horton Cooley, with whom he worked at the University of Michigan prior to going to the University of Chicago. Cooley, discussed in the previous chapter, offered to Mead an understanding of the self as a looking glass which reflects the social relations of others, and that influence had a profound effect upon Mead's own development of social psychology.

George Herbert Mead was born in South Hadley, Massachusetts, on February 27, 1863, during the heat of the Civil War, but unlike his forerunner in American sociology, William Graham Sumner, he missed the profound influence that the war had upon the reconstruction of social class and economics at the end of the 19th century. Not social turmoil but social stability constituted the matrix within which he developed his system of social analysis called social psychology. Raised in a Protestant, middle class family with both parents and an older sister, he enjoyed the stability of a Congregationalist pastor's home with a heritage of New England farmers and clergymen reaching generations back in time. His father became a professor of music at Oberlin College's theological seminary in Ohio where his mother also held a professorship. Eventually, she became the president of Mount Holyoke College in South Hadley, Massachusetts. In 1890 she was presented with an honorary A.M. degree from Oberlin, and in 1900 Smith College granted her an honorary L.H.D. degree. Mead himself was a graduate of Oberlin College, having entered at the age of sixteen, and upon graduation taught school briefly following which he worked for three years as a surveyor for the Wisconsin Central Rail Road Company. While working for the railroad during these three years as a surveyor, he also worked as a tutor in the winter months while springs and summers were involved in laying the first line from Minneapolis to Moose-Jaw, Canada. He was a good worker with skills requiring precision which resulted in his being appointed engineer-in-charge at the tender age of twenty.

Not completely satisfied with surveying work and desiring strongly to increase his knowledge required for a university teaching career to which he was quite naturally drawn, given both parents being college professors, Mead entered Harvard University in 1887 with plans to pursue both philosophy and psychology under the tutelage of Josiah Royce and William James, each internationally acclaimed scholars, Royce in philosophy and James in psychology. While Mead was completing his master's degree in philosophy, which he received in 1888, he was the personal tutor of the children of William James, with whom he failed to become close personally, preferring Royce as the focus of his intellectual interests. As was common at the time, upon completing his graduate studies at Harvard University, Mead journeyed to Leipzig, Germany, to work specifically with Wilhelm Wundt (a teacher of Sigmund Freud, among many others) where he developed the concept of "the gesture" which was to play a major role in the development of his social psychological theories of interpersonal relations.

Three years after graduating from Harvard and upon his return from Germany, Mead married the sister of a college classmate, Helen Kingsbury Castle. Mead never completed his doctoral thesis at Harvard but, owing to his growing reputation and support from James and others, he secured a teaching post at the

University of Michigan the year of his marriage. Mead's friendship and collegial working relations at Michigan, namely, with Charles Horton Cooley and John Dewey, proved to be major influences in the development of his sociological theories of personal relationships. And, three years later when Dewey moved to the University of Chicago to establish a department of philosophy in which psychology was to have a major place, Mead went with him where he taught the remainder of his life, eventually becoming the chairman of the department of philosophy while teaching sociology and social psychology courses. Influenced but not controlled by Dewey's theory of pragmatism, Mead gradually shifted his interests and developed his own theories of mind, self and society which proved his making as a leading voice in American sociology and psychology. Like Sumner, Mead was not a disengaged social theorist but rather was actively involved in Chicago politics and its social life and public affairs including major work for the City Club of Chicago in the areas of public concern for the poor and unemployed. Social science, he contended, must and should be involved in dealing with social problems and must play a role in public policy. He demonstrated how that might be done with his work in research dealing with the settlement houses of Chicago. Mead died of heart failure on April 26, 1931, at the age of 68.

The fundamental infrastructure of Mead's system of social analysis rested upon his commitment to pragmatism which grew out of the influence of James during his Harvard years. This wide-ranging philosophical perspective profoundly influenced Mead and the development of what became a major school of sociological analysis, namely, *symbolic interaction*. The development of the self is a major focus of philosophical pragmatism based upon the objective reality of the world as experienced within the social matrix of human relationships. Mead once said that "the individual mind can exist only in relation to other minds with shared meanings." This thread will follow throughout his work and will eventuate into the profoundly important interpersonal psychotherapy school developed by a colleague of his, namely, Harry Stack Sullivan, the recognized father of modern American psychiatry. The relevance of Mead's contribution to the philosophical underpinnings of the self-concept cannot be over emphasized given that the inevitabilities of a damaged self and diminished life occurs when the child's best interest is not served in the teaching of personal interactional social skills.

Without a self-consciously developed philosophical perspective and orientation, social theory was necessarily adrift and no one was more aware of that fact than Mead. His attraction to Royce and James at Harvard centered around his dual interest in philosophy and psychology and by embracing pragmatism as his philosophical orientation and perspective, Mead positioned himself to make a major contribution in both social and psychological theory. Four essential characteristics of pragmatism should be noted here as they bore heavily upon Mead's sophistication as a social theorist. First, for the pragmatist reality is a human creation rather than an external reality to be objectively encountered. What we experience as real is consciously created within the human mind and social matrix of experience. Second, remembered knowledge gained from personal experience constitutes the basis upon which individuals act toward the future and when a thing works, it is retained as real, and when it fails, it is discarded as useless, i.e., meaningless. Thirdly, objective reality is based upon those things which work, which serve effectively the need of the individual. "If it works, it is good; if it doesn't, it isn't." Finally, pragmatism suggests that to understand human action is to understand what individuals actually do because their behavior or action indicates their reality. This perspective is central to an understanding of the practice of psychotherapy for the behavioral matrix of the troubled patient can be traced to the psychopathology of the damaged self resulting in a diminished life.

Mead's pragmatism constituted the philosophical foundation upon which his major contribution in social analysis was based. Symbolic interaction drew heavily from pragmatism and the following ideas are the direct product of that relationship. First, symbolic interaction focuses upon the interaction between the individual actor and the world as experienced. Second, this interactive relationship between the individual and the world, between the "actor" and "objective reality" is dynamic rather than static, it is a process rather than a given. Thirdly, this interactive process constitutes the basis upon which the individual is able to interpret the social world, to make sense of human relationships. Given this reality, social psychologists have demonstrated that interactive consciousness or self-awareness constitutes the validation of both mind and object, the individual and the observable reality of the world. Human action or behavior cannot therefore be separated from interaction for they are conjoined in their pragmatic reality. The final product of this system of analysis became known at the University of Chicago and then throughout the country as a school of thought called "symbolic interaction."

Mead's focus upon the relationship between the emergence of mind and self from within the matrix of human communication became known as social behaviorism, a broadly defined area (not really a school) of research which proved to be the context within which symbolic interaction among sociologists emerged. His book, now a classic in the field, entitled *Mind, Self and Society*, was the outgrowth of his researches. The concept of how the human mind and the self evolved from within the social matrix of human communication could trace its initial impetus back to Herbert Spencer and then subsequently to William Graham Sumner. The emphasis upon the biological evolution of human consciousness linked strongly with this interest in the interaction between mind and self appearing within the framework of society. Hegel's dialectic constituted a backdrop to Mead and Dewey (Mead having moved somewhat away from James at this point) who based their philosophical concepts upon the dynamics of action and reality. Mead, with Dewey, argued that human action is based upon the criterion of truth as evidenced and validated through interactive communication with other individuals. The self evolves through the process of interactive communication with others and within interpersonal relationships, the self is either stifled or fails to appear. Harry Stack Sullivan will expand this exponentially in his interpersonal psychotherapy which we will later consider in depth. It is within this contextual framework of the developing self, when damaged, produces mental disorders.

The brilliance of Mead's construction of an analytical mechanism for studying the mind and self in interrelationship centers upon his differing from the current wisdom of his day regarding brain function and human physiology as the behavioral matrix of the mind. The mind, Mead argued, is not merely a complex of ideographs ponderously meandering through cellular paths producing random behaviors in a separated configuration of mind versus body. No, says Mead, for the emergence of the human is directly contingent upon the interaction between the human person – mind and self – and the social environment, namely, interpersonal relationships produce symbolic behavior expressive of individual action and thought. The human mind is then, says Mead, the individualized construct of the process of communication. This process of the emerging mind and self is predicated upon the utility of language, a linguistic imperative necessary for human relationships. Mind and thought cannot exist in the absence of language and language can only develop within the matrices of interpersonal communications between individuals. And mind, reasons Mead, is the direct product of this social interaction. In his classic, *Mind, Self and Society,* Mead points out that the human mind is then not simply reducible to the neurophysiology of the individual but emerges within the context of the "dynamic, ongoing social process" which characterizes human relationships in verbal communication.

Because Mead is insistent that the human mind emerges from the "social act" of interpersonal communication, this social act for Mead is then both a hermeneutical tool for social analysis and the indispensable ingredient in his theory of mind. His tripartite matrix of mind, self, and society constitutes a philosophy of the act involving a social process of interpersonal relationships between individuals similar to his theory of knowledge being the experiential encounter of the individual with the objective environment. The mind as well as the self, Mead explains, can only emerge within the context of social action radiating from interpersonal communication. What that relationship is negative or demented within the social context of the growing child, damage to the self is almost inevitable.

In the tradition of Weber and staying true to his pragmatism and social behaviorism, Mead is keen to emphasize that the core of his social theory centers around the human "act," an intentional effort at interpersonal communication wherein the individual engages with both his environment and other individuals within society. His analysis of the act is a key ingredient in his social psychology and the emergence of symbolic interaction. Mead, drawing from his relationships at the University of Chicago with other behavioral scientists, especially anthropologists, and in consort with his friendship with the psychiatrist, Harry Stack Sullivan, engaged in a carefully constructed minute delineation of the meaning and nature of the social act. The initial characteristic and presenting feature of the social act is the social "gesture." Gestures are preliminary and preparatory movements that enable individuals to become aware of the intentionality of the other in a relationship. Fundamentally elementary to the act is its conversational nature wherein an initial gesture on the part of one person elicits a responding gesture from the second individual which, in turn, precipitates a counter response from the initial gesture of the first person. Gestures themselves are without actual content as such and their meaning and, therefore, value depend solely upon the knowledge of the communicating individuals of the set of gestures employed in interaction. When this knowledge exists, then the symbols become significant to communication. Significant symbols are those gestures to which both communicating parties attribute the same meaning and value. This interaction constitutes what Mead considers to be meaningful communication and, therefore, all meaningful human interaction is based upon this "action-nexus," such that all human perceptions are couched in an action-based understanding.

Mead's social psychology and its subsequent product, symbolic interaction, opposed the notion promoted by the positivists that the individual is merely a product of society. Rather, Mead would have us understand that the "self" emerges within the matrix of interpersonal communication and that our movement from being objectified by others to becoming subjects in interaction constitutes the environment wherein humanity and individuality concurrently emerge. First, the individual is an object to others, then becomes an object to himself by taking the others' objectified perception of the self. It is our verbal communication skills, our language, which allows us to objectify ourselves in the same manner as we objectify others when we speak of "me" and "them." In the social act, therefore, we learn to see ourselves as others see us. Owing to this skill of self-objectification, we learn to engage in what Mead calls "position exchange," that is, we can imagine ourselves from the point of view of others and can imagine ourselves being someone else as well. Children's games constitute an early and meaningful experiment with and experience of this role playing and position exchange. It is here that the child's self-concept emerges wherein each component – self-esteem, self-image, ideal self – either is nurtured into a fully functioning and positive life or an injured and diminished life.

Mead has very carefully refined his notion of the "social act" so as to go beyond merely "the act" of John Dewey and the pragmatists. For Mead, the social act is not merely a human action but a social event. This social act allows the individual to take the perspective of the others in the interaction and, thus, see himself as others see him. This taking the perspective of others is not only applicable in interpersonal relationships but in relationship to the external world, our physical environment, so that we learn through the use of language and non-verbal communication skills which enhance our capacity to see things as our peers see them. This constitutes a community of identity, facilitating a profound sensitivity to the subtleties of interactional relationships, namely, what Mead called "reading one another."

Mead's obsession was in the study of the mind, not the brain, that complex phenomena wherein the human person becomes self-consciously aware of himself and wherein he develops a capacity, both linguistically and non-verbally, to communicate information and to share interpersonal dynamics with other people. The self and the mind work together, he tells us, in a social process, using gestures as meaning symbols. This grid of meaning gestures allows for genuine understanding of meaning and purpose between individuals in interpersonal communication. For Mead, the "I" and the "Me" constitute the ingredients required for this symbolic communication to occur and have meaning. The "Me" is the social self, he explains, and the "I" is the response the individual has to the "Me." The "I" is the responder to others, Mead explains, while the "Me" is the organized set of attitudes of others which the "I" takes on as personal identity. The "Me" is how an individual imagines his peers think of him, whereas the "I" is the individual's response to that imagined self as viewed by others. Put simply, the "I" constitutes the self as the subject whereas the "me" is the self as the object. The "I" is the knower, in other words, and the "me" is the known. The profundity of this insight is in the formation of a theory of cognition developed by Mead in which the thinking process of the individual is the internalized dialogue between these two features of the human mind, the I and the Me. The sociological infrastructure of the human mind and society which have conspired in the production of the self is clearly explicated by Mead in this design. Self-reflective awareness is the product of this dialogue with one's self within the matrix of society.

Not simply play but the game played by children constitutes the matrix, explains Mead, within which the self becomes fully self-aware. Personality begins to take shape and emerge with the playing of games. Children begin to function in organized groups, learning where and how to function in consort with others sharing the same idea of goal and purpose, namely, the point of the game. This, Mead calls the awareness of "the generalized other," is a central concept in Mead's social psychology and a key ingredient in symbolic interaction. This "generalized other" grows out of the child's understanding of the activities of others within the framework of a mutually agreed upon agenda, a corporate direction with a shared goal. By identifying this generalized other, the child develops the capacity to understand what is expected of him, what others are expected to do, and what the corporate outcome of cooperation is to be. In failed maturation situations, the child's personality is damaged and the life prospects are diminished due to the inability of the child to make the subtle yet crucial identifications and distinctions in relational interactions.

The pragmatism implicit in Mead's social psychology is predicated upon a perception of the human person and society itself as essentially rational, self-conscious, and self-reflectively mindful of the human quest for meaning and purpose in life. He was understandably a strong proponent, like Spencer and Sumner before him, of human freedom, but a freedom wherein ambivalence was ever present in the form of both social and antisocial human impulses found throughout the human community. This ambivalence characterizes all human organizations, Mead argued, and is paralleled within the behavioral matrix of the individual human as well. Conflict is inevitable, he noted, even within highly sophisticated social matrices and it is working in and through these conflicts, brought on by conflicting self-images, which constitutes the nature of the human struggle for individual and social survival. Joining with Spencer and in the company of Sumner, Mead would have us know that the ideal society is one in which the quest for perfection is ever present with all efforts being expended to continually nurture the evolutionary trajectory towards a fully functioning society based upon a self-actualized constituency of fulfilled individuals. There is always implicit within an emerging self-actualizing society a sense of "revolution," a revolution based on the recognition that change is necessary for survival and that this revolutionary change may and can occur within a democratic process of legislation and amendment, without the need for war and violence, producing what Mead chose to call "an open society of open selves."

From the beginning of his interest and passion for philosophy and psychology which led him to pursue graduate study at Harvard with Royce and James, Mead was insistent that the focus of his life's work was the study of behavior within the social matrix of human interaction and communication, the study of human relationships combined within the tripartite framework of *mind, self, and society.* It is no wonder that his major work bore this title and his students, recognizing this passion of his for a particularly characteristic sociological and psychological perspective on human relationships, were led to edit this collection of his essays under the subtitle of "From the Standpoint of a Social Behaviorist." Mead was eager to differentiate and distance himself from other behavioral scientists such as John Watson and B. F. Skinner who were both locked into a positivistic behaviorism which Mead felt diminished to inconsequential importance the human dynamics of social behavior. Mead was convinced of the uniqueness of the human mind and its emergence within the context of social interaction. The human mind could not fairly be reduced merely to behavioral responses to external stimuli. Evidence of this uniqueness, Mead believed, was most explicitly demonstrated in the linguistic acuity of the human person.

In opposition to deterministic behaviorism, Mead was eager to demonstrate empirically that the nature of human behavior was creatively dynamic and interactive within the interplay between the mind and the social environment. The role of contemplation, for example, Mead believed was key to the development of an individual's capacity to decipher and interpret social experience. Rather than dismissing this interest as too subjective and devoid of empirical verification as did the behaviorists, Mead believed that an individual's actions elicit the same responses in others by virtue of a shared symbolic reality. And, this being the case, social behavior and human interaction are subjects for legitimate scientific study. Mead's fascination with the concept of mind within this tripartite constellation of mind, self, and society was based on his firm belief that mind is in reality a social phenomenon which develops within the interactional process of social relationships, with, as he put it, "the empirical matrix of social interactions." The human mind is the product of this interactive process emerging out of and from within the utility of significant symbolic configurations embodied in human communication. The mind is developed as a process of systemic interaction within oneself and in communication with others. Symbols, then, dominate this emergent process of mind development for the most distinctive symbolic communication is language itself. As Mead put it, "out of language emerges the field of mind." Clearly, the child who is the victim of limited verbal communication with parents inevitably suffers psychic damage such that mental acuity is stifled and the self-concept is damaged.

Because, Mead said, the mind is a process rather than a mere product means that human consciousness is more than a mere manifestation of behavioral responses initiated by physiological stimuli. The mind is a dynamic and creative composite of self-reflective interactional forces emerging and changing with the increase in social and environmental experiences. Rather than a container into which data is stored, the mind is a discriminating enterprise of categorizing and interpreting signals and situational data being presented to it. It is the "self," Mead points out, which emerges within the social matrix of interactional experience. The self is aware of itself and constitutes a social structuring of receptivity to human community. The self of the individual is an evolving process of awakening, discriminating, and initiating of experiences which nurture the communication skills of the individual within the social arena. Self-consciousness is the result of this interactive relationship between self and society and that awareness is embodied in the functioning of the human mind. Grasping the dynamics of symbolic communication, the self is able to raise the question and reply to it, "Who am I?" Herein lies the key to the self-concept's development of the child's self-image and self-esteem.

As we have noted earlier, the development of the self

necessitates the capacity of the individual to take the role of the other, to imagine who the other is through a selective analysis of symbol usage in interpersonal communication. This role-taking is possible only because of our linguistic capacity and our interpretive skills at symbol reading. Role-taking is facilitated by the emergence of a self continually in the process of maturing. This maturation process is dependent, Mead suggests, on three phases, namely, a period of imitation prior to understanding the behavior being copied, the play-acting world of the child, and finally the emergence of a capacity to imagine what the other is thinking, doing, and expecting, called by Mead "the generalized other." Whereas playing among the very young simply means doing what others are doing, the gradual appearance of the "pretend" stage, when children often use the term "play like," there is a gradual but profound shifting from merely copying to taking on the role of the other, what eventuates in a movement from play to gamesmanship. In the game, rather than in play, the child learns to see himself and others from various perspectives and therein arises a consciousness of the self -- of both "I" and "Me" -- in a manner not previously experienced. In the process of this capacity to imagine the perspective of others, the individual matures into a socialized being grasping the meaning and use of symbolic interaction as the central mechanism for social living.

As we have seen, for Mead the "I" emerges in consort with the child's development of an identity "in response to the attitudes of others" while the "Me" emerges when the child has the capacity to assume the "organized set of attitudes of others." To play with others is one thing, but to engage in playing a game is quite indicative of a maturation of a consciousness of the self. In Mead's world, society is the extension of the "organized self" which comes with interactive communication skill development. Society, for Mead, is essentially common responses grounded in shared symbols of individuals who feel themselves integrated within a social matrix of commonality of meaning and purpose in life. Sounding more like Freud than one might expect at this juncture, Mead would have us know that both the self and society are products of the mind. This free, active and unique self is monitored and controlled by a corporate synthesis of wishes, rules and roles of others comprising society. But, eventually and inevitably, the ideal society evolves as an interacting order of self and others such that society's primary role is not simply or merely behavioral control of the masses but also functions to facilitate the emergence of a dynamically creative and positive interplay between self and society. From within this coagulating cauldron of self-concept, self-image, and self-esteem emerges the child's ideal self against which he perpetually judges and asses his behavior in society.

Though often overlooked or purposefully sidestepped, it is important for us to note here that the core of Mead's social psychology has much in common with Freudian psychoanalytic theories of personality formation and development and particularly as further advanced in altered form by the psychiatrist Harry Stack Sullivan, a colleague of Mead at Chicago. Personality in this trajectory of thought arises and develops from the inter-personalization of the role of other people, that is, interpersonal relationships constitute the base and core of personality development. Sullivan suggested that virtually all psychogenic mental illness and disorders derive from a failure of the personality to develop in childhood owing to a breakdown in interpersonal relations. When individuals are stifled in the development of interpersonal skills due to a breakdown in communication or a failure of the social environment to produce constructive and positive feedback relationships, mental illness develops. Mead believed that social psychology could play a role in further understanding this reality and offer some guidelines for improvement in the mental health of society through the application of social theories emerging from within symbolic interaction.

Mead explained that social psychology "studies the activity or behavior of the individual as it lies within the social process. The behavior of an individual can," he argued, "be understood only in terms of the behavior of the whole social group of which he is a member." No self exists without society according to Mead, and he was joined in this belief by Freud and Sullivan and the psychoanalytical school of thought at the time. No self, no consciousness of the self, and no interpersonal communication can exist without the social matrix provided by society. Furthermore, society, in turn, cannot exist in the absence of an on-going communication among individuals sharing a symbolic set of meanings relevant to the stability and perpetuity of that social grouping, that is, their society. Mead believed that consciousness can only be understood in terms of a "thought-stream" which develops within the dynamic relationship matrix existing between an individual and the social and physical environment. Arguing against the positivists and behaviorists of the time, Mead contended that mental activity cannot be merely reduced to biological reflexes nor can it be understood merely in terms of individualized concepts of the ego as Descartes would have us believe. Human experience is not, says Mead, first personal and then social, but rather every individual is perpetually involved in a succession of interactions with others for, says he, consciousness is not static but rather a process and continues its emergence within the matrix of individual and social interaction.

Mead believed that the historical emergence of society is always characterized by novelty and the unpredictability of events fostered by the workings of human consciousness. Mead was convinced that social change embraced an identifiable trajectory and "directionality" towards a more positive, fuller, more complete and near perfect social reality. Employing the notion of a "universal society" as explicated in the closing essay of his classic work, *Mind, Self and Society,* Cooley explored somewhat romantically the notion of a society realizing its potential for a fully realized world unity. In such a society, he mused, every person would be cooperatively involved with all others thereby forming a collectivity of fulfilled realization of the human spirit's greatest achievement of collaboration. There is, Mead argued, a destiny for humanity, an emergent goal towards which a grand union of human effort will be, can be, must be, realized. In such a romanticized society, the damaged self would not exist for the self-concept within every individual would inevitably be positive assuring no injured life.

There is a detectable harmony of thought between the dialectical world of Hegel and the evolutionary biology of Darwin, Mead believed, for whereas Hegel stressed the fact that reality is in a constant process of evolutionary emergence, Darwin described life as an evolutionary process giving rise to emerging new forms of structural variations offering new *speciel* possibilities for the biosphere. Neither Hegel nor Darwin, contended Mead, were determinists as they both identified that undetermined element within evolutionary processes wherein the new and creative expressions of possibilities for the future find expression. The flexibility of life is owned and validated by Darwinian evolutionary biology in which species are not immutable but fraught with possibilities of variation. Whereas Darwin treated natural selection and the survival of the fittest as biological givens, Mead's dialectic of the self and society, the "I" and the "Me," mediated by the functioning consciousness of the human mind, found a sympathetic parallel. Mead's commitment to adaptation of the individual within the social matrix of human society was not just a passing notion but constituted a major focus of his social psychology, and the debt to Darwinian evolutionary biology is self-evident. For Mead, the human mind, the self, and society were all adaptive mechanisms which nurtured the perpetuation of life itself. With Darwin, Mead believed in on-going adaptation and strategic adjustments to the social environment needed for the survival of the individual as well as society.

We cannot conclude this discussion of Mead without giving some passing tribute to the sociologist who had the greatest influence on Mead's system of thought. Certainly Royce, James, Hegel, Freud and Darwin have shown their rightful place in Mead's developmental theories of personality, the self, the mind, and society but no one became as crucial to Mead's mature development as did Charles Horton Cooley, his colleague at the University of Michigan when they were both young and aspiring novices. Cooley's now famous idea of the "looking-glass self" set the trajectory to Mead's own thought in the development of personality, the self, and social relations. Cooley's emphasis upon the central role of self-conceptions as emergent phenomena without the matrix of interpersonal relationships led Mead to see that the self was an emergent phenomena within social activity. Cooley's study of the process of socialization whereby the self appears within the individual's maturation process set the stage for Mead's further study of that reality. Mead was the first to acknowledge his indebtedness to Cooley and he did so without restraint in his now famous 1929 essay, "Cooley's Contribution to American Thought." From Spencer to Sumner to Cooley to Mead is a trajectory of increasingly mature understanding of the self's emergence and, from a psychopathology perspective, the profound relevance of this accelerating understanding relevant to psychotherapeutic treatment of the damaged self.

SELECTED PRIMARY SOURCES OF GEORGE HERBERT MEAD

In a career spanning more than 40 years, Mead wrote almost constantly and published numerous articles and book reviews in both philosophy and psychology. However, he never published a book. Following his death, several of his students put together and edited four volumes from records of Mead's social psychology course at the University of Chicago, his lecture notes, and his numerous unpublished papers. The four volumes are:

The Philosophy of the Present (1932), edited by Arthur E. Murphy.

Mind, Self, and Society (1934), edited by Charles W. Morris.

Movements of Thought in the Nineteenth Century (1936), edited by Merritt H. Moore.

The Philosophy of the Act (1938).

CHAPTER EIGHT

ADLER and the Function of the Inferiority Complex in Personality Development

Adler's humanistic theory of personality was in direct opposition to Freud's conception of human nature. Characteristics such as altruism, humanitarianism, cooperation, creativity, uniqueness, and awareness utilized by Adlerian psychology flew in the face of Freud's materialistic, instinctually driven, unconsciously motivated person. Whereas the Freudians were scandalized by the apparent naïve optimism about the human person, Adler's hopefulness toward the future range clear in the public eye. Adler's system had arrived in America at a time when it was most welcome.

Adler was concerned primarily with the fundamental goal in an individual's life, that for which a person strives and results in a kind of consistency of personality, a unity of purpose and person. Even before he left Freudian psychoanalysis behind, he had come to the conclusion that "aggression" rather than "sexuality" was the driving force to the human person seeking fulfillment. These aggressive impulses of the human person result in what became known as the "will to power." A child of the time, Adler believed that masculinity was a sign of strength; femininity a sign of weakness. He developed a concept out of this called the "masculine protest" which simply meant that men develop a behavioral mode of response to life's situations called "overcompensation." This is the standard mode of operation when either a man or woman feels helpless or inferior or inadequate. This will to power notion was given up in deference to a more sophisticated concept of the "striving for superiority." From aggression to power to superiority, Individual Psychology evolved into a more refined system of analysis. Not social distinction, leadership, or even a pre-eminent position in society, superiority for Adler in this analytical scheme simply means an endemic drive towards perfection, the "great upward drive" as he called it which characterizes every person, healthy or ill. "I began to see clearly in every psychological phenomenon the striving for superiority" Adler said. "It lies at the root of all solutions of life's problems and is manifested in the way in which we meet these problems." The drive is innate to the human animal.

What we have said about Freud's Vienna can likewise be said of Adler's Vienna as they were essentially contemporaries (Freud 1856-1939; Adler 1870-1937). And, they were both Jews and eventually physicians and psychotherapists. Adler's father, Leopold was born in 1835 in the Burgenland but at the time Leopold married Adler's mother, Pauline Beer, in 1866, they became residence of Pauline's hometown. The Beers were Czechoslovakian Jews from Moravia, not unlike Freud's family, and were by the time of the marriage of Leopold and Pauline successful business people operating the firm of Hermann Beer and Sons, dealing in bran, oats, and wheat. The first child of this marriage of Leopold and Pauline was Sigmund (1868) followed two years later by Alfred, born February 7, 1870, in the village of Rudolfsheim, a near suburb of Vienna.

Unlike the miserable days of Maslow's childhood, these were happy days for Adler as he says: "As far as I can look back, I was always surrounded by fiends and comrades, and for the most part, I was a well-loved playmate. This development began early and has never ceased. It is probably this feeling of solidarity with others that my understanding of the need for cooperation arose, a motive which has become the key to Individual Psychology." His outgoing and gregarious personality and the ease with which he made new friends he himself traced this ability back to his blissful days of youth. Yet and alas, he failed to maintain such friendships into adulthood.

The preference shown Adler's older brother, Sigmund, and the unhappy death and circumstances of Adler's little brother Rudolf both conspired, in his mind, to rouse an interest in medicine. Never religious and no identifiable interest in the religious side of Judaism, the Adlers deemed Judaism an encumbrance to their progress in society. Yet, little Alfred did find the Biblical stories a source of insight into human nature not unlike Freud's use of the Kabbala. Living in Leopoldstadt, the most Jewish district of Vienna, the Adlers were immersed in the Jewish culture from dawn to dusk throughout Alfred's childhood and adolescence. Being an eager assimilationist, Alfred Adler would eventually become Protestant, with little regrets to hear he tell it.

Adler's pursuit of a medical career was indicative of the aspirations of many modern Jews of the time. Dominated by his older and more outstanding brother, Adler later would suggest that he was, to use a formalized term later in his theories, "compensating" for physical weakness by achieving success in the profession of medicine. In the spring of 1888, he graduated from the Hernals *Gymnasium* and, at the age of eighteen, he was accepted into the University of Vienna's school of medicine. He completed the entire course of study in seven years, average for the time, taking only the minimum courses and examinations and passing with the lowest possible grades from the medical school and, interestingly enough, received no training in psychiatry.

Because of Adler's parentage, he held Hungarian citizenship and, therefore, in Austria the only medical experience available to him was working as a volunteer medical worker in the Viennese Poliklinik, a free medical hospital for working-class families. During these years of service and growing out of the experience in the public hospital, Adler became an enthusiastic socialist and a member of the Social Democratic Party. Because of the financial success of his older brother, Sigmund, the entire Adler clan lived better than most during these economically and politically troubling years.

In 1897, everything changed for Alder because he fell in love for the first, and only, time in his life with a Russian immigrant wife named Raissa Timofeivna Epstein. Alder never spoke nor wrote about how they met and the history of the relationship was forever veiled in mystery. She was born in Moscow in 1873 into an affluent Jewish family. Her mother died when Raissa was very young and her childhood was not happy. She attended the University of Zurich, the University of Moscow barring women from attending, studying biology, zoology, and aiming for a degree in the natural sciences.

At age twenty-seven and twenty-four respectively, Adler and Raissa were married on December 23, 1897, with a full complement of families on both sides in attendance in the city of Smolensk, Russia. Though she desperately missed her large family after the wedding when they returned to Vienna to Alder's medical practice, she gave birth the following year to their first child, Valentine Dina. In the meantime, Adler's medical practice and reputation was growing by leaps and bounds and he was already working on some theories of his own which included such formalized terms as *organ inferiority*, *compensation*, and *overcompensation* (about which more later).

At twenty-eight years of age, Adler published his first in what would be a long series of scholarly articles. It was a short monograph entitled, *Health Book for the Tailor Trade*, and reflected his passion for the working-class medical conditions, a concern which would characterize his entire professional career. During these years, domestic tranquility seemed to elude them as Adler had virtually no contact, by choice, with his two sisters and two brothers, and Raissa likewise had little family interaction. Yet, Adler's career continued to thrive and he continued to publish right along. Alder naturally came in contact with Freud as they both practiced medicine and psychiatry in Vienna and the history and complexity of that on-again off-again relationship we will only mention in passing later. Suffice it to say here that, at Freud's personal invitation, Adler was asked to join Freud's Wednesday Psychological Society as the youngest member of this small group of young psychiatrists and physicians.

In 1904, Adler published the most important article of his young career, an article that would set the stage for his climb to fame in Europe and America and a topic which would characterize the duration of his professional career. It appeared in *Aertzliche Standeszeitung*, entitled, "The Physician as Educator," with the overriding emphasis being upon the physician's role as "preventer" rather than "curer" of illness among children with special attention to their psychological health. That same year and without his wife, Alder and his daughters converted to Protestantism. Not an unusual occurrence at the time among Jews of his status in Vienna, he became a nominal Christian at best but they all celebrated Christmas enthusiastically. And, another bridged crossed and burned was the break with Freud, a long and tedious and never-to-be-clearly understood topic. Adler relied upon the "drive for assertion" rather than Freud's emphasis upon "sexual gratification" and, thus, since both were strong willed and strong minded, they broke at the same time Carl Jung was leaving as well. To counter Freud's Vienna Psychoanalytic Society, Adler founded in Vienna his own independent Society for Free Psychoanalytic Study. The break was clean and final and issued in the most productive period of Adler's professional life.

His domestic life seems to have settled down quietly and the recollections of his adult children confirm that impression. Emphatically opposed to physical punishment, both Adlers chose to explore deprivation as a punishment rather than hitting. All the while, he worked on with what he had chosen to formally label Individual Psychology, the Society publishing a new monograph series and him publishing his most important book to-date, namely, *Ueber den nervosen Charakter*, in 1912 and simultaneously in the United States as *The Neurotic Constitution.* Two years later, his colleagues launched with him their own journal, the *Journal for Individual Psychology* which set in motion the development of a whole school of psychotherapy called "Individual Psychology."

With the coming of World War I and the raging hostilities between Russia and the Austro-Hungarian Empire, the landscape seemed bleak in Europe and, naturally, Individual Psychology as a movement began to languish. In 1915 and after waiting for years for the appointment, Alder was finally being considered for an appointment as a Lecturer (without stipend) to the University of Vienna School of Medicine. But, where Freud had enjoyed for years a professorial appointment there, Adler was finally rejected even for this lowly honor. Because Europe (and it seemed the entire world) was falling apart with strife and hostilities, Adler argued that what was needed was "not more individualism" but what he called more "social feeling" (*Gemeinschaftsgefuhl*), meaning more compassion, altruism, and selflessness. He argued that social feeling was the infrastructural support of his newly developed Individual Psychology. In this notion, he was strongly supported by the American William Alanson White, founder of the White Institute of Psychiatry and Psychotherapy, and Harry Stack Sullivan who became a colleague. What struck a common cord with White and later Sullivan was Adler's contention that psychiatric disorders offered new evidence that "behind every neurosis is the existence of a weakling whose incapacity for adapting himself to the ideas of the majority calls forth an aggressive attitude taking on a neurotic form." This was particularly true of soldiers returning from the front lines of battle. At the war's end, some 15,000,000 soldiers and civilians had died in Europe and the face of western culture would forever be changed because of the carnage.

Following the war, there was a strong and growing movement towards Socialism and Adler found himself in the very midst of that activity. Arguing eloquently that "capitalism is inherently inequitable in the distribution of goods and services," he would eventually embrace a political position which suggests that socialism is the moral barometer of capitalism. However, Adler never embraced the use of violence by the Communists to gain their goals, saying, "Human nature generally answers external coercion with a counter-coercion. It seeks its satisfaction not in rewards for obedience and docility, but aims to prove that its own means of power are stronger … When in the life of man or the history of mankind has such an attempt ever succeeded? … No blessing comes from the use of power." Finally, in 1920, Adler published a major collection of essays designed to establish Individual Psychology as a school of thought within psychotherapy, entitled, *The Practice and Theory of Individual Psychology.* These twenty-eight essays did the job. Acclaimed throughout Europe and America, Individual Psychology came into its own, particularly in the field of child psychology.

Coming immediately on the heels of this major collection was the reestablishment, following the ravages of WWI, of the movement's periodical, called the *Journal for Individual Psychology*, in 1923 with an internationally distinguished board of editors including the renowned American psychologist G. Stanley Hall of Clark University and President of the American Psychology Association. Yet and still, Individual Psychology as a school of thought, not unlike psychoanalysis of the Freudian camp, came under severe criticism from certain quarters. First, Adler and Adlerians were criticized for their casual if not indifferent attitude to statistics and their use in assessments and evaluations of treatment and counseling results, particularly as relates to children. Furthermore, this school of thought seldom if ever provided a systematic follow-up of their interventions when dealing with psychological problems of children and youth thereby leaving them open to criticism for failing to actually demonstrate effectiveness.

Also, Adler's personal indifference to experimental work would eventually haunt him throughout the remaining years of his practice. Finally, Adler's inordinate emphasis upon environmental factors with a disregard to inherited behavior proved extremely problematic to establishing this school of thought as a major player in 20th psychotherapy. His naively employed motto when dealing with children was "Anyone can learn anything" and therefore and inevitably made the movement seem thin and simplistic.

Yet, his involvement in child psychology and educational psychology did not go unnoticed in the wider profession. For example, in 1924 Adler was made Professor of Psychology with special interests in child developmental and educational psychology at the Pedagogical Institute's Division of Remedial Education. The Institute was a part of the University of Vienna and worked in consort with Karl and Charlotte Buhler's Institute of Psychology. But in America, Adler and Individual Psychology were becoming a major point of interest within both the professional community and the general public at large. Emphasizing the two fundamental principles of his theory, Adler was always quick to point out that "two factors affect all human relations, namely, the inferiority complex and the striving for social feeling." The New York Times described this "new psychology" of Adler this way: "One of the most important schools of this new science of the soul is individual psychology, founded by the Viennese scholar and neurologist, Dr. Alfred Adler. Laymen sometimes make the mistake of regarding individual psychology as a mere subdivision of the psychoanalysis of Freud. It is no more that than is Protestantism a subdivision of Catholicism." Such praise went far to establish Individual Psychology as a major player on the American stage.

In anticipation of and as a lead up to the publishing of his next major work translated into English in 1926 entitled, *Understanding Human Nature,* Adler gave a cryptic summary for the press of what he means by Individual Psychology. Individual Psychology regards the craving for power on the part of the individual and of nations as a reaction to deep feelings of inferiority. "Individual Psychology," he said, "could rally all the latent forces for good which are inherent in groups, just as it is already rallying such latent forces in individuals. Wars, national hatreds and class struggle -- these greatest enemies of humankind -- all root in the desire to escape, or compensate for, the crushing sense of their inferiority. Individual psychology, which can cure individuals of the evil effects of this sense of inferiority, might be developed into a powerful instrument for ridding nations and groups of the menace of their collective inferiority complex."

Adler's coming to America on the heels of this publication was fortuitously beneficial for his school of psychology. America was experiencing a major decline in religious attendance which was coupled with major upheavals in the social values as regards marriage, romance, and sexuality. The popularity of the automobile was on the exponential rise as a portable living room for eating, drinking, smoking, gossiping, and sex. The liberation of American sexual mores centered in Hollywood and the coming of psychiatry and psychoanalysis as the new fads among the rich also served well the Adlerian agenda.

Freudian psychoanalysis, which was for a time the ruling school of thought among the top professionals and the wealthy in America, began to feel competition from Individual Psychology. Freud's anti-Americanism became increasingly known and unwelcome as the lead up to McCarthyism. The radically subjective nature of his therapeutic treatment, its unending demand for weekly visits over many years, the overall expense, etc., all conspired to create an atmosphere of welcome for Adlerian psychology as a radically different approach to mental health. Freud's criticism, first off the record then in later years on the record, of Americans as an uncouth, money-grubbing lot did not serve well his cause. Freud even went so far as to tell Ernest Jones, his famous biographer, that "America is a mistake; a gigantic mistake, it is true, but nonetheless a mistake." And, the fact that both Adler and Jung were experiencing a massive boost in their financial situations thanks to American interest grated hard on Freud and he didn't keep it to himself. A few clips from Freud's later statements about Americans and America will serve: "It often seems to me that analysis fit's the American as a white shirt the raven." "What is the use of Americans if they bring no money?" "America is useful for nothing else but to supply money." "Is it not sad that we are materially dependent on these savages (Americans) who are not better-class human beings?"

America was ready for Adler thanks, ironically and in part,

to the earlier arrival of Freud and psychoanalysis. Freud set the stage in America but Adler produced a more pragmatic approach to mental health. To professionals and the general public, Alder emphasized the concept of "inferiority" as a central theme in his understanding of human nature. "The behavior pattern of persons," he would say in all of his lectures, "can be studied from their relation to three things: to society, to work, to sex. The feeling of inferiority affects a man's relations to these." Again, he said: "The three great questions in life that require answers by each individual have to do with occupation, society, and love. ... (and the role of parents and teachers is to) help the child to create a style of life that is profitable for himself, for society, and for posterity." This was, indeed, well received in American audiences of professional counselors and teachers alike. His lecture series at the New School for Social Research in New York City in 1928 went a long way to further his reputation. The profound relevance of this behavioral insight relative to child development and parenting cannot be over-emphasized for its significance in analyzing the damaged self of an emotionally injured life.

Adler never stopped emphasizing the need to stimulate in the child a sense of confidence, to evoke his cooperative dispositions, to socialize and humanize his ego, especially to teachers and parents. He was becoming the darling to the teaching profession and to educated parents concerned about the raising of their children in a "modern" world. In the *Saturday Review of Literature*, S. Daniel House of Columbia University wrote: "The Adlerian approach to the problems of disharmony and maladjustment resident in human nature constitute a new chapter in psychology and, what is more important, a fresh beginning in education.... We might refer to Adler's work as educational sociology and compare him in his general social philosophy and creative attitudes towards education with John Dewey. ... he might be referred to with considerable accuracy as the pioneer in the comparatively new field of educational psychiatry."

Benefiting from such praise and desiring more and more to distance himself from both Freud and psychoanalysis, Adler spoke specifically to the issue in his lecture series at the New School for Social Research. In speaking of the differences, he said that "Freud takes as premise the fact that man is so constructed by nature that he wishes only to satisfy his drives but that culture or civilization is antagonistic to such satisfaction. However, Individual Psychology claims that the development of the individual, because of his bodily inadequacy and his feeling of inferiority, is dependent on society. Hence, social feeling is inherent in man and bound up with his identity." This did it for the American audience. Leading up to the occasion of him receiving an honorary doctorate from Wittenberg College in America, Adler said: "the most important single factor in personality development is the relative presence of the inferiority complex ... This feeling of inferiority forms the background for all our studies. It ultimately becomes the stimulus among all individuals, whether children or adults, to establish their actions in such a way that they will arrive at a goal of superiority." He subsequently learned that the Soviet Union had elected him an honorary member of the Leningrad Scientific-Medical Child Study Society, an accolade he was not willing to refuse.

Returning to America for the third time in 1929 to promote his latest book, *The Technique of Individual Psychology,* he continued to lecture at the New School on optimism and human nature to the delight of the professionals and students who flocked to hear him. That year, he made the decision to relocate permanently to America and New York, but without Raissa who was most disinclined to leave her European home and roots partly because of her increasing involvement in Austrian Communist Party activities. Alder, nevertheless, settled into his new residence, a suite at the Windermere Hotel on Manhattan's West End Avenue and Ninety-Second Street. The New York years saw his national reputation grow even while he continued relationships, mixed as they were, with the New School and Columbia University, taking a visiting professorships in medical psychology at the Long Island College of Medicine.

As the war mongering continued to accelerate in Europe leading up to the inevitable World War II, Adler was very concerned about his European family, none of whom were willing to consider coming to America in spite of his pleadings. Adler never returned to Austria following his last visit. At his leaving, he gave a book to a little boy who cared greatly for him. Adler later reported that as he left, the little boy ran down the road crying out to him: "Come back, and stay forever!" With this, Alder turned his back forever on

Europe, save for a visit to England where he traveled with his wife, Raissa, for the last time. He returned to New York and continued to lecture, teach, and practice individual psychology until his death of a heart attack at the age of sixty-seven. Freud was reported to have rejoiced that he outlived Adler but many accolades from professional colleagues were published from such as Maslow, Rogers, and Frankl.

As Adler began to feel the power and strength of his own theory-building enterprise, he commenced, at first quietly and subtly but gradually both aggressively and outspokenly, to move away from Freud's fundamental argument that sexual conflicts in early childhood caused mental illness. Adler gradually begin to consign sexuality to a symbolic role in human strivings to overcome feelings of inadequacy, what he came to call the inferiority complex. By 1911, Adler was speaking out loudly and publicly against Freud's fundamentally erroneous mistake regarding the centrality of sexuality in child development. Adler and a group of colleagues eventually disassociated themselves from Freud and the classical psychoanalytic school of sexual dominance in mental illness and began the eventual development of what became Individual Psychology, best and most thoroughly developed in Adler's 1927 book, *Menschenkenntnis* (English translation, *Understanding Human Nature)*. Without question, "This book is an attempt," wrote Adler, "to acquaint the general public with the fundamentals of Individual Psychology. At the same time, it is a demonstration of the practical application of these principles to the conduct of one's everyday relationships, not only to the world, and to one's fellowmen, but also to the organization of one's personal life. ... The purpose of the book is to point out how the mistaken behavior of the individual affects the harmony of our social and communal life; further, to teach the individual to recognize his own mistakes, and finally, to show him how he may effect a harmonious adjustment to the communal life."

It is this work of Adler's, *Understanding Human Nature*, which captures the attention here for it was this book, more than any other, which commended his optimistic worldview and hopeful approach to the study of human development, especially of children, to America and the world. We will take excerpts from this great classic and our comments upon them we will each citation. This perspective applied to child mental health proved most attractive in dealing with the damaged self-concept of the emotionally injured child within professional circles of psychiatry.

"We have often drawn attention to the fact that before we can judge a human being we must know the situation in which he grew up." These are Adler's opening words when speaking of *"The Family Constellation."* He continues: "An important moment is the position which a child occupied in his family constellation. Frequently we can catalogue human beings according to this view point after we have gained sufficient expertness, and can recognize whether an individual is a first-born, an only child, the youngest child, or the life."

Adler was the first to place a major emphasis up what later became commonly called within psychotherapy "birth order" of the child. He was himself one of several children and always felt confident that the order a child in born into the family would/could/should have a major, and not always positive, impact upon his development. He spent a great deal of time researching and writing upon this factor even though, ironically enough, there is nothing anyone can do about the order of their birth in a family. His concern was for both the parents need to take full cognizance of the fact and to directly address that point in the childrearing practices employed in dealing with each child as well as the child, in adulthood, taking full cognizance of that reality as he reflects upon his childhood and how that reality may have affected his worldview. A diminished life is frequently the result of parental failure in addressing compassionately and sympathetically the unspoken needs of the child.

"People seem to have known for a long time," explains Adler, "that the youngest child is usually a peculiar type. ... Not only is he the youngest, but also usually the smallest, and by consequence, the most in need of help. ... Hence there arise a number of characteristics which influence his attitude toward life in a remarkable way, and cause him to be a remarkable personality. ...One group of these youngest children excels every other member of the family ... But there is another more unfortunate group of these same youngest children ... which have a desire to excel, but lack the necessary activity and self-confidence, as a result of their relationships to their older brothers and sisters."

147

Adler was keen to place a great deal of emphasis upon the first child, the youngest child, and the only child as being of particular types and quite susceptible to both analysis and study as well as themselves being personally susceptible to certain psychological dysfunctions. As an educator as well as psychotherapist, he was especially concerned that full awareness of these realities be integrated into the educational system of the day. "We are really tired of having nothing but the first and best people," explains Adler. "History as well as experience demonstrates that happiness does not consist in being the first or best. To teach a child such a principle makes him one-sided; above all it robs him of his chance of being a good fellow man. The first consequence of such doctrines is that a child thinks only of himself and occupies himself in wondering whether someone will overtake him. Envy and hate of his fellows and anxiety for his own position, develop in his soul. His very place in life makes a speeder, trying to beat out all others, of the youngest. ... This type of the youngest child is occasionally to be found as a clear-cut type example, although variations are common. ... Another type, which grows secondarily from the first, is often found. When a youngest child of this type loses his courage, he becomes the most arrant coward that we can well imagine. We find him far from the front, every labor seems too much for him, and he becomes a veritable "alibi artist" who attempts nothing useful, but spends his whole energy wasting time. ... He will always find excuses for his failures. He may contend that he was too weak or petted, or that his brothers and sisters did not allow him to develop."

Adler wished to call attention to these two types of "youngest" personality options, the high achiever at any price and the low achiever at no price. Though parents could sense these characteristics in their children, Adler was the first to elevate the discussion to a clinical investigation, to an analytical study of data based upon observed behavior. He became recognized as the master in dealing with children in these situations and always with an eye towards their constructive education, thus becoming the darling of American educators.

"Both of these types are hardly ever good fellow human beings," Adler continues. "The first type (the strong youngest child) fares better in a world where competition is valued for itself. A man of this type will maintain his spiritual equilibrium only at the cost of others, whereas individuals of the second (the weak youngest child) remain under the oppressive feeling of their inferiority and suffer from their lack of reconciliation with life as long as they life. The oldest child also has well-defined characteristics. For one thing he has the advantage of an excellent position for the development of his psychic life. History recognizes that the oldest son has had a particularly favorable position. Even where this tradition has not actually become crystallized ... the oldest child is usually the one whom one accredits with enough power and common sense to be the helper or foreman of his parents. If his development in this direction goes on without disturbance then we shall find him with the traits of a guardian of law and order."

Adler was especially sensitivity, owing to his own personal life story, to the reality of this dominance of the first son as he was himself the subject of such an older brother. His further remarks regarding the "second-born child" are most insightful and led him to the development of one of his most important contributions to psychotherapeutic practice, namely, the concept of the inferiority complex. He says of the second born son: "The second born may place his goal so high that he suffers from it his whole life, annihilates his inner harmony in following, not the veritable facts of life, but an evanescent fiction and the valueless semblance of things."

"The only child, of course, finds himself in a very particular situation," reasons Adler. "He is at the utter mercy of the educational methods of his environment. ... Being constantly the center of attention he very easily acquires the feeling that he really counts for something of great value. ... Parents of "only" children are frequently exceptionally cautious, people who have themselves experienced life as a great danger, and therefore approach their child with an inordinate solicitude."

Birth order, as we have said, played a major role in Adler's child psychiatry and whether dealing with youngest or oldest child or the only child, he was most sensitive to the personality developmental issues which arise from the birth order phenomenon both as it relates to the individual child's self-understanding as well as that of the child's nurturing environment controlled by parents and teachers. "We see, therefore," counsels Adler, "that the very position of the child in the family may lend shape and color to all the instincts, tropisms, faculties and the like, which he brings with him into the world. ... (therefore) it would seem to us that the theory of inheritance of acquired characteristics is based upon very weak evidence. ... From our previous descriptions we may assume that whatever the errors to which a child is exposed in his development, the most serious consequences arise from his desire to elevate himself over all his fellows, to seek more personal power which will give him advantages over his fellow man." Unlike Freud's rather positive emphasis upon the inevitability of the "will to pleasure" which he felt was the fundamental driving force in human life, Adler is keen both to point out that the "will to power" is, rather, the driving force but, rather than being merely positive about this drive, Adler believes that the social environment, particularly the parents and educators of small children must assert themselves for the controlling and direction of this power-surge for superiority over the child's peers.

"In our culture," reasons Adler, "he is practically compelled to develop according to a fixed pattern. If we wish to prevent such a perilous development, we must know the difficulties he has to meet and understand them. There is one single and essential point of view which helps us to overcome all these difficulties; it is the viewpoint of the development of the social feeling. If this development succeeds, obstacles are insignificant, but since the opportunities for this development are relatively rare in our culture, the difficulties which a child encounters play an important role."

Adler is painfully aware of the developmental obstacles placed in the child's path by his social environment and he rails against parental practices of feeding the drive to dominant which our culture seems to cherish and perpetuate. In *Understanding Human Nature*, Adler is eager for the informed parent and educational system to be aware of the drive or will to power which characterizes human nature and the absolute necessity of guiding and educating that drive for the welfare of human society. The notion of "social feeling," which Adler has so emphasized in his work, is central to an understanding of this concept of Adlerian guidance.

Individual Psychology, as we have seen, maintains that the overriding motivation in most individuals is a striving for what Adler early on called "superiority" but later modified to "compensational behavior" for feelings of inferiority. This human quest, commencing in early childhood, for self-realization, completeness, and perfection, is usually frustrated by feelings of inadequacy, or incompleteness arising from physical defects, low social status, pampering or neglect during childhood, and not infrequently birth-order. Compensational behavior relative to these feelings of inferiority can include the development of personal skills and abilities.

Here is the arena for the parent and the educator to take the initiative in nurturing positive responses to the child's need for a sense of fulfillment even in the face of stifling environmental and physical handicaps. Over-compensation for inferiority feelings can, says Adler, take the form of an egocentric striving for power and self-aggrandizing behavior at other's expense. This led Adler to propose an alternative to Freud's short-hand notion of the "will to pleasure" with his own idea of the "will to power." Simplistic and unfair to his own system of thought, this notion nevertheless emphasized the prominence in child development of feelings of inferiority and compensatory behavioral responses to assert jurisdiction over one's own life and destiny, namely, the will to power.

Adler was internationally recognized and acclaimed for his creative and innovative response to the need for the cultivation and monitoring of mental health among children. He established a series of child-guidance clinics in Vienna in 1921 for this purpose and international figures including Maria Montessori called attention to is outstanding efforts in this regard. Though the Nazi influence on the Austrian government forced the closing of these Adlerian child counseling centers in 1934, his reputation preceded him to New York in 1926, joining first the Columbia University faculty the next year and eventually the faculty of Long Island College of Medicine in 1932.

It is the contention within Individual Psychology that there is a direct relationship between the human person and the world around him as relates particularly to a few biological principles operative within human nature. Psychoneurosis, then, is seen as a disturbance in the relationship between the individual and his social environment. Therefore, therapeutics based on individual psychological data must be an etiological therapeutic in the proper sense of that word. Given the social etiology of mental disease, it is the intention of the psychotherapist in the modality of Individual Psychology to address the need for a readjustment of the interpersonal relationship between the patient and his social environment, the community and social circle within which he lives and works and loves. Tracing mental disorders back into childhood and parental care was, of course, inevitable and greatly enhanced the professional understanding of the nature and significance of the damaged self-concept in child development. And, though Freud is due the credit for early on calling attention to these maturation issues, Adlerian psychology has offered an additional modality of treatment which has stood the test of time.

The term "Individual Psychology" was chosen by Adler specifically to identify his system of theory and analysis because of his radical emphasis upon the essential subjective nature of the individual's striving, the innate creativity of human psychological adaptation, and the wholeness of the individual's unified personality. The drive for superiority in the face of compensatory behavioral response to personal feelings of inferiority constitutes the matrix of human development. "The goal of superiority, with each individual," says Adler, "is personal and unique. It depends upon the meaning he gives to life; and this meaning is not a matter of words. It is built up in his style of life and runs through it like a strange melody of his own creation." If individuals have developed a healthy social life through creative and responsible interests, their strivings for superiority will be shaped into a style of life that is warmly receptive of others and focused on friendship and interpersonal ties. If not, neuroses and psychoses will develop as the individual attempts to adjust his will to power, his personal agenda, to the conflicting demands and expectations of society.

Individual Psychology is built upon the notion of a fundamental unity of the human personality. All apparent dichotomies and duplicities of life are organized in one self-consistent totality. No definite division can be made between mind and body, consciousness and unconsciousness, or between reason and emotion. All behavior is seen in relation to the final goal of superiority or success, of the will to power. This goal gives direction to the individual within his social matrix. If he has developed strong "social feelings" for his social environment, he will thrive. If not, mental illness awaits him as he struggles unsuccessfully to assert his demand for superiority in the absence of a capacity to get along in his social environment due to the failure to have cultivated this strong social feeling.

In contrast to Freud and psychoanalysis, which places so much emphasis upon the assumption that man is motivated by instincts, and in contradistinction to Carl Jung's Analytical Psychology which emphasizes above all else man's dependence upon inborn archetypes, Adler believed that the human person is motivated by social urges. We are inherently social beings and our very nature is interpersonal, requiring cooperation in social activities. Whereas Freud relied upon sexuality and Jung upon primordial thought patterns, Adler stressed social interest or, what we have seen him call, "social feeling."

Furthermore, with respect to the emergence and development of personality, Adler placed emphasis upon the concept of the "creative self," the notion that the human is a highly personalized, subjective entity which interprets his social environment and tries to make sense out of it for his survival and betterment. Whereas Freud would have us believe that personality relies upon inborn instincts for self-aggrandizement, Adler believes that the human person seeks for experiences which will aid in fulfilling the individual's unique style of life. This concept of the "creative self" was new to psychoanalysis but over time has become a major conceptual framework in analyzing personality and behavioral disorders.

A primary distinction of Individual Psychology over against psychoanalysis was Adler's insistence upon the absolute "uniqueness" of each personality. Each person is a composite of his own personalized motivations, traits, interests, and values and each person, then, carries a distinctive style of life unique to his experiences and situation in the social environment. Adler minimalizes Freud's emphasis upon sexual instinct as the dominant dynamic in human behavior, rather calling attention to man's social character, his experiences of inferiorities not sexually derived or driven. Adler's "dethronement" of sexuality was for many professionals and the laity a welcome relief from the monotonous pansexualism of the psychoanalysts in the Freudian camp.

It was upon personal consciousness as the center of human personality which Adler emphasized, studied, and was fascinated by. The human person is a conscious being, ordinarily aware of its reasons for his behavior. Fully cognizant of his inferiorities and well aware of his personal goals for which he strives in life, man is a being capable of planning and guiding his behavior, fully conscious of the meaning of such plans as relates to his self-realization as a person. Freud was completely at odds with this concept of personality and image of human nature for Freud and his school felt that human consciousness was a minimal component of human behavior with the individual primarily victimized by his unconscious.

Adlerian psychology is quite splendidly simple in terms of the minimal use of conceptual terms developed in his theories of personality. Six major concepts are operative within Individual Psychology and we will quickly review them here. They are (1) fictional finalism, (2) striving for superiority, (3) inferiority feelings and compensation, (4) social interests, (5) style of life, and (6) the creative self.

Once Adler and the Individual Psychology school of professionals distanced themselves from Freud and the psychoanalytic school of psychotherapy, they moved to adopt a rather well-developed philosophical optimism, a kind of "idealistic positivism" over against Freud's rather dark notion of "historical determinism." Man, Adler argued, is motivated more by his hopes and aspirations about the future than he is by suppressed experiences of the past. The hopes and aspirations are not teleological, that is, they are not predestined or subject to fate, but rather are quite decidedly subjective, mental constructs of the hopeful personality. Adler called these "fictional goals," because they are subjective causations which may or may not be realized but are, nevertheless, ever present in the human heart. Rather than teleological in nature and, thus, the result of causation, the fictional nature of hopes and aspirations are based on the principle of finalism. Adler spoke to this issue decisively: "Individual Psychology insists absolutely on the indispensability of finalism for the understanding of all psychological phenomena. Causes, powers, instincts, impulses, and the like cannot serve as explanatory principles. The final goal alone can explain man's behavior. Experiences, traumata, sexual development mechanisms cannot yield an explanation, but the perspective in which these are regarded, the individual way of seeing them, which subordinates all life to the final goal, can do it."

The etiology of this innate drive, Adler believed, was located in the feelings of inferiority which characterize every person in some form or another and in varying degrees of intensity. Early on in his medical training and beginning clinical work, he links the notion of what he called "organ inferiority" with "overcompensation." He later broadened the concept to include any feelings of inferiority which arose from subjectively felt psychological or social disabilities as well as from physical insufficiencies. Adler believed that feelings of inferiority are the basis for all human improvements and creativity in the world. When these feelings are exaggerated, mental illness is the results. When they are held at bay or educated into a viable self-understanding, they lead to success and leadership, superiority of deed and person. Though not inevitably or even commonly leading to pleasure, such development was designed to lead the individual toward perfection which, he believed, was the ultimate goal of life.

The idea of social interest, or social feeling as we discussed earlier in this chapter, came later to Adler and in response to pervasive criticism from the professionals in the field of counseling and therapy. The criticism was due to Adler's early emphasis upon aggression and the will to power at the expense, it was thought, of human cooperation. Because in his own life he was an outspoken proponent of social justice and social democracy, he worked tirelessly to broaden his understanding of human nature to include this sense of social interest and social feeling toward one's fellow man and fellow creatures. Cooperation, he began to say, is a fundamental characteristic of the human person. In this development, he moved further and further away from his earlier emphasis upon aggression and selfish interest, arguing, in his mature years for the centrality of social feeling as an indispensable component of personality.

"Style of life" became a slogan for Adlerians of the day. His whole theory of human personality was summed up in this one expression. Though every person has the goal of superiority (defined in the Adlerian sense of personal pursuit of perfection) as his foremost agenda, there are countless ways in which this superiority might be realized in one's life. The style of life one lives is early formed in childhood. Based upon social encounters with the outside world as well as birth order and family life, the style of life is constructed. His attitudes, feelings, apperceptions, and aspirations are set in motion. One's sense of inferiority in various aspects of life are contributing factors in the development of one's style of life always within the context of self-aware inferiorities and the self-administered pressure to seek perfection and personal fulfillment in one's life. It was the concept of the "creative self" which proved to be the crowning achievement of his theory of personality. All of his other concepts and notions about personality development fell into place when the idea of the creative self was discovered and expanded upon in his clinical work and theoretical writing. It is this creative self which gives a person meaning in life. It is the active principle of humanity. In essence, the doctrine of a creative self asserts that man makes his own personality. This was Adler's major contribution to personality theory and the one which assured the prominence of Individual Psychology.

SELECTED PRIMARY SOURCES OF ALFRED ADLER

The Practice and Theory of Individual Psychology (1927)

Understanding Human Nature (1927)

What Life Could Mean to You (1931)

In his lifetime, Adler published more than 300 books and articles. The Alfred Adler Institute of Northwestern Washington has recently published the first ten of the twelve-volume set of *The Collected Clinical Works of Alfred Adler*, covering his writings from 1898-1937. An entirely new translation of Adler's magnum opus, *The Neurotic Character*, is featured in Volume 1.

Volume 1 : The Neurotic Character — 1907
Volume 2 : Journal Articles 1898-1909
Volume 3 : Journal Articles 1910-1913
Volume 4 : Journal Articles 1914-1920
Volume 5 : Journal Articles 1921-1926
Volume 6 : Journal Articles 1927-1931
Volume 7 : Journal Articles 1931-1937
Volume 8 : *Lectures to Physicians & Medical Students*
Volume 9 : *Case Histories*
Volume 10 : *Case Readings & Demonstrations*
Volume 11 : *Education for Prevention*
Volume 12 : *The General System of Individual Psychology*

CHAPTER NINE

ERIKSON and the Quest for Personal Identity

Though a trained and never rebellious psychoanalyst in the true Freudian school of thought, Erikson nevertheless never ceased to claim allegiance to Freud while boldly asserting the further development and contribution of his thought to the Freudian school of psychotherapy. His psychosocial theory of personality development relied upon a strong argument for the centrality of ego psychology, developmental changes throughout the life cycle, and an understanding of personality against the background of social and historical forces. Contrary to Freud, Erikson held that the ego was an autonomous personality structure and he concentrated his efforts, therefore, upon ego qualities that emerge during the fundamental stages of maturation.

Many distinguished scholars have established themselves on the strength of one great book such as Frankl and Adler and Rogers, while others wrote and wrote and wrote, leaving behind a library of research and scholarship such as Freud, Jung and Maslow. It can be argued that Erikson's name and reputation was established and secured with the publication of his first book in 1950, *Childhood and Society*. Erikson's fascination with the study of children, their personality development and their maturation, resulted in the writing of his major text. Here, he elaborated his approach of "triple bookkeeping," as he called it, namely, that understanding a person or behavior involves taking into account somatic factors, social context, and ego development, each in relation to the other. To unpack the somatic aspect of child development, Erikson developed and helpfully expanded Freud's theory of psychosexual development. Erikson chose to explore the power of social context in relation to child-rearing practices and their effects on later personality through some fascinating anthropological and psychoanalytical analysis of the Native Americans, particularly the Sioux and the Yurok cultures.

Erik Homburger (Erikson) was born on the 25th of June, 1902, in Frankfurt-am-Main in Germany and died in Harwick, Massachusetts, on May 12, 1994. His mother was a young woman named Karla Abrahamsen from a prominent Jewish family in Copenhagen and his natural father, a Dane named Erik Salomonsen, deserted his mother before Erik was born. At the time of his birth, his mother was "officially" married to a Jewish stockbroker and at his birth, he was registered as Erik Salomonsen. She later trained as a nurse in Karlsruhe and in 1904 married a Jewish physician named Dr. Theodor Homburger who was, at the time, serving as Erik's own pediatrician. In 1909, Erik Salomonsen became Erik Homburger and in 1911 he was officially adopted by his stepfather. Personal identity was an obsession with Erik throughout his childhood and adolescence for at the temple school the children teased him for being "Nordic," owing to his blonde hair and blue eyes, and at public school he was teased for being a Jew.

Upon Erik's eventual arrival and adoption of America as his homeland, having fled Germany with the rise of Nazi proliferation, he changed his surname to Erikson when he took U.S. citizenship. Personal, racial, and religious identify seemed to have plagued Erickson from his earliest memories and haunted him throughout his childhood, adolescent, and adult life. It has been suggested that possibly this life experience itself was a significant ingredient in leading him to the development of his now famous eight stages of development.

Following public school in Germany where his first love was quite clearly art, Erikson studied at a variety of places in Munich and Florence and eventually arrived at the door of what was then still a newly emerging discipline in psychology, namely, psychoanalysis. It should be pointed out here that Erikson did not ever pursue formalized educational training beyond the high school diploma, relying rather upon his own confidence and insights into the field of which he was most interested. He did attend a humanistic gymnasium in Karlsruhe, Germany, where he was not a particularly good student while, nevertheless, doing quite good work in ancient history and art as he records showed. Refusing to heed his step-father's urgings to pursue medicine, Erikson left home to travel across central Europe and within the next year enrolled in an art school and, for a brief time, accepted the fact that even an aspiring artist could learn something in an educational setting. Becoming restless yet again, he left that school and set out for Munich to study at the famous art school, the Dunst-Akademia. Two years there, he then moved to Florence while generally wandering aimlessly around Italy "soaking up sunshine and visiting art galleries." He later would write that he finally came to realize that "such narcissism obviously could be a young person's downfall unless he found an overweening idea and the stamina to work for it."

In 1927 at the age of twenty-five, Erikson took up a teaching post at an experimental school for wealthy American children living with their parents in Vienna. This school, called the *Kinderseminar*, was founded to serve the needs of American professionals studying in Vienna to become psychoanalysts and was under the directorship of a psychoanalyst Dorothy Burlingham who was the daughter of the internationally acclaimed New York jeweler, Charles Tiffany. She was herself a professionally trained psychoanalyst and not reluctant to promote this school of thought to all with which she came in contact. Needless to say, the young Erikson fell under her spell from whom not only did he study and learn as well as undergo psychoanalysis but also was introduced to the Montessori education method and to Anna Freud herself, a lifelong collaborative friend of Dorothy Burlingham. Erikson also and quite naturally was welcomed into the Vienna Psychoanalytic Society which was Sigmund Freud's center of teaching and training psychoanalysis to medical professionals and selected layman alike. Besides undergoing psychoanalysis at the hands of Anna Freud herself, Erikson also took the Certificate from the Maria Montessori Teachers Association in Vienna, his only academic credential throughout his entire professional life.

Naturally, young man Erikson was greatly influenced by these heady relationships and professional experiences which, undoubtedly, were instrumental in fostering his passion for analytical studies of childhood maturation. From a modest teaching appointment, Erikson managed to squeeze out an incredibly provocative life experience which led to his now famous ideas and theories about human personality development. In 1929, he married Joan Serson, an American teacher and dancer who was at the time a member of Anna Freud's and Dorothy Burlingham's experimental school in Vienna where Erikson himself taught. By 1933, they had two sons and the whole Erikson family then attempted to immigrate to Copenhagen where he had hoped to secure citizenship based upon his natural father's nationality. He had hoped to establish a psychoanalytic practice there, little known in Denmark at the time, but the effort failed and they were forced to look elsewhere to begin again, having feared Hitler's rise to power. That same year he completed a course of study at the Vienna Psychoanalytic Institute.

His enthusiasm for this general field of work and study eventually led him to immigrate to the US in 1933 where he was, quite fortuitously, provided study and teaching opportunities at some of America's most distinguished centers of learning including Harvard, Yale, and the University of California at Berkeley. Upon his arrival in Boston in 1933, he set up as one of the very few child psychoanalysts in the country and carried out research on children at the prestigious Harvard Psychological Clinic where he enjoyed a close friendship and working relationship with both Henry Murray and Kurt Lewin. From 1933 to 1935, he held an appointment as a clinical and academic Research Fellow in Psychology in the Department of Neuropsychiatry at Harvard Medical School. He enrolled in a Ph.D. in psychology at Harvard but quickly, within months, withdrew never again to make such an attempt. From 1936 to 1939, he served under an appointment in the Department of Psychiatry in the Institute of Human Relations at the Yale University Medical School where he thoroughly enjoyed continuing his work and interest in personality development and cross-cultural studies.

Erikson's early work concentrated primarily upon psychological testing with special attention to the ways and means of extending Freudian psychoanalytic theories in relation to the effect of social and cultural factors upon human development and personality. He was particularly fascinated with the impact of these insights upon how society affects childhood and development. It was at this early stage in his own professional development that studies of child psychopathology became paramount in his research agenda. Because of his driving interest in multi-cultural studies of childhood and society, he became a great student of cultural anthropology, especially as relates to the study of children and personality development cross-culturally. As with Maslow, the works of Margaret Mead and Ruth Benedict proved pivotal to his own conceptual framework and subsequent theoretical development in this area. To further deepen his understanding of cross-culturalism and child development, he journeyed to the Native American communities of the Oglala Lakota (Sioux) and the Yurok peoples where he stayed for an extended time of observation, interviews, etc. The richness of these experiences fed his ambitions in theory and conceptual development while also demonstrating to him some of the apparent deficiencies of Freudian theory as relates to personality development. This encounter with psychoanalytic shortcomings coupled with the richness of his cross-cultural experiences eventually led to his development of what came to be called the "biopsychosocial" perspective on childhood and society. Within this stimulating matrix of behavioral science and psychoanalysis that substantive issues involving the damaged self-concept in children and the diminishment of their life prospects occupied much of his clinical attention.

Eventually migrating with his family to the University of California at Berkeley in 1939, he continued his concentrated efforts in the study of child welfare and personality development and practiced as a clinical psychologist at the San Francisco Veterans Hospital where he treated trauma and mental illness. By 1942, Erikson had risen to the position of Professor of psychology at the University of California at Berkeley where he enjoyed assisting Jean MacFarlane in the Child Guidance Study. During the McCarthy era, he moved back to Massachusetts from whence he had come owing to his refusal to sign a loyalty oath which was now being required of all teachers in the State of California. In 1951, he joined a group of mental health professionals at the Austen Riggs Center in Stockbridge, Massachusetts, which was a private residential treatment center for mentally ill young people. He also, and amazingly, continued to maintain a part-time teaching appointment at the Western Psychiatric Institute in Pittsburgh, Pennsylvania while also teaching at the University of Pittsburgh and the Massachusetts Institute of Technology.

From 1951-1960, he taught and worked in New England, but in the summer of 1960, he spent a year at the Center for Advanced Studies of the Behavioral Sciences at Palo Alto, California, and was the following year rewarded by being invited to teach at Harvard University from which he retired in 1970 from his clinical practice but not from his busy schedule of research and writing. He died in Harwick, Massachusetts, on May 12, 1994 and was followed three years later by his Canadian wife, Joan, whom he had met and married while still living and teaching in Vienna. She was herself an academic and particularly fascinated with the study of childhood development and became a major collaborated with Erikson in his research and publications.

A prolific writer, it has been suggested that all research and publication subsequent to his first and indisputably his most famous book in 1950, *Childhood and Society*, was merely a continuing commentary on that book. He continued to push his interest in the life cycle (eight stages of development) during which time he introduced the concept of the "identity crisis" within adolescence. A gradual movement away from psychoanalytic theory and practice was seen as he moved closer to the Third Force and humanistic interests within psychological research and writing. This shift was reflected in his subsequent books such as *Young Man Luther* (1958), *Identity and the Life Cycle* (1959), *Insight and Responsibility* (1964), *Identity: Youth and Crisis* (1968), and *Gandhi's Truth* (1970) which won for him the Pulitzer Prize. In 1974, he published *Dimensions of a New Identity*, and with the editorial revisions made by Joan Erikson, his 1982 book, *The Life Cycle Completed: A Review*, was republished in 1996 which happily extended the stages of old age within the life cycle model, thus completing Erikson's contribution to developmental psychology.

Though trained by Anna Freud and within the psychoanalytic tradition of Freudian psychoanalysis, Erikson was not disinclined to move in his own sphere of thought just as he had chosen not to pursue a traditional university education. Erikson looked at ego development in particular through an analysis of the significance and role of "play," for it was in child's play that he was able to emphasize the need for integration. These three processes, somatic, social, and ego development, are interdependent and that each is both relevant and relative to the other two. This was quite decidedly an advance over traditional Freudian concepts of personality development and child sexuality and elevated Erikson in the field of child psychopathology.

Before we go further in our appreciative assessment of his work, let us simply here recite the primary contributions to the understanding of child development which Erikson has brought to the table of psychological insight. First, he elaborated and modified the theory of psychosexual development as produced by Freud; second, he drew from his own clinical experience in working with ego development among children for his theory construction; and third, he employed anthropological data to emphasize the significance of the social context for child rearing and cultural process for personality development.

A fundamental component of Erikson's theory of ego development is the assumption that the development of the person is marked by a series of stages that are universal to humanity. This was, of course, a very bold claim. The process whereby these stages evolve, he explains, is governed by the "epigenetic principle" of maturation. By this Erikson is asked to explain: "(1) that the human personality in principle develops according to steps predetermined in the growing person's readiness to be driven toward, to be aware of, and to interact with, a widening social radius; and (2) that society, in principle, tends to be so constituted as to meet and invite this succession of potentialities for interaction and attempts to safeguard and to encourage the proper rate and the proper sequence of their enfolding."

In his great classic, Erikson outlines a sequence of eight separate stages of psychosocial ego development, commonly called "the eight stages of man." Far from the speculative mysticism of Jung and his genetically inherited "archetypes," Erikson is keen to postulate that these stages are the result of the epigenetic unfolding of a "ground plan" of personality that is genetically transmitted, and this is a "universal phenomenon." By epigenetic (*epi* means "upon" and *genetic* means "emergence"), Erikson has proposed a concept of development which mirrors the notion that each stage in the life cycle has an optimal time, i.e., "critical period," in which it is dominant and hence emerges, and that when all of the stages have matured according to plan, a fully functioning personality comes into existence.

Going further, Erikson is eager to emphasize that each psychosocial stage is accompanied by a "crisis," that is, a critical turning point in the individual's life that arises from physiological maturation and social demands made upon the person at that stage. The various components of personality are, in his theory, determined by the manner in which each of these crises is resolved. Conflict is a vital and integral part of Erikson's theory, because growth and expanding interpersonal radius are associated with increased vulnerability of the ego functions at each stage. However, it is important to keep in mind that, according to Erikson, each crisis connotes "not a threat of catastrophe but a turning point and, therefore, the ontogenetic source of generational strength and maladjustment."

In a review of Erikson's *Childhood and Society* over fifty years ago, the now famous Dr. Eric Berne wrote a critically appreciative assessment of Erikson's book for the *New York Times*. We will quote extensively from that review to give an idea of the impact Erikson was having on the psychological professional at the time. Berne himself at the time was being established as a major force for what he called "transactional analysis." He was extremely complimentary of Erikson's pioneer spirit in the study and treatment of children as relates to psychoanalytic understanding of ego development. Erikson, Berne points out, early emphasized the importance of early frustrations and leniencies on the development of adult anxieties and actions, believing that while sexual conflict was at the basis of most neuroticism in Freud, the main reason for emotional disturbances in America today lies in the lack of "an emotional integration." This harps back to emotional immaturity caused by a prolonged period of childhood and to certain unique characteristics of American culture and family training. Erikson, of course, and due to his study of cross-cultural childrearing practices, was very cognizant of the fact that personality development is deeply imbedded in the social mores of the child's own culture. This constituted the fundamental starting point of Erikson's monumental work, *Childhood and Society.*

Without doubt, Erikson was one of the leading 20th century psychologists working in the area of personality development, what he called the psychosocial growth of the ego. Interestingly and not particularly to his credit nor benefit, Erikson always insisted that he was not a creative thinker but rather a commentator and, possibly, an elaborator of the psychoanalytic theories of personality development introduced by Freud. He claimed simply to have complimented Freud's work with further investigations of sociological, anthropological, and biological data relevant to personality. In spite of his protestations to the contrary, there are four distinct areas in which Erikson moved away from and beyond Freudian psychoanalytic theory of personality which profoundly advanced on-going research in child psychopathology.

First, Erikson shifted the emphasis from the prominence of the id in Freudian theory to the ego which Erikson believed to be the center and basis of human behavior. Called "ego psychology," this shift proposed an understanding of the ego as an "autonomous structure of personality" which follows a course of social-adaptive development that is distinct from but parallels the id and the instincts. Second, Erikson distinguished himself with his emphasis upon the child's relationship to parents and the socio-historical matrix within family life in which each child's ego develops, for good or ill, emphasizing the relevance to the origins of mental illness linked to the maturation experience of child personality development. Third, Erikson's ego development theory covers the entire span of psychological growth and development throughout the individual's life. Freud's theory was woefully brief after adolescence. Finally, there was a great divide between Freud and Erikson when it comes to the nature and resolution of psychosexual conflicts within an individual's life. Whereas Freud wished to resolve these issues by delving into the unconscious reservoirs of the adult through dream analysis and word association, Erikson wish to focus upon the adult's capacity to move forward by assessing life's situations and embracing a mode of operation designed to foster healthy living.

The fundamental ingredient in Erikson's theory of ego development is the assumption that the development of the individual is marked by a series of "stages" that are universal to every person throughout the world. The process whereby these stages evolve is governed by the fundamental principle of maturation, what he called the "epigenetic" principle. Hear him:
This concept means "(1) that the human personality in principle develops according to steps predetermined in the growing person's readiness to be driven toward, to be aware of, and to interact with, a widening social radius; and (2) that society, in principle, tends to be so constituted as to meet and invite this succession of potentialities for interaction and attempts to safeguard and to encourage the proper rate and the proper sequence of their enfolding."

In his highly acclaimed, *Childhood and Society,* Erikson identified and extensively elaborated upon a sequence of eight separate stages of psychosocial ego development, what was usually in shorthand fashion referred to as the "eight stages of man." These eight stages he carefully identified, in his clinical practice and in his laboratory research, as the epigenetic unfolding of a "ground plan" of personality that is genetically transmitted. Whereas Jung would have us believe that archetypes are genetically transmitted (against all scientific evidence to the contrary), Erikson is keen for us to see that the stages of life are genetically transmitted throughout the human species. The fully matured human person arrives on the scene when each of these eight stages have been allowed to mature and function in their own time within the personality of each individual. However, it must be pointed out that Erikson was also eager for us to understand that each stage of development carries with it a "crisis," that is, a critical turning point in the individual's life that arises from physiological maturation and social demands made upon the person at that stage. Each component of the individual's personality develops in relationship to the method in which and the success with which each crisis is met and handled. Conflict, in Erikson's psychosocial theory of development, is crucial and indispensable for healthy development of the ego in each person.

For Erikson, the psychosocial stages of ego development were chronologically sequenced and each was companioned with a "crisis" component which could work either positively or negatively. Though accused of being "too mechanistic" in his developmental stages, he was insistent throughout his career that these stages were, indeed, sequential, and most definitely universal to the human animal. We will discuss briefly each stage of psychosocial development and its corollary crisis.

Corresponding only somewhat with Freud's "oral stage" of infant development, Erikson's first stage (Infancy) placed "trust" and "mistrust" in juxtaposition to each other with the psychosocial strength gained by the individual to be that of "hope." He believed that a sense of trust was essentially the cornerstone of a healthy personality. This sense is sometimes thought of as "confidence," and it grows out of an infant's "inner certainty" about the world as a safe, stable place and people as nurturing and reliable. It all stems from the infant's earliest experiences with mother and feeding rituals. Erikson explains: "Mothers, I think, create a sense of trust in their children by that kind of administration which in its quality combines sensitive care of the baby's individual needs and a firm sense of personal trustworthiness within the trusted framework of their culture's life style. This forms the basis in the child for a sense of being 'all right,' of being oneself, and of becoming what other people trust one will become...." The first major psychological crisis for the child wherein mistrust emerges is related to the quality of maternal care which is unreliable, inadequate, and rejecting, thus fostering a psychosocial attitude of fear, suspicion, and apprehension in the infant. Erikson believes that the development of a healthy personality is not just based on the rise of trust versus mistrust in the infant's earliest maternal experiences but rather of the dominance of trust over mistrust. The psychosocial strength gained from this successful management of trust over mistrust, says he, is the emergence of "hope" in the child's attitudes towards the future and his social relations with others. Failure to foster such hope in the child constitutes the basis for a damaged self-concept and potentially producing mental illness in adulthood.

By a year and a half, the child is ready to move to the stage of "autonomy versus shame and doubt" and the personality skill to be learned here is that of "will power." As the child gains in neuromuscular maturation, verbalization, and social discrimination, he begins to explore and interact with his environment more independently and the parents are, therefore, confronted with decisions regarding balancing "holding on" with "letting go." The meeting and handling of this psychosocial crisis, both for the child who wants to "let me do it" and the parent who wants to "let me help you," will set in motion wheels of positive or negative development which not only with encourage or stifle autonomy and shame but will both inculcate a sense of "will power" while affecting the earliest stage of life's sense of trust and mistrust. Each stage of ego development is linked to the previous one and a kind of building block phenomenon occurs such that strong ego boosters grow while weak ego boosters stifle personal development. Failure to inculcate and nurture a sense of autonomy in the child, Erikson believes, will instill in the child a sense of shame, something Erikson believes to be akin to "rage turned upon himself" because he has not been allowed to exercise his personal freedom. Shame grows in the personality traits as autonomy is stifled and, thereby, the curtailment of a responsive feeding of the child's "will power." Erikson goes on to say: "Will power is the unbroken determination to exercise free choice as well as self-restraint in spite of the unavoidable experience of shame, doubt, and a certain rage over being controlled by others. Good will is rooted in the judiciousness of parents guided by their respect for the spirit of the law." Parental guidance at this stage must be firm, Erikson says, but protective of that sense of trust achieved during the previous oral stage. He continues, "Firmness must protect him against the potential anarchy of his as yet untrained sense of discrimination, his inability to hold on and to let go with discretion. As his environment encourages him to 'stand on his own feet,' it must protect him against meaningless and arbitrary experiences of shame and of early doubt."

From trust to autonomy to a sense of "initiative" is the developmental process of the four- to five-year-old child. The resolution of the conflict between initiative and guilt is the final psychosocial experience in the preschool child's personality development, during what Erikson calls the "play age" of childhood from about four years old to the beginning of formal schooling. This resolution of conflict versus guilt produces in the child a deep sense of purpose or, if negatively resolved, the loss of direction and purpose towards the future. "Initiative," explains Erikson, "adds to autonomy the quality of undertaking, planning, and 'attacking' a task for the sake of being on the move, where before self-will, more often than not, inspired acts of defiance or, at any rate, protested independence."

At this time, a child begins to experience the feeling of being a person who actually counts, one who thinks for himself, "I am what I will be." The balancing of this sense of initiative with the experience of guilt is very much dependent upon how parents handle this last pre-school developmental stage in the child's life. Successful development of this sense of initiative produces what Erikson calls a "goal-directedness" in the child. "The child begins to envisage goals for which his locomotion and cognition have prepared him. The child also begins to think of being big and to identify with people whose work or whose personality he can understand and appreciate. 'Purpose' involves this whole complex of elements." A sense of guilt, on the other hand, is fostered by parents who employ excessive amounts of punishment (verbal or physical) in response to the child's urge to love and be loved. The child's future potential to work productively and achieve self-sufficiency within the context of his or her society's economic system depends markedly upon the ability to master this psychosocial crisis of "purpose" produced by the initiative versus guilt dialectic.

At stage four, the school age years, the child moved to another major level of ego development and personality. This "school age" period covers the years between about six and eleven and in classical psychoanalysis is referred to as the "latency period." Here, industry versus inferiority appears and the crisis produced by this tension is that of a sense of competency. We have now moved, in the positively developed personality, from trust to autonomy and initiative to industry or, contrariwise, for the negatively developing personality of the child from mistrust, shame, and guilt to a sense of inferiority. Hope, will power, and purpose as character traits developed in response to the psychosocial crises of each developmental stage now give rise to what Erikson calls a sense of competency on the part of the healthy child. Erikson has summarized these developmental stages as a movement from "*I am what I am given*" to "*I am what I will*" to "*I am what I can imagine I will be*" to, now at the fourth stage, "*I am what I learn.*" "In school," Erikson explains, "with varying abruptness, play is transformed into work, game into competition and cooperation, and the freedom of imagination into the duty to perform with full attention to the techniques which make imagination communicable, accountable, and applicable to defined tasks." Learning, demonstrating, moving forward in one's capacity to perform, to compete, and to demonstrate ability is now in full sway. The danger at this stage, of course, lies in the potential of failure which will inculcate a sense of inferiority or incompetence. The child's sense of competency and industry is, in modern society, primarily affected by and determined by his educational successes. Yet, cautions Erikson, a genuine sense of industry involves more than simply one's educational achievements and occupational aspirations for it also includes a feeling of being interpersonally competent, the confidence, if you will, that one can exert positive influence on the social world in quest of meaningful individual and social goals. This fundamental strength, namely, competency, is the basis for participation in the social, economic, and political order of one's culture and society.

The fifth stage of ego development falls between childhood and adulthood and is a pivotal period in the development of the individual. Adolescence is that period in a person's development where "ego identity" and "role confusion" come face to face with the resulting psychosocial crisis of "fidelity." This stage in Erikson's developmental scenario is the most well developed in his overall schema. He elaborates on the nature of "ego identity." "The growing and developing youths, faced with this physiological revolution within them, are now primarily concerned with attempts at consolidating their social roles. They are sometimes morbidly, often curiously, preoccupied with what they appear to be in the eyes of others as compared with what they feel they are and with the question of how to connect the earlier cultivated roles and skills with the ideal prototypes of the day ... The sense of ego identity, then, is the accrued confidence that one's ability to maintain inner sameness and continuity (one's ego in the psychological sense) is matched by the sameness and continuity of one's meaning for others." Three fundamental elements characterize ego identity. First, individuals must perceive themselves as having inner sameness and continuity. They are the same person over all. Second, the individual's social milieu must also perceive a sameness and continuity in the individual, so group affirmation is crucial. Third, the adolescent must have gathered confidence in the relationship between his world and that of his social group by having a sense of who he is and having that affirmed by others. However, when this mutuality of ego identity affirmation is absent, adolescents will encounter what Erikson calls "role confusion." In the absence of a personal identity which is strong enough to see a youngster through these developmental years, an identity crisis is inevitable. This crisis is most often characterized by an inability to select a career or pursue further education with the added deficit of a deep sense of futility, personal disorganization, and aimlessness. The feeling of inadequacy, depersonalization, alienation, and even a negative identity may result. When the adolescent has confronted the challenge and ego identity has finally emerged sound and operational, "fidelity" emerges and this, says Erikson, refers to the individual's "ability to sustain loyalties freely pledged in spite of the inevitable contradictions of value systems." Being true to one's own ego identity while remaining loyal to the social matrix within which that ego identity has developed and emerged is a characteristic of fidelity and prepares the adolescent for the next stage of development.

By virtue of a well-established ego identity characterized by fidelity or loyalty to oneself and one's social *milieu*, the individual, says Erikson, is now "ready for intimacy, that is, the capacity to commit himself to concrete affiliations and partnerships and to develop ethical strength to abide by such commitments, even though they may call for significant sacrifices and compromises." This is the stage in which courtship, marriage, and early family life come on the scene. By "intimacy," Erikson has in mind the sense of intimacy most of us share with a spouse, friends, brothers and sisters, and parents or other relatives. He also, however, speaks of intimacy with oneself, that is, the ability to "fuse your identity with somebody else's without fear that you're going to lose something yourself." This two-pronged sense of intimacy is crucial in a well-developed relationship -- intimacy with others within the framework of intimacy with oneself. The inevitable danger in this developing sense of intimacy is, of course, a sense of isolation where neither intimacy nor social involvement are possible or productive. The inability to enter into positive and intimate personal relationships leads the individual to feelings of social emptiness and isolation. Merely formalized and superficial social relationships are inadequate to meet the developmental needs of these individuals, however, and given the fact that they may be suffering from an over dependence upon self-absorbing behavior to relieve their sense of loneliness, they drift further and further away from realistic opportunities to experience and nurture feelings of intimacy. Their behavior, then, becomes inevitably counterproductive. The psychosocial strength being sought here and the one which is realized in the healthy development of a sense of intimacy is that of love. In addition to its romantic and erotic qualities, Erikson regards love as the ability to commit oneself to others and abide by such commitments, even though they may require self-denial and compromise. "Love," explains Erikson, "is mutuality of devotion forever subduing the antagonisms inherent in divided function."

The "middle years" of an individual's stages of life are fraught with prospects of creative activity or degenerative stifling. What is not possible is for nothing to happen to the individual's ego development and psychosocial maturation. This process continues throughout life, it does not stop for age and only ends with death. The countervailing options for the middle age adult is either what Erikson calls "generativity" or "stagnation" and the psychosocial crisis produced is that of "care."

"Generativity" occurs, says Erikson, when an individual begins to show concern not only for the welfare of the next generation but also for the nature of the society in which that generation will live and work. This developmental stage in life has to do with the willingness, or not, of the individual to meet the challenge of assuming responsibility for the continuation and betterment of whatever is instrumental to the maintenance and enhancement of the society in which the individual lives. It represents the older generation's concern in establishing and guiding those who will replace them. Failure to assume this responsibility, to assert oneself into the mainstream of social betterment and improvement leads to individual and societal stagnation. The sense that one does not wish to be involved, not participate in teaching the next generation the values necessary for successful and fulfilled living, all lead to a failure of courage and a diminishment of one's social worth and the worth of society at large. Those in their middle years who embrace and nurture generativity will produce a sense of "care" needed for the ongoing contribution to the improving quality of life for the next generation. Individuals lacking generativity cease to function as productive members of society, live only to satisfy their needs, and are interpersonally impoverished. This is often called the "crisis of middle age" where the person has a sense of hopelessness and tends to feel that life is meaningless. Caring for oneself, for others, for society at large is the benefit and reward to those who develop and nurture a sense of contribution to the wider society.

The "mature years" constitutes the last stage in life's journey. Every culture has this stage well developed according to its own social values, history, and composition. It is a time when the individual's ego is confronted with the option of "integrity" or "despair" and the crisis which comes with this confrontation can lead to a general sense of "wisdom" about life and how to live it. "Only in him who in some way has taken care of things and people," says Erikson, "and who has adapted himself to the triumphs and disappointments adherent to being, the originator of others or the generator of products and ideas -- only in him may gradually ripen the fruit of these seven stages -- I know no better word for it than ego integrity." With the inevitable demands brought on by these declining years of the need to adjust to deterioration of physical strength and health, to retirement and reduced income, to the death of a spouse and close friends, and the need to establish new affiliations with one's age group, there is a marked demand for shifting one's attention from a focus upon future life to that of one's past life.

The sharing of past experiences, of days gone by, with those who are younger characterize this stage in life and often, depending on the culture, is perceived by the listeners and observers of these older persons as a sense of "wisdom," a kind of helpful knowledge about what is important and how to live a meaningful and fulfilled life. "The wisdom of old age," explains Erikson, "involves an awareness of the relativity of all knowledge acquired in one lifetime in one historical period. Wisdom is a detached and yet active concern with life in the face of death." On the other hand, the lack or loss of ego integration in older individuals is earmarked by a hidden dread of death, a feeling of irrevocable failure, and an incessant preoccupation with what might have been." "Fate," he explains, "is not accepted as the frame of life, death not as its finite boundary. Despair indicates that time is too short for alternate roads to integrity: this is why the old try to "doctor" their memories." Ego integration leads to a sense of real and practical wisdom worthy to be shared with the young and in that process the individual comes to a deeper sense of self-fulfillment and contentment with life as he has lived it with hope for the future.

Erikson argued that the ego continues its development throughout life and identified eight stages in which that development occurs. These psychosocial stages characterize the human life cycle, as he called it, and he contended that the individual's personality is determined by the resolutions of the conflicts which emerge in each of these developmental stages. His theory is, of course, rooted in his basic assumptions concerning human nature itself, namely, (1) a strong commitment to the assumptions of holism and environmentalism, and (2) a moderate commitment to the assumptions of determinism, rationality, objectivity, pro-activity, heterostasis, and knowability.

Though some have registered concern over the relationship between the personal life of Erikson, his family life and his failure to come to both an emotional and professional embracing of the life of his mentally challenged child, and the profundity of his thought, most psychotherapists today are, however, indebted to Erikson for calling attention to the eight stages of the life cycle. Granted, they are mechanistic, sometimes even antiseptic, they have, nevertheless, spawned a whole new way of viewing human maturation and have nurtured a deeper appreciation for what a modified psychoanalytic theory of personality can still offer to the modern practice of psychotherapy. Particularly, the relevance and utility of his insights into child personality development is universally applaud and have stood the test of time.

SELECTED PRIMARY SOURCES OF ERIK ERIKSON

Childhood and Society (1950)

Young Man Luther. A Study in Psychoanalysis and History (1958)

Identity: Youth and Crisis (1968)

Gandhi's Truth: On the Origin of Militant Nonviolence (1969)

Adulthood (edited book, 1978)

Vital Involvement in Old Age (with J.M. Erikson and H. Kivnick, 1986)

The Life Cycle Completed (with J.M. Erikson, 1987)

Identity and the Life Cycle. Selected Papers (1959)

A Way of Looking at Things: Selected Papers 1930-1980 (Editor: S.P. Schlien, 1915)

The Erik Erikson Reader (Editor: Robert Coles, 2001)

Erikson on Development in Adulthood: New Insights from the Unpublished Papers (Carol Hren Hoare, 2002)

Erik Erikson Worked For His Life, Work, and Significance (Kit Welchman, 2000)

Identity's Architect: A Biography of Erik H. Erikson (Lawrence J. Friedman, 1999)

Erik H. Erikson: The Power and Limits of a Vision, N.Y., The Free Press (Paul Roazen, 1976)

"Everybody Rides the Carousel" (documentary film) (Hubley, 1976)

John H. Morgan

Erik H. Erikson: the Growth of His Work (Robert Coles, 1970)

Ideas and Identities: The Life and Work of Erik Erikson (Robert S. Wallerstein & Leo Goldberger, eds., [IUP, 1998])

CHAPTER TEN

KAREN HORNEY and a New Approach to Child Psychoanalysis

That Karen Horney has been one of the most prolific theorists in 20th century psychoanalytic theory is indisputable, whether one is insistent upon calling her an adulterated Freudian, a neo-Freudian, or a psychoanalytic innovator. Both her creative genius in appropriating psychoanalytic theory to new realms of application as well as her ingenuity in creating a whole new world of theory development in relationship to Freudian criticism and Feminist psychology have contributed profoundly to her reputation, both among her many antagonists and her countless protagonists. That she questioned, even occasionally challenged, traditional Freudian theories and practices is well known, especially as relates to psychoanalysis' early emphasis on infantile sexuality and this, as we shall see, led to her establishing what eventually became commonly known as Feminist Psychology. Freud was wrong, she believed, in his over emphasis upon the differences between men and women preferring *vis a vis* Freud to trace such differences to social and cultural bias rather than to a biological determinism. Moving the argument for the etiology of mental illness away from deterministic biogenics to the psychogenics of socio-cultural environmental circumstances and situations as the origin of most mental illness proved both liberating and empowering to the therapist who was not solely dependent upon either pharmacology or psychoanalytic probing of the unconscious through dream analysis and free association. Horney's approach has been subsumed within the broader school of humanistic psychology called the Third Force but her unique composition of a school of thought best labeled psychoanalytic social psychotherapy encompasses both the best of Freudian theory and the best of the humanistic school of psychology in emphasizing the centrality of interpersonal relationship skills development as the source of both mental illness and mental health. She has become a giant in her own field and an admired practitioner and theorist in the broad field of psychotherapy and particularly relevant to child psychopathology. In the following essay, we will attempt to identify and delineate the scope of her creativity and the depths of her contribution to a therapeutic theory and practice best known as psychoanalytic social psychotherapy particularly as it relates to child psychopathology.

Karen Horney is classified as a modern psychologist because she lived more than have a century as an adult in the 20th century. Born Karen Danielsen in Blankenese, Germany, on the 16th of September, 1885, the daughter of a noted sea captain, Berndt Wackels Danielsen, known by his children as "the Bible-thrower" owing to his traditional patriarchal ideas and ways of living. Her mother Clotilde of the van Ronzelen family was called "Sonni" and, unlike her husband, was an open-minded woman of the time. Karen's own elder brother Berndt was a favorite of hers but she also cared deeply for her four step-siblings from her father's first marriage. Her recollections of childhood as regards the memory of her father were not good as she characterized him in the diary of her youth as a cruel disciplinary figure. He was, she recalls, particularly inclined to favor her brother over herself all the while her father chose rather to disregard such feelings as she reported. Nevertheless, her clear and public preference was for her mother.

Even in pre-adolescence, Karen made a conscious determination to cultivate her intellect rather than her beauty which was, as all agreed, rather inconsequential. Her ambition was fed by this realization of not being beautiful but quite possibly intelligent. Though not everyone discounted her lack of beauty, she was affirmed by all in her intellectual ambitions and acumen. Whether the precipitating cause or not (this she pondered throughout her life), depression appeared not infrequently during early adolescence and plagued her throughout her life, the origin of which, she believed, was the rejection of her older brother's puppy love crush she had for him. He pushed her away owing to understandable embarrassment and consequently the first early appearance of life-long depression.

When she was nineteen years of age, her mother separated from her father and while never divorcing, her mother took all of the children, her own two and her husband's four by the previous marriage. While only a mild and intermittent factor in the family's life, the father opposed Karen's entering medical school though she enjoyed the support of her mother in this venture. The German universities precluded women from entering medical studies until 1900, but by 1906 she was able to enter the medical school of the University of Freiburg which had pioneered the way for women early on in the century. At the time, this now famous university was small with only 2,400 students of which only 58 were women. Within two years of commencing her studies, she transferred to the University of Gottingen and subsequently to the University of Berlin, finally graduating in 1913. Attending multiple universities in Germany before taking one's degree was and somewhat still is a common occurrence, students following individual scholars in their field of study from one university to another to broaden their exposure to a variety of ideologies.

During these medical school years, Karen Horney met and married Oscar Horney in 1909, the following year giving birth to the first of eventually three daughters. Brigitte was her firstborn in 1910 followed by Marianne in 1913 and Renate in 1916. She actually relied upon her Freudian studies of psychoanalysis to work through her own personal problems, thereby learning with a passion the efficacy of this method of psychotherapy. Besides marriage and motherhood, Horney had become fascinated with the newly emerging and soon to be burgeoning field of psychoanalysis, thanks to Freud and his professional society of psychoanalysts. Losing her mother two years after her marriage, she found that her husband Oscar was a duplicate of her own father but chose not to challenge his heavy-handed authoritarianism as she was consumed with both the task of mothering three daughters while completing her medical degree. Later, she would look back with regret for having permitted his paternalistic child rearing practices and would write extensively upon the topic. These early experiences certainly played a role in her fascination with the relationship of parenting skills to the child's damaged self-image and self-esteem.

Within seven years of graduating from medical school, Horney was offered a position in the Institute for Psychoanalysis in Berlin, a prestigious institution where she was able to cultivate her knowledge of the field where she lectured extensively for several years. She also had the opportunity of teaching at the New School for Social Research in New York City during this time. One of many notable colleagues of Horney's was Karl Abraham who was himself a friend of Freud's. Abraham kept it no secret that Horney was a gifted and talented psychoanalyst as well as a scholar in the field of psychoanalysis. To both practice as well as teach psychoanalysis provided a unique opportunity for Horney to cultivate her skills as well as her international reputation.

In 1923, just three years after Horney took the teaching position in Berlin, her husband's business failed during which time he had developed meningitis. Becoming depressed, bitter, and irascible, Oscar became increasingly problematic to the serenity of family life with his interventionist posture towards Horney and their children. Concurrently, Horney's brother died during this same year from a pulmonary infection, precipitating a severe strain on Horney's mental health. Another near debilitating bout of suicidal depression. Struggling through these dark years of depression while maintaining her role as both mother and researcher/teacher at the

Institute, she eventually made the decision to make a new start in life in a new place with her daughters.

Though early on and still loyal to the fundamentals of Freudian psychoanalytical theories and practice, true to her nature Horney began to venture out, challenging and questioning the domain assumptions of the orthodox practitioners particularly as related to the Freudian view of women and the implicit bias against female psychology which, according to Freud, was merely and solely a by-product of male psychology. "Penis envy" was the simple justification for such prejudice. Horney was solid and relentless in her criticism of such unquestioned assumptions about female psychology. Mental disturbances among women, she argued vociferously, was located within the matrix of male-dominated cultural prejudices which both fed and was fed upon by Freudian theory of sexuality. Countering Freudian bias, Horney proposed "womb envy" as the nexus of male envy towards pregnancy, nursing, and motherhood, i.e., the female capacity for creating and sustaining life, and this feeling of male inferiority spawned male superficial superiority in culture, society, and family relations.

Moving to the United States in 1930 at the age of forty-five, she had great fortune in having as her first American job that of Associate Director of the Chicago Institute for Psychoanalysis, a position she held for two years. Subsequently, she and her daughters moved to Brooklyn where she found a lively intellectual and professional community of Jewish refugees primarily from Germany. Here to her great joy and personal professional development and success, she became friends with both Erich Fromm and Harry Stack Sullivan. Though the intimate relationship which developed with Fromm ended in great bitterness, the friendships she cultivated within the professional psychotherapeutic community of New York at the time served her career splendidly. Sullivan was particularly credited with introducing her to the value and place of the behavioral sciences in psychotherapy and their relevance to the understanding of the etiology of mental illness traced to a failure of social interactional skills development during childhood. Here, again, constituted a fertile matrix for her deep interest in child psychopathology and the effectiveness of a modified psychoanalytic approach.

Horney's drift away from orthodox psychoanalysis and Freudian theory of sexuality came early in her career as she explored more substantively her fascination with what she thought of as lifelong growth and development. Though she continued for a while both practicing and teaching in the Berlin Psychoanalytic Society (at least until 1932), Freud had become increasingly distant towards her believing, as he did and rightly so, that Horney was moving away from his school of theory and practice towards a more female-expansive view of psychotherapeutic practice. Owing to her increasing fears of Nazi expansionism in Germany, she accepted an invitation from Franz Alexander to join the Chicago Institute of Psychoanalysis. Her marriage having come undone prior to this invitation and upon her immediate acceptance, she took her daughters to Chicago where she became increasingly convinced of the central importance of socio-cultural factors in psychological development. Besides Erich Fromm and Harry Stack Sullivan, she was befriended by such scholarly giants of the time as Margaret Mead, Paul Tillich, and Ruth Benedict, all representing the behavioral and social sciences as well as philosophy.

Unstoppable in her quest for a deepening and broadening of psychoanalytic theory and practice outside the pale of Freudian orthodoxy, Horney based her emerging theories upon her own clinical practice wherein the experience of working with patients allowed her the opportunity of exploring new methods, new insights, new approaches to previously established practices. Her confidence, as was true of Harry Stack Sullivan, in her patients' own ability to work out their neurotic causalities with an assisting practitioner was anathema to accepted practice but she found this approach rewarding to her patients.

Inevitably, her resistance to adherence to the Freudian received practice, to the orthodox interpretation of psychoanalytic theory, resulted in her being dismissed from membership in the New York Psychoanalytic Institute in 1941 following years of successful practice and a broadly established reputation as a scholar and therapist. The result of this dismissal was that she predictably created her own professional body called the Association for the Advancement of Psychoanalysis.

Eager to advance herself, she set about researching, writing and teaching upon a topic of genuine interest to her professionally, namely, a composite theory of neurosis and personality based on her own clinical experience in psychotherapy within the context of psychoanalytic theory. As noted above, while her first major career appointment was as the Associate Director of the Chicago Institute for Psychoanalysis for a two-year commitment, in 1937 she made a significant advancement in her American reputation, just seven years after coming to America, by publishing a major book titled, *The Neurotic Personality of Our Time,* which gained her a foothold in the field given its popularity as a readable book within psychotherapy. This book was followed two years later by another extremely popular work titled *New Ways in Psychoanalysis.* Here she explicated her argument that environmental and social conditions, not just instinctual or biological determinism as argued by Freud, constituted the basis for personal development. She insisted that these socio-cultural factors must be taken full account of in both the development of human personality and in the etiology of mental illness. One of her major disputes with orthodox psychoanalysis was over the inordinate use of the concept of libido as well as the death instinct and the whole matrix embodied in Freudian Oedipus complex theories. Drawing from the insights learned from her behavioral science colleagues, particularly Fromm and Sullivan, she was convinced that the socio-cultural matrix of personality growth and development had been underplayed by psychoanalytic theory and must be corrected.

Agreeing with Harry Stack Sullivan, Horney was convinced that the etiology of neurosis could be traced to the infantile experience of anxiety in which the child experiences acute isolation and helplessness in a hostile world. Coping strategies can and do become the basis for the emergence of neurotic behavior and personality disorders. Within four years of the publication of these books, she had become the Dean of the American Institute of Psychoanalysis, a major training center in the U.S. During this time, as mentioned above, Horney also established her own organization, the Association for the Advancement of Psychoanalysis, owing to her growing dissatisfaction with the restrictive and overly orthodox practice of psychoanalysis within the established medical community of committed Freudian psychoanalysts. Again, in 1945 she published a major work on interpersonal relationships titled *Our Inner Conflicts* and within five years followed it with *Neurosis and Human Growth.* Much later, her ideas regarding female psychoanalytic theories relevant to sexual development were expounded extensively in her now classic in the field titled *Feminine Psychology* released in 1967. As she was influenced by Fromm and Sullivan, so those who followed after Horney would become the founders of the Third Force of Humanistic Psychology, namely, Abraham Maslow and Carl Rogers, who were always quick to credit the influence of Horney in the development of their own work.

As we have said, this breach between her innovative approach and that of the orthodox practitioners eventually led to her resignation as the Dean of the AIP. Taking a teaching post at the New York Medical College, she ventured out into the scholarly world of publishing by launching her own professional journal, *The American Journal of Psychoanalysis.* She continued in this professional matrix of teacher/scholar/practitioner until her death on

December 4, 1952, in New York City at the age of 67. In 1952, the year of her death, colleagues and friends proposed the establishing of a clinic in her name dedicated to the practice of her expanded type of psychotherapy. She died of cancer that year, but The Karen Horney Clinic opened as a research, training, and low-cost treatment center three years later on May 6, 1955. This Clinic was dedicated to research and the training of medical professionals with special emphasis upon psychiatric practice as well as providing an inexpensive treatment facility for the people of New York City. Patients were treated with psychotherapeutic modalities such as supportive psychotherapy and psychoanalytic social psychotherapy based upon the fundamental teachings and principles of Horney's system of analysis and patient care.

The contributions of Karen Horney to psychology are well known and greatly valued. Her particular insights regarding the psychology of women and the adjustments made to the resulting practice of psychoanalysis have withstood the test of time. Still and unquestionably considered one of the most important and first psychologist to establish the general field of feminine psychology, her adjustments made to Freudian psychotherapeutic theory based on her own clinical practice and critique of that school of thoughts' inordinate emphasis upon the masculine nature of the psyche has endured and thrived. Drawing from her exposure to behavioral and social sciences in the U.S., Horney has demonstrated the centrality of socio-cultural factors in personality development and their relationship to the etiology of mental health and mental illness. Counter balancing the so-called *penis envy* of Freudianism with her concept of *womb envy*, she argued persuasively with clinically empirical evidence for the uniqueness of feminine psychology and its necessary and equal status within the broad field of clinical psychology and psychotherapy. The culturally mandated dependence of women upon men for love, money, security, and protection has driven the female population in western society to the over emphasis upon personal beauty thereby elevating the male population to an inordinate and superficial level of power and authority over society generally and women specifically. Her contributions to both the Third Force of humanistic psychology, particularly as created by Maslow and Rogers, and to Gestalt psychology are well known. But also, her work in the field of what is now respectfully labeled self-psychology as well as neo-Freudian psychoanalytic social psychotherapy must be acknowledged. The rational emotive therapy of Albert Ellis, feminism generally, existentialist thought in a post-Sartrean world, and the clinic named for her all bespeak her enduring legacy.

Horney's theory of neurosis is based upon her own personal life experience and situation and draws from her own knowledge of how she navigated through her childhood and adolescence where interpersonal relationship dysfunctions were common and pervasive. That which distinguishes her theory of neurosis and psychoanalytic practice involves her awareness of inner conflicts occurring within the social matrix of family and society. Neurosis, she contended, is the mechanism whereby individuals are able to cope with interpersonal relationship dysfunctions, events which occur in everyday life for children and adults alike. And many professionals in the field today would argue that Horney's theory of neurosis is still the most insightful and productive theory available for psychotherapists in practice. As with Harry Stack Sullivan, she contended that neurosis was much more contiguous with normal daily life than practitioners of the past were willing to admit or acknowledge. Neurosis itself, she suggested, was a survival mechanism, an attempt to make an otherwise unbearable life livable. It essentially constitutes a coping technique for survival, essentially an effective technique for the damaged self to endure diminished life prospects.

Differing from Freud and the psychoanalytic contention that mental illness generally and neurosis specifically was a result of childhood abuse or neglect, Horney contended with Sullivan that it was parental indifference wherein interpersonal relationship skills were neglected or denied the child during personality development and this constitutes the etiology of mental illness. The key to understanding this perspective, she explained, was to grasp deeply the fundamental characteristic of the child's own perception of his life situation rather than that of the parent's presumed intentions in child care. What a child feels is what is important for it is the determining variable in accounting for the child's sense of a lack of warmth and affection, for instance, from a parent who too frequently is also suffering from a neurosis. Such failure in parenting results in broken promises and insensitivity to the child's purported sense of abandonment.

Understandably, given her personal life story, Horney was particularly interested as both a researcher and a therapist in the meaning and nature of neurosis and though trained in psychoanalysis, her inclinations reached far beyond the orthodox approach to analysis and treatment. Her extensive clinical records based on patient reports constituted the basis for her innovative approach to neurosis, treating it not as a biogenic dysfunction of mental processes but rather tracing its etiology to environmental conditions particularly in childhood and adolescence. Agreeing with Harry Stack Sullivan that mental health and mental illness are more commonly traceable to social environmental events, situations, and interactional relationships between children, parents, siblings, and playmates, Horney placed much more emphasis upon the child's perception and interpretation of events and relationships, whether those perceptions and interpretations were correct or not. It is the child's feelings about these events which matter in personality development and, naturally, in the emergence of mental illness if there is a negative assessment of these relationships on the part of the child wherein self-esteem and self-image fall short of the child's ideal self.

In her book on the neurotic personality, Horney suggested that neurosis consists of a psychic disturbance which is brought on by fears and defenses against these fears and by the inevitable attempts on the part of the neurotic to identify a compromise solution between conflicting inclinations. A neurotic individual struggles with mechanisms for coping and managing psycho-social environmental stressors which occur commonly in everyday life. These individuals, as neurotics, cannot, however, have been diagnosed and treated in the absence of a thorough assessment of their socio-cultural behavioral matrix, i.e., their social environment involving interpersonal relationships. Neurosis emerges out of the dysfunction of interpersonal relationships and, whereas Freud believed that instinctual drives and biologically determined behavior constitute the generative *milieu* for mental illness, Horney, on the contrary, agreed with Harry Stack Sullivan and others that the socio-cultural matrix of interpersonal relationships constituted the fundamental arena for the etiology of both mental health and mental illness.

According to Horney, the neurotic has come by his fears through the medium of the culture and social environment. In orthodox Freudian psychoanalysis, the neurotic person's real self is determined by the individual's concept of the ego, an ego without initiative or power. Horney, on the other hand, argues that the neurotic person is driven by emotional forces generated by the social life of the individual, the social and cultural as well as interpersonal environment. Rather than agreeing with Freud that neurotic behavior is essentially instinctual and, thus, biogenic, Horney argues to the contrary that neurotic behavior is generated psychogenically through the influence of the social environment and interpersonal relations. Neurotic behavior, then, constitutes a matrix of compensation and coping mechanism to permit life to continue in the face of fears and anxieties, stress and self-doubt.

Not out of character with most theory-builders in psychotherapy, Horney, like Adler, Erikson and Maslow, believed in itemizing components of a system of theory. So, her "ten patterns of neurotic needs" were based on her psychiatric and psychotherapeutic experience in clinical practice. Successful living, she believed, required these basic ingredients, adjusting them according to individual idiosyncrasies and, though theoretically possible that a single individual might manifest all of these needs, it was her clinical experience which led her to suggest that only a few of these were necessary in an individual to manifest neurosis. Classified as "coping strategies" in her nomenclature, they are as follows:

Moving Toward People (*compliance needs*)

1. The need for affection and approval; pleasing others and being liked by them.

2. The need for a partner; one whom they can love and who will solve all problems.

Moving Against People (*aggression needs*)

3. The need for power; the ability to bend wills and achieve control over others—while most persons seek strength, the neurotic may be desperate for it.

4. The need to exploit others; to get the better of them. To become manipulative, fostering the belief that people are there simply to be used.

5. The need for social recognition; prestige and limelight.

6. The need for personal admiration; for both inner and outer qualities—to be valued.

7. The need for personal achievement; though virtually all persons wish to make achievements, as with No. 3, the neurotic may be desperate for achievement.

Moving Away from People (*detachment needs*)

8. The need for self-sufficiency and independence; while most desire some autonomy, the neurotic may simply wish to discard other individuals entirely.

9. The need for perfection; while many are driven to perfect their lives in the form of well-being, the neurotic may display a fear of being slightly flawed.

10. Lastly, the need to restrict life practices to within narrow borders; to live as inconspicuous a life as possible.

Horney found that this listing provided a quick and meaningful reference point in her therapeutic practice. And, with further use, she realized that by combining these into three more broadly conceived classifications, the analysis and treatment plan could more readily be employed. *Compliance Needs, Aggression Needs,* and *Detachment Needs* became her three categories for classifying neurotic behavior. "Moving towards people" constituted her description of compliance needs, a behavior pattern characterized by self-effacement where, for example, children are confronted with difficulties in interacting with parents. In such situations, the fear of abandonment or general helplessness are lumped into a sense of basic anxiety. Such children often demonstrate a conspicuous need for affection and approval from parents, siblings, and/or peers and identifying a friend or confidant in whom reliance fosters a false sense of enduring security. These individuals, both children and adults suffering from this basic anxiety, usually fail to place demands on others in their relationships, often denigrating themselves to a self-state of inconsequentiality.

The second classification of coping strategies Horney labelled "Aggression Needs," or more commonly characterized as aggressive behavior "moving against people." Somewhat more elaborate and expansive than the first category of compliance needs, the neurotic individual, child or adult, commonly manifests anger and hostility towards his social environment. The sense of a need for power, control and even exploitation is conspicuous and there is a recognizable veneer of omnipotence in social situations. Within this behavioral matrix, Horney is quick to suggest that social recognition, if not outright social approval, is very much sought by such an individual. Popularity seems not to be the driving force but rather acknowledgment and possibly being feared as the desired effect. This aggressive neurotic type produces an avoidance behavior of others within his social arena for this type of individual is perceived by the social group as willing to do whatever it takes for personal happiness even at the cost of hurting or alienating members of the social peer group.

Horney was particularly keen on exploring what she chose to call "Detachment Needs" for it was within this matrix of behavior that she found an opportunity to explore child/parent relationships in a detailed fashion. She called this category "moving-away-from" and sometimes "resignation solutions" which characterizes the detached personality of the abandoned or overlooked child. There are those children for whom the social environment has fostered a sense of self-sufficiency which distinguishes them from both the aggressive as well as the compliant behavioral categories. This withdrawal characteristic is more non-aggressive in nature, seeking rather solitude and personal independence as the preferred behavioral posture towards the social group. The driving desire, however, for perfection can become an inordinately motivating behavioral pattern such that a high level of intolerance for others and for oneself in the face of behavior assessed as less than perfect. Because of this driving force towards perfection, tolerance of others is often a low priority and the suppression of such feelings as love and hate become paramount in this type of personality.

Never willing to stand still when work in theory development was needed, she continued to refine these categories of assessment throughout her professional career. Just two years before her death in 1952, she published what became the most commonly quoted summary of her latest theories regarding personality development in a book titled *Neurosis and Human Growth: The Struggle Toward Self-Realization* (1950). More than merely a summary of her ideas regarding neurosis and neurotic needs, she further clarified and extended her concepts of the three neurotic solutions to the stress and anxiety of living. Herein she proposed a tripartite combination of narcissistic, perfectionistic, and arrogant-vindictive approaches to life which essentially constituted a rethink of these concepts which had first appeared in print in her 1939 book *New Ways in Psychoanalysis.* Using clinical case studies from her own practice, she developed a concept called "morbid dependency" which addressed those individuals suffering from the neurotic characteristics of narcissism and resignation. In a concluding statement, she emphasizes that where non-neurotic individuals may act out components of these three needs categories, the truly neurotic person will inevitably display deeper, stronger, more willful drives to fulfill these needs. This last book was acclaimed by both her protagonists and antagonists as her finest work.

Whereas Freud and the orthodox school of psychoanalysis placed a great deal of emphasis upon the central function of narcissism within the context of psychoanalytic theory, Horney preferred, and said so emphatically, to view the narcissistic personality as having been produced by social environmental situations and circumstances rather than the biogenic features.

Whereas her concept of self-idealization was thought of as compensatory in the behavioral matrix of the developing personality (as are all defense strategies), she argued that the narcissistic personality is inclined to self-indulgence even and essentially in the absence of a genuinely merited self-esteem. Therefore, she contended that weak self-image produces narcissistic behavior. Furthermore, whereas Freud was not indifferent to the reality of inner conflicts within the neurotic or narcissistic patient, he merely saw them as illustrative of repressed anxiety. He regarded the individual's inner self with a sort of disbelief in the essential goodness of the human person and in personality growth and development.

With Jean-Paul Sartre, Freud was content with the idea that individuals are condemned to destroy themselves through self-induced suffering brought on by unrealistic desires and ambitions. Horney was not satisfied with this pessimistic view of the human condition but strove for a reason to hope for a better world in the nurture of the human spirit's drive for self-fulfillment. That is to argue that the damaged self is not inevitable. This position put her front and center of the humanistic tradition called the Third Force created by Carl Rogers and Abraham Maslow. The conflict in life between contradictory neurotic tendencies, Horney suggested, and the attitudes embodied in the individual who is suffering from neurosis towards the self, personal qualities, and social values, constituted a life situation which could, with effort and intentionality, be directed towards personal fulfillment and self-actualization. The prospects for such a corrective in behavior for the neurotic narcissist suffering from inner conflicts is to be found within the individual himself, confident that the human person embodies the very source of his own mental health. This comes, of course, from the cultivation of meaningful and enriching interpersonal relationships wherein lies the prospects for a deepening of a sense of self-esteem and self-worth and a divestiture of narcissistic self-indulgence and inner conflict.

For Horney, psychoanalysis consisted of a theory of assessment and description as well as a modality of treatment based upon the centrality not in the Freudian psychoanalytical tradition of the biogenic etiology of mental illness but on the meaning and relevance of interpersonal relationship skills development beginning in early childhood and progressing throughout adolescence. The socializing factors of the individual child in relationship to the parent proves crucial in the development of mental health or the appearance of mental illnesses such as narcissism and personality dysfunction. Self-image as well as self-esteem and self-worth all constitute the challenge to the healthy maturation process of children into adolescence. Childhood neurosis finds its origin precisely here in the early skills development of interpersonal relationships, says Horney. It is here that the child's self-concept is nurtured or damaged. As in childhood, so in adulthood, neurotic individuals are those persons who have struggled against the odds of an emotionally poor social environment to gain a sense of self-worth, rather losing their capacity to make good decisions, gripped by fear of relationships and the unknown as well as obsessive-compulsive behaviors, anxiety, and depression. The goal of psychoanalysis, according to Karen Horney, is to facilitate a systemic change in the individual's personal assessment of his life situation, changing opinions and perceptions of and about life by assisting the individual in reaching deep within his own sense of self-worth towards a looming potential found in self-realization and self-actualization.

Horney's work led her to believe that neurotic behavior is spawned by social environmental conditions and provides the foil for understanding the etiology of mental illness itself. Individuals, at whatever level of self-actualization, should have the capacity, opportunity, and responsibility of seeking to realize their full potential through personal relationships and self-understanding.

Psychoanalysis in the form of Horney's understanding cannot, she explains, solve the world's problems, such as they are. However, self-analysis can lend itself to a deepening of one's own sense of self, the real self, a self which has the capacity of seeking greater fulfillment. Psychoanalytic therapy, Horney contended throughout her professional life, lends itself to the development of a deeper sense of self and a greater capacity for self-fulfillment. Transference or love for the therapist by the patient Horney downplayed *vis a vis* the orthodox Freudian notion of transference and counter-transference being the glue that binds the patient to the therapist and *vice versa*. Rather, says Horney, the patient's fear of others, the unknown, the outside world of conflict, constitutes the drive towards the therapist rather than a Freudian notion of "love for the therapist." Facilitating the patient who suffers from feelings of helplessness and naturally a sense of dependence upon the therapist, psychoanalysis in the Horney tradition, is designed specifically to foster a sense of self-confidence and self-reliance within the framework of a clinical relationship built upon trust.

Though initially a cause of anxiety and stress, eventually Horney came to view her departure from the orthodox Freudian psychoanalytic school of analysis and therapy as a good thing, joining Alfred Adler and many others later in the formation of what became known, ironically, as the Neo-Freudian school of psychoanalysis. While Adler despised the use of Freud's name and his school of thought avoiding it with a passion, the emergence of the Neo-Freudian school by name, theory, and practice could not finally be ignored or denied. With less rancor and more critical acumen than Adler seemed capable of, Horney was able to delineate the points of subtle as well as significant variances in theory and practice between the orthodox Freudians and the neo-Freudians and did so without rancor.

Carl Jung would eventually join the ranks of Horney in her aggressive disputing with Freud over the centrality of sex and aggression as the primary determiners of personality. Furthermore, Freud's inordinate emphasis upon the nature and function of "penis envy" proved to be a significant point of departure in these two competing schools of psychoanalysis. Freud's naïve assessment of female jealousy of what he thought of as the male's natural power and dominance was, according to Horney, indicative of an overly inflated masculinity rather than a truly natural assessment of the male-female relational matrix. Whereas a neurotic woman may be susceptible to penis envy, Horney believed that "womb envy" occurs just as frequently among insecure men owing to a natural male tendency to resent woman's ability in child birth, mothering, and nurturing of the young. The male drive to success, Horney contended, may actually be a reflection of the substitutionary character of the absent womb in men. She further extended this, at the time, controversial assessment of male vulnerability by suggesting that men have a tendency to envy women, unconsciously, for their capacity for simply "being" in society rather than, as with men, having to prove themselves worthy of their elevated place in society.

Horney was somewhat baffled by the Freudians' inordinate emphasis on the centrality of the male sex organ and found it necessary to reformulate the psychoanalytic concept of the Oedipal complex by suggesting, based on her own personal experience as a child and her clinical experience as a therapist, that the child grasping and holding tight to one parent over the other and jealousy towards one in favor of another was merely the inevitable result of anxiety produced in a dysfunctional interpersonal relationship with one or the other parent. Socio-cultural etiology rather than a biogenic etiology constituted the best explanation for such behavior according to Horney. Not early willing to separate herself professionally or ideologically from the Freudian school of psychoanalysis, Horney struggled admirably in an attempt to reformulate concepts, theories, and modalities of treatment which had been produced by Freud and his psychoanalytic group of practitioners, seeking all the while for a more comprehensive, socio-culturally sensitive and informed theoretical matrix based on a behavioral science awareness of personality development.

The humanistic school of psychology called the Third Force by Maslow and Rogers, the First Force being Skinner's Behaviorism and the Second Force being Freud's psychoanalysis, was very attractive to Horney and the relationship was mutually complimentary of both theory and practice within her own school of *psychoanalytic social psychotherapy*. With Maslow, she believed that all people fundamentally seek "self-actualization" in which she defined the self as an individual's own personal being and potentiality. The individual who has a comprehensive grasp of his own self, that individual is thereby at liberty to seek his full potential in the achievement of reasonable goals. The healthy person realizes self-actualization through this process of quest and achievement rather than, in a Freudian sense, a neurotic individual's inevitable search for self-interest and pleasure based on a set of key needs.

Individuals essentially have two separate views of themselves, according to Horney, viz., the "real self" and the "ideal self." The former is the actual person as he really is and the latter is that type of person each individual feels they should be or desires to be. The former has the capacity for growth, development, and maturity towards a self-fulfilling happiness through the employment of will power and the utilization of personal gifts. The ideal self, however, is used as a "model" in guiding the real self towards self-actualization. Knowledge of the difference is a sign of personal maturity and a healthy self-image. Horney was convinced that the neurotic person's self was divided between an idealized self and a real self. However, the neurotic person finds himself being self-critical for having not been able to live up to the standards of the ideal self. Anxiety rises in these persons in relationship to the rising awareness of a "flawed nature," having failed themselves by not meeting their ideal standards. Unfortunately, the goals for self-actualization set by the neurotic person are unrealistic, not attainable, and therefore the individual is set up for failure by producing a diminished self-esteem boarding on self-contempt. Furthermore, this diminished self-image becomes, then, in the mind of the neurotic person the true self thus creating an oscillation between the ideal perfect person and the diminished flawed person. Fluctuating between narcissism and self-contempt, the neurotic person continues to fall deeper and deeper into neurotic behavior. Horney chose to call this "the tyranny of the shoulds" in which the neurotic person's quest for perfection leads to a demented self-image. Unless this "cycle of neurosis" can be broken, the individual is doomed to a perpetual state of mental disorder.

Though clearly a pioneer in more ways than one, Horney has specifically characterized her reputation and scholarship as that of being one of the first female psychiatrists and the credited founder of what has become established as feminine psychology. Between 1922 and 1937, she wrote fourteen papers on various aspects of the topic which were published in a single volume titled *Feminine Psychology*. With so very few women recognized or even accepted into the psychoanalytic society of medical practitioners at the time, Horney was determined both to call attention to that void in the profession and to offer a substantive contribution as a psychoanalyst to the professional practice. In an essay entitled, "The Problem of Feminine Masochism," for example, she set out to demonstrate that cultures and societies globally encourage women to be dependent on men for love, wealth, and protection. Concomitantly, these societies have balanced this directive to women towards masculine dependency by emphasizing male dominance in power and authority. This diminution of the role of women as creators, nurturers, and bearers of the species to the satisfaction for men as women being merely the embodiment of beauty and self-absorption has reduced both the role of men as well as women. Women as objects of grace and beauty with men as objects of power and authority serve neither the potential of women nor men in their quest for self-actualization.

Within this same collection of essays, Horney scoped out the complexities of the conflict. Women have historically been valued based on child birth and the mother/wife figure in the family. The husband-wife relationship too often and historically compares to the parent-child relationship, i.e., the conflict of authority and power, miscommunication and misunderstanding, all of which have fostered a debilitating neurosis of family members – for all are involved including husband, wife, mother, father, and children. And finally, her essay on monogamy became her most notable essay in the collection titled "The Problem of the Monogamous Ideal." Here she explicated the complex and unbalanced relationship between husband and wife, men and women as perpetuated by the male-dominated society in western culture.

Horney contended that both men and women are possessed of a drive to be productive with women satisfying this need normally yet interiorly through pregnancy and childbirth while men through externality such as work and constructive creativity. Horney, to the disbelief of male psychoanalytic practitioners, contended that this externality of male ingenuity was motivated by the male's attempt to compensate for not being able to give birth, namely, womb envy!   Such a notion, not well received by the established professional community, nevertheless launched Horney into the public eye resulting in a practical publication of a "self-help" book in 1946 with the title *Are You Considering Psychoanalysis?*   Extremely controversial within the orthodox profession of psychoanalysis specifically and psychotherapy and psychiatry generally, she suggested that for the normally healthy man or woman there is the possibility of them being their own personal psychotherapist! Self-treatment for the self-helper was the theme with heavy emphasis upon the notion that an awareness of the self can and should foster self-esteem producing stronger, more confident, and more fulfilling lives for both men and women. This drift towards the popularization of psychotherapy was, in the minds of many professionals, a downward trajectory of her otherwise distinguished career as teacher, researcher, and clinician.

Throughout her professional career, Horney was keen to emphasize the central role of parenting in the personality development of children. She believed that the etiology of mental illness could be traced, as did Freud and the whole school of psychoanalysis, back to childhood. However, rather than child sexual abuse or physical neglect as the cause of neurosis, she believed, based on her own personal experience and her clinical practice, that the fundamental root cause of mental illness could be traced to parental indifference during a child's early formative years. Horney was eager to acknowledge the profound impact the work of Harry Stack Sullivan had upon her with his theory of interpersonal psychotherapy's emphasis precisely upon this point of parental guidance and its role in precluding or predicting mental illness in adulthood. This notion was so very central to her theory of personality development and the etiology of neurosis that she labelled it the "basic evil," namely, parental indifference wherein there is a lack of parental warmth and affection towards the child. In the absence of warmth and expressive love, children develop a plethora of neuroses which can plague them throughout their adult lives.

Understanding what was thought of as this "basic evil" of parental indifference was key to Horney's psychotherapeutic assessment and treatment of mental illness, particularly neurosis. This understanding is based upon the child's perception of the meaning and nature of the parental relationship and with emphasis upon perception rather than what objectively may be thought of as the real situation. A well-intentioned parent who thinks of themselves as trying their best to be a good mother (or father) may very well fail in the effort by presenting a style of parenting which is perceived by the child to exemplify indifference. Gifts and favors, for example which Horney experienced from her father, do not substitute for warmth and nurture regardless of the intention of the parent. Again, as in her case, preferential treatment of one child over another or falsely blaming one child for another child's misdemeanors can constitute the basis for a perception of indifference. Furthermore, such things as on-again off-again favors and affirmations, warm one moment, cold another, failed promises, inordinate teasing about a child's appearance or ideas or attitudes all can converge into a matrix of neurosis-producing parental behavior. Whether exemplified by a neurotic parent or merely a parent periodically (and understandably) distracted by the demands of life, the results can be disastrous for the child.

The self-survival instincts of children Horney was quick to identify and applaud. Again, as in her own life, there are response mechanisms endemic to child maturation which can work for their benefit in a survival mode of interpersonal relationships. Often and to their credit, a child's response to the "basic evil" of parental indifference is anger giving rise to a persistent hostility which manifests itself most commonly as protesting against the injustices characterizing the indifferent parent's parenting behavior. The effectiveness of this hostility can, if it proves beneficial to the child's coping with the family situation, becomes a habitual response to many of life's difficulties which, Horney explains, can and does often become an aggressive coping strategy throughout adulthood. However, and Horney is quick to make this point, many children rather find themselves overwhelmed by the experience resulting in an often-debilitating anxiety about life and relationships. Such anxiety produces a persistent experience and fear of helplessness and even abandonment in the face of parental indifference. Horney notes that an alternative to anger and hostility is the realization by the child that if stability is to be maintained in the relationship with parents, then anger and hostility must be replaced by a copying mechanism she has called compliance. In the absence of love, at least the child can avoid in his own perception parental hatred. When neither aggressive nor compliant behavior can produce the desired relationship between child and parent, then the only apparent solution is withdrawal from family interaction and activity. This Horney called the third coping strategy.

That Karen Horney was a pioneering psychoanalytic social psychotherapist has been shown without question. The first woman psychiatrist to venture into the troubled waters of modifying Freudian psychoanalytic theory, Horney's courage both as a professional in the field and a woman in a man's world cannot but be admired and applauded. And, to put a fine point on it, the correctives as well as elaborate improvements to many of the orthodox theories and concepts within psychoanalysis which she developed have stood the test of time. Combining a thorough training in traditional Freudian psychoanalysis with her not reluctant readiness to spot a weakness and address it with creative improvements, Horney demonstrated the unique insights which a woman psychiatrist could and did make to the male dominated professional practice of psychotherapy at the time. Her critique of Freud's overly enthusiastic fascination with the sexual origins of mental illness and her dismissive posture relative to female penis envy and the introduction of the profoundly important concept of male womb envy all converged to make her insights both attractive and viable. Furthermore, and to her profound credit, she joined Abraham Maslow and Harry Stack Sullivan in their embrace of the behavioral sciences and the application of the insights of social psychology to psychotherapeutic theory and practice.

SELECTED PRIMARY SOURCES OF KAREN HORNEY

Neurosis and Human Growth, Norton, New York, 1950.

Are You Considering Psychoanalysis? Norton, 1946.

Our Inner Conflicts, Norton, 1945.

Self-analysis, Norton, 1942.

New Ways in Psychoanalysis, Norton, 1939.

The Neurotic Personality of our Time, Norton, 1937.

Feminine Psychology (reprints), Norton, 1922–37 1967.

The Collected Works of Karen Horney (2 vols.), Norton, 1950.

The Adolescent Diaries of Karen Horney, Basic Books, New York, 1980.

The Therapeutic Process: Essays and Lectures, ed. Bernard J. Paris, Yale University Press, New Haven, 1999.

The Unknown Karen Horney: Essays on Gender, Culture, and Psychoanalysis, ed. Bernard J. Paris, Yale University Press, New Haven, 2000.

Final Lectures, ed. Douglas H. Ingram, Norton, 1991.—128 p.

John H. Morgan

CHAPTER ELEVEN

MELANIE KLEIN and Object Relations Therapy in Child Psychotherapy

Melanie Klein's brand of psychoanalytic theory and practice represents one of the major schools in the broad field of psychotherapy. Followers of her system of theory and practice referred to as Kleinian psychoanalysts are recognized members of the International Psychoanalytical Association which has a distinguished following in the United Kingdom, Latin America, and throughout Western Europe. However, within the United States, the Psychoanalytic Center of California is presently the only major center for training in Kleinian psychoanalytic practice owing, possibly, to the fact that the Kleinian practice of psychoanalysis still follows the traditional orthodox Freudian system of the proverbial couch and four to five sessions a week style of treatment. Rather than focusing upon the patient's ego development, Klein's approach is to focus on the deeper and more primordial emotions and fantasies of the patient. While questioning some of the fundamental components of traditional Freudian psychoanalysis, she with Erik Erikson and Karen Horney and somewhat with Harry Stack Sullivan still very much considered herself a psychoanalyst in the Freudian tradition. Emphasizing that allegiance, Klein was recognized as the first orthodox psychoanalyst to employ Freudian theory and practice in the treatment of children. Modifying and patenting her methodology in the treatment of children, such as play therapy using toys and childhood props, she cultivated a whole system of treatment and theory relative to infant personality development and, most decidedly like Freud himself, she was extremely demanding of her students requiring loyalty to her theory and modality of

205

treatment out of which grew a highly refined and respected training program in psychoanalysis. Its distinguishing feature centered around the development and use of *object relations theory*.

The wide spread pervasiveness of object relations theory in the modern practice of child psychology and psychotherapy in western countries and particularly the United States is counter balanced by the common absence of knowledge within the general population of the creator of that theory. Ironic it is that Melanie Klein has been one of the most important theoreticians in modern psychotherapy while both name recognition and credit for her pioneering work in the field are singularly absent. With Karen Horney and Anna Freud, Klein is considered within the hallowed halls of the academy and in the clinical setting of therapeutic practices one of the most important psychologists of the 20th century. While Anna Freud and Karen Horney are universally heralded as key figures in modern psychology owing particularly to their profoundly important contributions to female psychology and feminine psychotherapy, Klein is held up within the professional community as a brilliant theoretician and clinician owing to her development of object relations theory and its expansive application and relevance to child psychotherapy. She is recognized not only as a major female psychologist but as a major psychologist in the field of a modified application of neo-Freudian psychoanalysis. Credited rightfully as the major force in the development of a new school of psychoanalysis known as object relations therapy, she demonstrated the effectiveness of this system of thought in her work with mother-infant-child relationships as related particularly to personality development. The influence of this profoundly insightful modality of analysis and treatment has been felt and reflected by and in the work of John Bowlby and Donald Winnicott to name only two of a plethora of prominent psychotherapists. Though indirectly through her psychoanalytic psychotherapy, she has, nevertheless, made and her work continues to make major contributions to the general fields of social psychology and developmental psychology, especially in the sub-fields of parent-child relations and personality development theory.

Born in Vienna on March 30, 1882, into a middle-class Jewish family, Melanie was the youngest of four children. Her father, Moriz Reizes, was a general practitioner of medicine in Galicia. Her mother, with whom she had a troubled and complicated relationship, Libussa Deutsch Reizes, was never a real source of nurture or encouragement. Melanie's closest family tie was with her only brother, Emanuel who died at an early age in 1902 when Melanie was just twenty years old. Melanie Reizes took her education in the local city gymnasium, but her childhood dreams of pursuing the study of medicine were not realizable at the time owing to a serious decline in the family fortune. The alternative was marriage and so she married Arthur Klein, an industrial chemist, and they began their family life together eventuating in the birth of three children. Understandably, she suffered early on in her marriage from depression and a nervous disorder resulting from, as she explained it many years later, a difficult relationship with her overly domineering mother. First living with him in Rosenheim, in 1910, she moved with her husband and children to Budapest and there she was fortunate to have the opportunity of entering psychoanalysis with the famous Sandor Ferenczi, one of Freud's most faithful and favored supporters. This analysis and relationship proved of monumental importance in her future development professionally as well as personally. Her therapist, Ferenczi, recognized her intellectual acumen and was fully cognizant of her passion for psychoanalytic theory, so he encouraged her to employ her growing understanding of psychoanalysis in the care and treatment of her own children. Extremely unorthodox, if not unprofessional, this trajectory of psychoanalysis applied to children was the first instance of such practice to occur and, fully aware of the originality of this approach, Klein began to develop a schema of techniques in child analysis which has endured the test of time and is still employed today virtually unchanged. In what she early on chose to call her "play technique," Klein would note the child's play activities and interpret them as symbolic of unconscious data within the child's psyche, interpreting this data in the same orthodox and traditional way as was applied in adult analysis. Eventually, she became the first practicing psychoanalyst to approach children's play as providing meaningful data in their analysis and treatment. This concept of play technique naturally contributed to a more formalized development in America of what we commonly think of today as play therapy in child counseling.

Klein's own personal life was full of tragedy and the scars of such were seen and carried throughout her professional and personal life. She learned even as a child that she was unwanted by her parents who showed her little affection. This experience, of course, resonates closely with Karen Horney's notion of the emergence of anxiety, fear, and anger within the child who has experienced parental indifference as a developmental phenomenon. Klein had an older sister whom she dearly loved but who died when Klein was only four years old. The result was that she was felt responsible for the death of both of her siblings.

Klein attended the International Psycho-Analytic Congress in Budapest in 1918 at age 36 and there for the first time had an opportunity to meet Freud himself. She once said she remembered vividly how impressed she was and how the wish to devote myself to psychoanalysis was strengthened by this impression. She was very eager to become a member of that professional body of psychoanalysts in Hungary based on the scholarly strength of a paper she presented before that professional assembly dealing with the application of psychoanalytic practice to the treatment of children. She eventually did, and to her great professional advantage, become a member of the Hungarian Psycho-Analytic Society. However, her marriage to Arthur Klein was rapidly declining and as a result she left him, taking the children with her to Berlin where fortunately she was welcomed into the Berlin Psycho-Analytic Society. At age 38, the separation for Klein was wrenching and the move to Berlin was seen as a real opportunity to immerse herself into the most exciting training center at the time for psychoanalytic study. Little money and few friends did not deter her as she believed deeply that her future lay within the practice of child psychoanalysis. As we will see later, she pleaded with Karl Abraham to take her on as a trainee analyst. One of the leading voices in Berlin in the field of psychoanalysis, he was not afraid to challenge some of the theories and practices of Freud himself. They were of kindred spirits for it is reported that Abraham himself once said that the future of psychoanalysis rests with child analysis.

It was in Berlin that Klein began to blossom both as a student and theorist. While studying with Abraham, she began to study and analyze children's behavior which was to become the basis of her own developing theory of object relations. The approach in the studying of children as young as two years old was too radical for the orthodox establishment of psychoanalytic practitioners in Berlin and she understandably met with great hostility. Being both a divorced woman in conservative Berlin and without even a college degree to show for credentials to practice psychoanalysis, she found the environment stifling and counter-productive to her professional desires as a woman in a male dominated medical community. She would later find quite the opposite reaction when she made her move to London. When Abraham died suddenly in 1925, she was essentially cut off from professional access to the practice of psychoanalysis and her theory-developing enterprise suffered severely. The end of the following year saw her determined to immigrate to England and establish herself (and her young family) in London where she would spend the rest of her life.

Without question, her arrival in London as a practitioner of psychoanalysis and a theory builder related to the treatment of children met with much interest. Personally very beautiful, according to all reports, and rather young to be a practicing therapist, Klein became quietly referred to as "the black beauty" and being Jewish simply added to her mystique. The professional community, primarily made up of older men, became intrigued with her. Klein was unquestionably committed to her work and set about to further, through clinical experience, her deeper understanding of the nature of child development from a psychoanalytic perspective. Besides the standard texts in psychology and Freudian analysis, she was an enthusiastic reader of the classics in Russian, French and English. The theatre and classical music were high on her list of interests and, of course, given her middle-class Viennese childhood education, she played the piano and was an inveterate concert patron and, indicative of her cultural refinements, even winning a wine tasting competition in the South of France. She was purported to hold her own with the highest level of professional practitioners in London in terms of both intellect and class.

But, alas, the picture was not all wine and roses. Klein experienced a great deal of sadness in her life, as a youngster, an adult, a professional, and as a mother. Owing to the early death of her older sister whom her mother made no secret of her being the favorite, Klein developed a periodic and near debilitating depression which persisted throughout her adult life. Subsequently when she was in her 20's, Klein's bother died which proved a real shock owing to their closeness as siblings in a troubled household. The death of Karl Abraham soon after she had begun her analysis with him and from whom she was receiving great encouragement in her theories of child development proved both personally and professionally devastating as well. Later losing a son to apparent suicide and with her daughter turning against her both personally and professionally during the highlight of her rising reputation in

London conspired to stifled her otherwise gregarious public pursuit of an ever-enlarging forum for her lectures on child neurosis and personality development.

As we have noted above, during her time in Berlin, she felt she needed to enter further psychoanalysis and she did so under the care of Karl Abraham, a noted and well-respected psychoanalyst in Berlin admired by Freud himself. Abraham was at the time working on the Freudian concept of the death instinct, developing his own understanding of this concept with ideas related to oral and anal sadistic tendencies he had identified in his treatment of children. We now see that Klein was early influenced by this insight and she soon and aggressively adopted and adapted these ideas into her own understanding and interpretation of children's play activities. Not all practicing psychoanalysts in Berlin either agreed with Abraham or approved of Klein's approach and when Abraham died in 1926, she chose to move with her children to England. There, she set up house-keeping in London, joining the British Psycho-Analytical Society at the personal urgings of Ernst Jones, the colleague and official biography of Freud.

Unlike her cool reception in Berlin excepting for Abraham, Klein found the British psychoanalysts enthusiastically welcoming both of her involvement in the Society and her energetic development of the treatment of children using her ideas of play therapy. For the duration of her professional life, Klein concentrated her efforts in this regard, eventually producing a system of child development theory within the psychoanalytic school of psychotherapy. This approach became so internationally recognized and endorsed that the emergence of an entire school of Kleinian psychoanalysis was the result. The training of these professionals constituted a major part of her work and these innovative insights employing play activities as the basis for analysis and treatment proved to be valued within the professional community as a unique and extremely valuable contribution.

Drawing from her early work with Abraham, she developed an interpretive approach to the death instinct Abraham had identified in early childhood conjoined with the emergence of an early superego construct within the maturing child which offers a corrective to Freud's notion of the Oedipus complex.

Naturally, this reinterpretation of Freudian theory of ego development combined with Klein's notion of play therapy as an analytical technique produced an international incident of controversy between the English therapists and the Viennese Society which at the time was headed by Anna Freud who was herself developing a whole construct of analytical theory of child therapy not in consort or agreement with Klein. Nevertheless, the 1927 Symposium on Child Analysis launched a periodical titled the *International Journal of Psychoanalysis* wherein both Anna Freud and Melanie Klein produced some of their most important work in the broad field of child psychology and psychotherapy. However, and it cannot be overlooked, Anna Freud, who had fled the Nazi persecution in 1938, and the Viennese Group consisting also of Edward Glover and particularly Melanie Klein's own daughter, the distinguished and highly respected psychoanalyst Melitta Schmideberg, were outspokenly critical of Klein's work. From 1927, she and Anna Freud had disagreed as to the proper interpretation and application of psychoanalytic theory to child therapy. This disagreement first became public in the 1927 London Symposium on Child Analysis wherein Anna Freud particularly challenged some of the key theories of Klein in Anna Freud's book titled *An Introduction to the Technique of Child Analysis*. The disagreement centered especially upon the origin of the super-ego within the child for both Anna Freud and her father argued that the super-ego superseded the Oedipus complex whereas Klein argued that the early primordial and harshly emergent super-ego occurred as a result of early experiences within the child's life and evolved out of the child's sadistic impulses, not, according to the Freuds, in identification with the parents.

Consistent with her whole system of child-world construction, Klein described the inner world of early childhood primarily as independent of and free from the influence and experience of the outer world. This inner world, as Klein saw and constructed it from within the perspective and interpretation of the child, was comprised of fantasies of good and bad objects which had their origin from instinctual conflicts growing out of the parent-child relationship. Drawing from Sigmund Freud's theory of the death instinct, Klein argued that these internal objects were essentially manifestations of the inevitable, natural, and fundamentally innate conflicts which emerge between parent and child as the child encounters the outer world from within the inner world construct of the psyche. The driving force for Klein in this matrix of child behavior was that of fear, fear which was an instinctual and naturally destructive impulse originating in the death instinct itself. For Klein the notion was that the etiology of the damaged self in childhood was endemic rather than externally linked to psychosocial and environmental factors which the Third Force psychotherapists like Maslow, Rogers, Sullivan, and Horney believed crucial.

In 1932, she took the opportunity to demonstrate the analytical effectiveness of this theory and application in her book titled *The Psycho-Analysis of Children.* She further explicated this theory and delineated its clinical effectiveness in a series of collected essays published in 1935 titled *A Contribution to the Psychogenesis of Manic-Depressive States,* in 1940 titled *Mourning and Its Relation to Manic-Depressive States,* and again in 1946 titled *Notes on Some Schizoid Mechanism.* She eventually finalized her overall theory of object relations therapy with the defining concept of the paranoid-schizoid position and the depressive position which included a serious accounting of the counter-balancing feelings within the child of love and hate. This refinement gained her much international attention and respect but the seriousness of the conflict with Sigmund and Anna Freud and the entire Freudian school, a debate subsequently referred to in the journals as the Controversial Discussions, occurring in the heat of the Second World War, led to the establishment of a competing school of thought within the British Psycho-Analytic Society. Some have suggested two while others have identified three separate schools of thought and practice – Klein, Freud, and the Independents.

The first major appearance of what would become the defining characteristic of Kleinian psychoanalysis, namely the term and concept "object relations therapy," was in her 1932 book titled *The Psychoanalysis of Children.* In this now classic text based on her own clinical work as a therapist, she suggested that every infant has a primary object relationship to its mother and in this relationship the infant experiences a psychic life which is essentially dominated by sadistic fantasies which originate from what most psychoanalysts, including Karen Horney, then and now recognize as an innate aggressive drive. Extending this what at the time was considered an extremely controversial proposal, she published a major paper dealing with the explication of this object relations theory titled "A Contribution to the Psychogenesis of Manic Depressive States" in 1935. The timing was suggestive of a personal passion and obsession as her son Hans had just recently died prior to the paper's appearance in the journal. Herein she explored and explicated the components of parental mourning and the sense of primitive defense mechanisms in the Freudian orthodox sense in which she introduced her fundamental idea of two phases of personality development.

The first phase of her system she called the *paranoid-schizoid position* and the second phase the *depressive position.* Her idea of the first phase centered round the concept of defense mechanisms within the child. However, this specific idea precipitated heated debate within the British Psycho-Analytic

Society itself, resulting in a series of discussions fraught with controversy occurring during the second World War years around the question as to whether or not what was now being called everywhere "Kleinianism," really constituted an operationally accepted use of the term psychoanalysis or whether, indeed, it was too far removed from orthodox Freudian theory as to preclude its acceptance as a theory and a practice within the British Society. Amazingly British in the resolution of the controversy was the decision to actually teach and practice two different schools of thought, viz., both the Kleinian school and the Freudian school. By doing so, Klein's system of psychoanalysis was the first nationally and eventually internationally recognized challenge to orthodox Freudian definitions of psychoanalysis while still remaining within the tradition of psychoanalysis. Clearly Freud would not agree, but the British sense of compromise facilitated this historic divergence in theory and practice without an actual brake within the professional community of practicing psychoanalysts!

"The book," as her friends and colleagues commonly referred to her 1932 collection of creative, provocative, and quite controversial essays, was very early on recognized and promoted as one of the most original pieces of clinical and theoretical work in the general field of psychoanalysis to date. Whereas Freud, the father of the movement, had proposed a construct of the human psyche which differentiated structures and developmental stages over time from infancy to adulthood, Klein proposed and illustrated a much more dynamic portrayal of psychic development. She contended, for example, that there were a set of processes operative within the human psyche which constituted a complex of emotions built upon a developmental operation concomitantly emerging with profound intensity within the developing child, an explosion of trajectory of consciousness she chose to call "a mosaic of turbulence." It was within this matrix of developmental coalescence within the child psyche that led her to experiment with play through the use of children's toys as a hermeneutical tool for probing the child psyche. This, she argued, was not dissimilar to the function of free association analysis with adults used by Freud.

Interestingly, Klein began to report in her clinical studies that children's play often was characterized by violent fantasies which were acted out within the context of severe and acute anxiety and fear. No clinician had yet engaged in the systematic and laboratory study of child behavior from the psychoanalytic perspective and orientation and her work quickly became both the topic of conversation within the profession and also the basis for ground wars among professionals, those both for and against this approach and interpretation. This psychoanalytic approach to probing the child psyche became the basis upon which subsequent child studies were conducted for she showed her colleagues how to open up the child's interior world for scrutiny and analysis. Child psychoanalysis thereby became a real and viable agenda for the professional practitioner who was willing to employ the Kleinian modality of analysis and therapy. Klein's emphasis was upon "listening to the child" as the child reported on the interior world of their daily experience, a world that for the child is as real as the external world of interactional encounter and personal experience for adults. Through these clinical encounters with the child's psyche produced by play therapy, Klein was able to probe more deeply and substantively the childhood experience of ambivalence, conflicted experiences of love and hate felt towards the mother. These insights led her to a more expansive grasp of the development of human consciousness and the mind itself in relationship to the mother/infant/child matrix of interactional relationships.

Not one to shy away from the problematic or disturbing complexes within human behavior and the psyche, Klein was eager to decipher the tendency, for example, within the human person to destructiveness and the resultant demand for coping with destructive behavior as a complex within social relationships and personality development. Furthermore, and not unrelated to this destructive tendency within the human psyche is the ever-present reality of pervasive envy in human relationships. Her developmental theory of adulthood required a kind of "depressive position" in which the individual is challenged to confront and manage polarization and discrimination. This depressive position or phase as she portrayed it emergences from within the individual's encounter with pain caused by or administered by the other, the "not me" in Sullivan's system. From infantile dependency emerges the individual, a trajectory of development from anxiety towards self-awareness and self-competency.

Needless to say, but worthy here of emphasizing, Klein had become a very powerfully influential professional within the British Psycho-Analytic Society for she was made a member of the prestigious Training Committee, made a training analyst herself, and became the designated and indisputable leader of what was now being called the Kleinian group which, incidentally, included such notable figures as John Bowlby and Donald Winnicott. Nevertheless, such powerbase building was not without its drawbacks as the price paid for the development and exercise of such power within the Society came dearly. Her daughter, the well-known and highly regarded psychoanalyst Melitta Schmideberg, had openly opposed her during these controversial years of struggle and fighting within the British Psychoanalytic Society. She became and remained estranged from her mother until the end of Klein's life. Having immigrated to America, Melitta was never reconciled with her mother and failed even to attend her mother's funeral.

Having lost two of her children already, Klein drove herself more deeply into her professional writing, research, and counseling. Her ideas regarding the early controversial theory of schizoid defense mechanisms she continued to pursue including the nuanced concept of "splitting" and the central role of play in what she began to call "borderline conditions" in mental illness. A major contribution to her psychoanalytic theories centered round the concepts of envy, gratitude, and reparation as exist within the mother-infant relationship matrix.   Clearly, these were intimate themes to herself personally as she was both an estranged daughter and an estranged mother. The 1961 book *Narrative of a Child* was her last major work and it consisted of a detailed case study of an analysis of a young boy during the war years and appeared the year following her death.   She died on 22 September 1960, at the age of 78.

Not surprisingly and without doubt, Klein's modifications and adjustments to orthodox psychoanalytic theory and practice have merited her many followers and not a few detractors. She never stopped working and even towards the end of her life she remained aggressively enthusiastic about clinical research.   Always attractive and never failing to dress with aplomb, she lived with a maid and always had a contract secretary to assist in her writing. Living in Hampstead in a spacious flat overlooking the rolling hills and meadows of the countryside, she continued to entertain, research, and write all with vigor and enthusiasm. Delighting in her grandchildren, the children of her son Erich, ironically her last paper addressed specifically the difficulties of old age and the loneliness it brings.

As with Adler, Jung, Erikson, Horney and so many other psychotherapists in the psychoanalytic school of Freud, Klein was not able and did not herself choose to completely separate herself from the work of Freud in the creating of her brand of psychoanalysis. She, like other practitioners, did, however, wish to extend and expand Freud's original work and this, too often, led to both a misperception of her intentions and a misplaced hostility to her work.   Her passion for psychoanalysis and particularly its potential application to the therapeutic treatment of children drove her to extend Freud's work even when Freud and his daughter as well as their immediate cohort of followers wished her not to do so.

Freud's emphasis upon the meaninglessness of life and, therefore, the need for an existential embrace of the moment constituted for the lay person a sense of life's anomaly, a sense of life with neither purpose nor direction. Yet, in Freudian terms, there was an inevitable call towards what he thought of and developed as the concept of the instinct to die, the death wish, of every person. That sustaining principle, what he called "Eros," which causes us to seek life is counterbalanced by an instinct towards death, what he called "Thanatos." This counterbalancing of life and death, an instinct to live and an instinct to die, Klein became fascinated with and wished to extend its application to the treatment of children in whom she, more than others, had found this counterbalancing phenomenon of life and death.

Klein was quick to point out that Freud's relative indifference to child psychoanalysis was the natural result of his having spent all of his professional career working with adult patients (and Horney would remind us that most of those patents were upper middle-class Jewish women in Vienna). Klein, on the other hand, was driven with a passion for the care and treatment of children rather than adults. She developed remarkable techniques for eliciting insights into the psyche of the child through the use of play wherein a child could feel free in emotional expressive behavior without fear of censorship from watchful adults. Today we would think of phenomenology as this method of allowing the individual to express their emotional feelings without censorship or judgment. This play therapy, as it would eventually be called, encouraged the child to communicate deep feelings of fear and anxiety, hatred and compassion, in a way that the talking therapy of traditional psychoanalysis could not do. Through the use of this posture towards child play Klein applied herself to the development of interpretive techniques of therapeutic intervention without stifling the child's exploration of his inner world. Observing closely but non-intrusively the play behavior of troubled children in a play environment including dolls, animals, pencil and paper, etc., she sought out effective methods of interpreting such behavior and its relative meaning in relationship to their personality disorders.

A failure in interpersonal relationships, as Horney and Sullivan have said earlier, constitutes the basis for the emergence of mental illness and Klein was keen to demonstrate the effective use of psychoanalysis in interpreting such disturbed behavior on the part of troubled children. This had not been done so far with the consistency of analysis and the drive towards operational theory which Klein brought to the subject. Just for example, Klein was able to demonstrate in her analysis how parental figures constituted a central role in childhood fantasies whereas Freud's Oedipus complex method proved consistently ineffective as an analytical tool. Klein was able, to the horror of the orthodox psychoanalyst, to identify evidence of the early emergence in the child psyche of the superego long before the appearance of the Oedipal phase of personality development. This proved to be a "deal breaker" in terms of her collegial relationship with orthodox psychoanalysis for it cut at the very heart of much of Freud's notion of personality development and the interplay between ego and superego.

In every school of psychotherapy, there must be a theory of the unconscious. Freud's psychoanalysis constituted the first serious attempt to explicate the nature and function of the unconscious through clinical research and counseling data. Klein proved to be one of the most important clinicians of the time engaged concurrently in theory-building, particularly the development of object relations theory as well as clinical practice. Klein's theory of the unconscious was informed by Freudian orthodoxy but she proposed to deepen and expand its applicability in the treatment of mental illness particularly among children. She was keen to point out that in object relations theory, the fundamental concern of the therapist is with how an individual's experience of other people from their past affects their present and future relationship with other people. Those early and initial experiences, in infancy and early childhood according to Klein, become a part of the individual's own self-image and are then projected onto future relationships. Object relations theory, then, suggests that an infant's primordially instinctual drives are inevitably directed towards particular objects of experience informed by their fantasies. Therefore, for example, an infant's orientation towards and relationship to an object such as the mother's breast is limited in its totality owing to the infant's present inability to distinguish the breast from the mother. Klein calls this a "partial relationship" and its significance, for the maturation of the infant, has to do with the fact that this relationship, limited and constricted as it necessarily is, functions as a prototype for future relationships with the totality of an object, such as the mother in her complete self.

Owing to this process of gradual development from partial objectivity to total objectivity, the initial experience of the infant is essentially unrealistic owing to its limitations. The fantasy does not completely convey the reality – mother is more than her breast. When this process is nurtured responsibly, the child gradually differentiates the fantasy from the reality and this capacity to differentiation leads to healthy relationships with others in the future. Where there is a failure in this maturation process, the infant as an adult is destined to suffer from a deficient capacity to cultivate meaningful and rewarding interpersonal relationships. This internalization of object relationships, from partial to completion, plays a key role in the nature of an adult's capacity to interact with others. These object relations in infancy, says Klein, are inevitably and necessarily internalized and subsequently unconsciously projected onto others in adult interaction. If the early experiences were positive and the movement from partial to complete recognition of object differentiation is meaningful, then the establishment of mental images of personal interrelationships will prove mature and nurturing. Where the experience has been negative and characterized by a failure to consistently move from partial to complete objectivity, then the individual is destined to suffer from the anxieties and fears of infancy and childhood, not having cultivated a differentiation capacity towards reality of object-fantasy coalescence. Herein, then, lies the matrix of the damaged self in childhood eventuating in adult mental illness.

Owing to her dauntless courage, Klein was able to press on with this trajectory of theory and analysis even in the face of professional criticism and attempted censorship. For example, she applied herself to the study of ultra-aggressive fantasies of such behavior as hate, envy, and greed within the very young troubled child wherein she proposed an interpretation based on her modified and expanded theory of the human psyche suggesting that in this complex behavioral matrix there is a constant oscillation between Eros and Thanatos, between life and death, love and hate. This became a very sophisticated and central theme in much of her therapeutic practice in the treatment of troubled children. The state of the child's psyche when being sustained by the will to live, when this feeling is dominant, she called the "depressive position," but when the emotional state is preoccupied with the destructive tendency towards death and disintegration of life, she called it "paranoid-schizoid position." This duality of concepts became a hermeneutical tool for analytical interpretation of disturbed child behavior. This approach was quickly adopted by her followers who consistently indicated its effectiveness in treatment. She always insisted on viewing aggression within the life of the child as a central factor when analyzing the troubled child and this posture towards aggression within child behavior precipitated a direct conflict with Anna Freud who, at the time, was considered the major voice in child psychology in the England of that day and, needless to say, this conflict constituted a pervasively hostile atmosphere in their continuing professional lives.

The "death instinct" as a central component of her approach to the psychoanalysis of troubled children was not a passing fancy and would not go away as a point of controversy with non-subscribers within the psychiatric profession. Klein believed firmly that she was incorporating the Freudian concept of what Freud had first called the "death instinct," which, as he carefully explained it early in his system's development, was an endemic component of all living things. All life had a tendency towards non-life, towards an "inorganic state" and, therefore by extension, there endures an inclination towards death. According to psychoanalytic theory, the "life instinct" called Eros constituted the *contra* tendency towards life rather than death and aimed at the embodiment of a unifying principle implicit in life itself. Eros, then as the life instinct, was counterbalanced by Thanatos, the death instinct with the former nurturing life, the latter seeking its destruction. Klein agreed with Freud that this bio-mental force of counterbalancing tendencies to life and death constituted the fundamental and foundational nature of the human psyche. These tendencies were human drives and were not reducible to animal instincts for they are primarily unconscious drives made up of the tripartite matrix of id, ego, and superego. These truncated terms – id, ego, superego – constituted a very sophisticated understanding and delineation of the complex nature of the human psyche. Freud's essential *psychocartography* of the human psyche was never abandoned by either Freud or Klein as they found this schematic design of the components of the human psyche useable and manageable as well as efficiently applicable in therapeutic analysis.

As the early psychoanalysts trained by Freud understood the concept of object relations, it was used to describe the bodily drives which serve to satisfy the infant's instinctual needs through the use of an object or focal point of attention and solicitation. Rather simplistic and narrowly applied was this concept in early psychoanalytic theory. However, when Klein came along seeking to extend and expand the concept in her work with mentally disturbed children, she saw the concept of object relations playing a much more central and decisive role in the development of personality in early childhood. She began to differentiate, on the basis of her clinical experience with children, what she saw as either "part-objects" or "whole-objects," that is to say, the difference between a single organ such as the mother's breast and the whole organ such as the mother in her entirety. Either object, partial or entire, can for the infant be the source of satisfaction depending on the drive being served. Two types of drives are operative within the infant at this stage, namely, the libido (recognized as Eros) and the death instinct (recognized as Thanatos). Therefore, argues Klein in her quest to expand the limited Freudian notion of the death instinct in object relations, the object being fixated on by the infant may receive both love and hate with the drive and situation dictating which emotion is being served at what time and under what circumstances.

Never content with the *status quo*, however, and to the disgruntlement of many of Freud's followers as well as himself particularly, Klein moved ahead in her further explication and application of the principle understanding in psychoanalysis of the unconscious particularly as relates to her work with children. Demonstrating how the analysis of children's play was not unlike Freud's analysis of adult dreams, Klein continued her adventurous exploration of the mind of the infant and early childhood during which time, to the great horror and chagrin of Freud and his orthodox followers, she claimed as we noted earlier to have discovered the roots of the superego prior to the emergence of the Oedipus Complex, the darling concept of the orthodox practitioners. By plumbing the child's deepest fears and anxieties through careful observation and analysis of the child's play, she was able to identify the mechanism employed by the troubled child to defend himself against such fears and anxieties and this became the great contribution she and her followers believed she had made to the refinement and extension of psychoanalytic practice in the care and treatment of the troubled child. These very insights constituted a means whereby through child therapy the origins of mental illness within the adult were identified. The etiology of adult mental illness, therefore, could be traced to the troubled mind of the child suffering from incomprehensible fears and anxieties too often perpetrated, sometimes unwittingly, by the indifferent or inattentive parent.

The origin of what eventually became the signature characteristic of Kleinian psychoanalysis, namely object relations theory, had to do with a revisionist approach to the traditionally used concept by Freud and his followers of what was called "splitting," namely, that procedure whereby the child was able to distinguish between love and hate, anger and compassion, particularly as applied to the parental relationship. The good mother/bad mother, good me/bad me binary self-understanding which had its origins in early personality development constituted a sore point of divergence between Klein and the Freudians. The splitting, it was argued, which produced in fairy tales the good mother and wicked mother or the good fairy and the evil witch constituted a mechanism where the child could separate out his feelings of anger and compassion, love and hate felt intermittently towards one parent or the other. The maturation process in personality development necessarily required the ability to distinguish, that is, to separate out, these conflicting feelings held by the child in an oscillating sway of emotional responses to divergent experiences and encounters with a parent. It is generally agreed among professionals in the field that Melanie Klein's major contribution in respect to this concept had to do with her use of the term good/bad objects and the splitting of the objects of encounter such that the child became able to distinguish between the good parent and the bad parent, the right object and the wrong object. In object relations theory, according to Klein, the early infant experiences call for a distinguishing between good objects and bad objects, "splitting" the whole experience of interpersonal encounter using this simple differentiation. This occurs acutely to the child attempting to make functionally viable the struggle between love and hate, creation and destruction, the good and the bad, the right and the wrong. The maturation process centered upon the child's increasing ability to relate these binary experiences, breaking down the false and dysfunctional distinction between each by "depolarization" of these two instinctual drives of life and death, love and hate. Where there is failure to make such distinctions without bifurcation, there is the matrix for the emergence of mental illness and the rise of anxiety and fear leading to neurosis and, when untreated, psychosis.

Ever eager to deepen and extend the relevance of psychoanalytic theory to her practice particularly with troubled children, Klein frequently introduced new terms and concepts or modified and altered older ones to mean more than originally intended. We have seen this with object theory and the death instinct, concepts developed by Freudians but extended by Klein and her school of psychoanalysis. The concept of "projective identification" was introduced by Klein as relates to children and their capacity or lack of ability to handle anxiety and fear. Projection, explains Klein, functions to facilitate the ego's ability to overcome anxiety by dislodging the ego from feelings of danger and evil. The inculcation of the good object, what she called "introjection," is employed by the young child's developing ego as a defense mechanism against this feared anxiety. Expanding Freud's notion, Klein believed that the process of "splitting off" parts of the self-image of the child and then projecting those split-off characteristics into external objects is a process and function profoundly important for the natural development of the child's sense of self. The fundamental effect of this process of introjection in object relations theory is the introduction or inculcation of the good object, whatever that might be. For example, the mother's breast, is, she argues, a precondition for normal personality development. This process nurtures the child's ego-development by focusing upon the good object characteristic of nurture which is anxiety free. This process Klein chose to call "projective identification."

The development of this capacity for self-defense, the creation of a functional defense mechanism, Klein believed was indispensable for the development of a normal ego within the infant including, she suggested, both ego structure and object relations capacity for integration of reality informed by infantile fantasy. The introjection of, for example, the good breast creates an environment wherein the infant can seek protection and hide from danger which, she suggested, constitutes an early step in the child's development of the capacity for self-soothing which is key to emotional stability within the infant and the early nursing child.

The stages in personality development, what Klein called interestingly enough "positions" rather than stages, are a central component as we have been emphasizing in her theory of maturation from infancy through childhood. With the unconscious fantasies as an infrastructural foundation upon which the reality principle of Freud must be encountered, Klein explored the relationship between ego structure, formation and development in terms of object relationships. As we have seen, these relationships carry within them their own set or matrix of defense mechanisms and organizational structures. The two positions which occur in Klein's analysis, contrary to the orthodox Freudian perspective, in the pre-Oedipal oral phase of personality development are the paranoid-schizoid position and the depressive position. As we have discussed earlier, Klein felt that the "introjection" (her word) or the inculcation of the sense of both good and bad as relates to object relations was natural to the infant and the development and internalization of good object experience was crucial for the development of a healthy ego.

The depressive position, she contended, constituted the most mature posture relative to ego formation and this orientation can and should continue throughout life. This depressive position orientation occurs, Klein argued from clinical experience, during the second quarter of the first year of a child's life. The paranoid-schizoid position precedes the depressive as the most primordial experience and orientation of the new-born infant. Persecutory anxieties and the splitting mechanisms of project, introjection, and omnipotence all characterize this stage of development and it includes such protective features as idealization and denial used to stave off anxieties and fears of the young infant. The stage called paranoid-schizoid is characterized by what Klein called the "part object relationship," namely, the part object function as a splitting mechanism which occurs in the infant's fantasy where experience can only be either all good or all bad as there is no room here for tolerance. The function of a part object is identified by the experienced self of the infant as the whole object. For example, the hungry infant is eager for the good breast to appear and feed it. In the absence of the good breast the frustrated angry infant experiences distress and anxiety precipitating destructive fantasies manifested in oral aggression towards the absent bad breast.

Splitting the object into good and bad objects is paralleled by the concomitant splitting of the ego. So, the infant who fantasizes the destruction of the bad breast is not distinct from the infant who is presented with the good breast owing to an inability to modulate the presence and absence of the desired object. When it is present, the infant is good; when it is absent, the infant is gripped by frustration, anxiety, and manifest anger. The development of the depressive position, however, brings with it tolerance allowing for the interplay between good and bad with the inculcation of both the capacity for remorse and reparations in interpersonal relationships which occur, for example, between mother and infant. Klein has emphasized that the anxiety precipitated during the paranoid schizoid period is essentially fear of the ego's destruction. Splitting, as Klein has redefined Freud's notion, provides a false sense to the infant and young child of allowing for the good to remain separate from the bad, a static bifurcation of the positive and the negative experience of the mother's breast, for example. The employment of projection is the use of a mechanism which attempts to repel the bad and embrace the good by assuming a mastery over one's social environment. Splitting, Klein counseled, is never completely or fully effective for the infant because the ego's agenda in the maturation of personality development is towards integration, not separation. The inculcation of tolerance and a ready willingness to live with the balancing act of good and bad constitutes a sign of the progress of maturation.

Whereas the paranoid-schizoid stage embodied splitting and the part object relations without the capacity to differentiate good mother/bad mother clearly and functionally, the depressive position (or stage) constituted an important further maturational development consisting of the operative capacity to perceive the real world of dual presentations, namely, the one who frustrates is also the one who satisfies. The good mother is also the bad mother and feelings of guilt, anger, grief and the desire to make amends in relationships begin to take precedence over the paranoid-schizoid stage. Unlike in the earlier stage where differentiation was not possible, in the depressive position the infant gains in the ability to actually encounter others as whole objects rather than part objects and this differentiation capability radically transforms the infant and early child's interpersonal relationships. The level of maturity in the depressive position is seen, Klein says, when it becomes evident that the early child is able to realize that the polar qualities of good and bad are integrated into the same object, not distinct and separate objects so that the good mother is the bad mother or the good breast is the bad breast, depending on the perceived situation and circumstance of need and response. The increasing awareness of the nearness of both good and bad fosters a resulting integration of the ego. Maturity is the result of the depressive position realizing that the polarization of characteristics are actually integrated into one reality.

One of the key results of this emerging integrated ego is the shifting on the part of the child from a fear of being destroyed to a fear of destroying the other. The realization that the ability to harm or repel the other, particularly in this case the mother who feeds and scolds, carries with it the price of repelling the one who is loved. Defenses cultivated by the child in confronting anxieties resulting from this maturation process include both repression and reparation, called by Klein the "manic defenses." Though having first become evident in the first position of infancy, these same defenses have now become activated so as to protect the child's psyche from a debilitating anxiety. As the ego becomes increasingly integrated, the defense mechanisms become less intense and foster a deepening sense of the awareness of the psyche and the real world of encounter.

Klein's clinical experience lead her to realize that as the infant works through this depressive anxiety it begins to reduce dependence upon projections and greater maturational characteristics begin emerging such as autonomy, awareness of the real rather than the imaginary world, and a sense of separateness from others. Whereas the young infant's destructive fantasies were directed towards the bad mother/bad breast which caused anxiety and frustration (even anger), this emerging sense of self with an integrated ego begins to realize that both bad and good, frustration and satiation, are always within the same mother. Klein agrees with Freud here in pointing out that unconscious guilt produced by the destructive fantasies swell up with the child in proportion to the love and nurture provided by the mother. Evolving out of this sense of guilt owing to a false sense of having hated the mother, there is a rising fear of losing the loved mother and this fear emerging from this sense of unfairness in judging the mother becomes a major step in child maturation. These feelings of guilt and distress now constitute significant components of a deepening capacity for love, becoming an indispensable part of love. Here both Freud and Klein have conjoined the experience of guilt and love as a major maturation step in the development of the personality and self-consciousness. It might even be argued within the context of this binary experience of guilt and love that the greater the feelings of guilt are balanced by a greater feeling of love. As guilt deepens and matures, likewise does love deepen and mature. And, as love and guilt mature, so does the self.

The amazing thing about this progression towards an interfacing of the child with the real world, explained Klein, is that the individual's capacity for such emotions as sympathy and a sense of responsibility towards others as well as an increasing ability to actually identify with the subjective experiences of other people for whom the child cares accelerates proportionately to this deepening sense of self. When the destructive projections of which Klein has spoken extensively began to recede there is a concomitant capacity and inclination to repress aggressive impulses which were so commonly employed in an earlier phase of development. Control over the child's reactions becomes a positively repressive preference to anxiety and anger towards the loved parent. Klein is keen to point out that in this process the child is much more willing to acknowledge the separateness of the other, whether parent or sibling or cohort, which then serves the on-going development of a functional capacity to distinguish and differentiate the inner self from the outer reality of the world of others. The sense, Klein explained, of the infant's omnipotence towards his emotional environment begins to lessen resulting in a decrease in his feelings of guilt and the fear of loss. The desired result is eventually realized through this maturation process when the child begins to understand that external others are actually free and separate people, autonomous of the child's governance, for the others have their own needs and wishes, their own subjectivity and their rightful place in the matrix of a social environment. This is, Klein reasoned, the desired result of a positive maturation process.

To elaborate further, what Klein called the "paranoid-schizoid position," as has already been pointed out, constituted a radical distinction in the child's mind between those things that are loved – the good parent, the gratifying objects of childhood -- and those things which the child hates – the bad parent, the frustrating and problematic objects of childhood. This polarization of extremes – everything, every object is perceived to be either good or bad, one way or the other, without the rational capacity to depolarize these objects thereby making them more compatible to the personality – constitutes the origin and basis of mental illness or mental health. Klein's favorite example of this conflicting object orientation, which we have discussed earlier, is that of what she called the "good breast" and the "bad breast," a split which occurs in the infant's mind but in reality are the same breast. However, and this was the driving interpretation of Klein's object relations theory, as the child grows and develops to the realization that things can be simultaneously good and bad, loved and hated, desired and despised, depending on the situation, the circumstances, and the interpersonal relationship matrix at any given moment, then maturation occurs. At this level of maturing, the child moves to the next phase called the "depressive position," which, as understood and explained by Klein, results in a gradually emerging sense of personal reality of oneself and of others. It is a painful, troubling, aggravating processual movement towards maturity but is inevitable if the child is to move beyond the mechanistically simplistic notion of everything being always strictly good or strictly bad, completely right or completely wrong. The mature person is more fully aware of the integration and connectedness of right and wrong, good and bad, than the infantile personality has the capacity to imagine.

Integrating this binary worldview and being, then, able to balance them in a creative and responsible fashion through life constitutes the differentiation between childhood and adulthood.

Illustrative of this good-bad spectrum in the maturation process versus the simplistic immaturity of the either good or bad spectrum with no ability to see the gray between the black and white is evidenced in religious fundamentalism. This, in the Kleinian sense, would be suggestive of the immaturity of the religious enthusiast unable to imagine a world not strictly composed of either the good or the bad wherein compromise and accommodation based on cultural and ideological difference are precluded. The inevitable inference from this analysis is that religious fundamentalism is incapable of maturity and is forever locked in a childish and undifferentiating judgmentalism which, as we know, frequently leads to neurosis and even psychosis.

To create a new concept within an already old and established school of analysis and therapy is no small undertaking. But, as we have seen, Klein was not inclined to demur from an idea worth pursuing merely because of the challenge or even the professional danger involved. Such is the history of the concept of the object relations theory. In such an august field as psychoanalysis to be known for having developed a theory which deepens and expands that field is what Klein has done. For, though she is known for having greatly expanded and elaborated the field of Freudian psychoanalysis, she is always and firstly remembered for her object relations theory. In psychoanalytic psychotherapy, we understand that social behavior and the unconscious are linked. This we credit Freud for first explicating demonstrably and clinically. And, we further know, thanks to orthodox psychoanalysis, that repeated experiences from within the matrix of infancy and childhood have resulted in internalized images of our parents and significant others and subsequent experiences and behaviors are a manifestation of those images as they have been modified in the unconscious mind over time. This we know from Freud. Object relations theory, however, extends this depth of understanding by suggesting that the infant mind early on engages objects, even minimally comprehends those objects, in terms of their functions and the maturation process fosters an expanding comprehension of the scope of these objects which manifest both good and bad characteristics held in the child's consciousness in a sort of tolerant ambiguity. Initially, this experience of the oscillation of good and bad fosters anxiety and fear within the child but gradually through maturation allows for a more tolerant acceptance of such ambiguity. To the extent that the child develops this tolerance, to that extent the child in adulthood will have avoided mental illness and fostered mental health. Where there is a consistent failure to cultivate a tolerant posture towards these ambiguities of life, neurosis looms.

As we know, Freud proposed a developmental *scenario* in which the ego developed later than Klein felt it did owing to her clinical studies of early childhood anxiety and fear. She wished to push back to infancy the child's first experience of the tensions arising from the oscillating ambiguities regarding good mother/bad mother. Here, she felt, anger and frustration were experienced within the context of good breast/bad breast complexes while other dynamics in the relationship produced such deep emotional response as dependence on the mother. At this time, this realization that mother is more than breast begins to take form in the child's consciousness. Klein contended that these emotional pulses, oscillating between positive and negative characteristics, could and often did overwhelm the child's developing individuality and the struggle to resolves these conflicting emotions were configured to reflect the parent's own personality. The emotionally troubled child, then, reflects the emotionally troubled parent -- the child is the reflection of the adult caregiver, for good or ill. This was considered at the time an original and profoundly insightful revelation in the etiology of mental illness. Nevertheless, and it must be pointed out here before we move on that within the London psychoanalytic community, there was a conflict of loyalties between those who favored Klein's new and expanded view of object relations theory (called by some at the time "id psychology") and that of Anna Freud and what she preferred to call "ego psychology." Understandably, Anna Freud dominated American psychoanalysis from the 1940s through the 1960s owing to both Sigmund Freud's having come early to America to receive an honorary doctorate from Clark University in Massachusetts and to the quick and enthusiastic embrace of Freud's brand of psychoanalysis by the psychiatric community in New York City particularly. In London, it was somewhat different with, in the English tradition, a tendency to walk the middle path between Anna Freud and Melanie Klein in what became amusingly called the "Middle School" with, however, such notables involved in it as Winnicott and Balint. Because the tensions between the two schools were so great in America, it was not until the 1970s that American psychoanalysts would acknowledge the influence of Melanie Klein in their own work.

True to both her independence and her imaginative creativity when it came to theory building and nomenclature, Klein was keen to reflect her own nuancing of Freud's concept of the unconscious and its relationship to instinct particularly as she used the term in child psychotherapy. Therefore, she began to use the term "fantasy" to indicate instinct within the context of the unconscious. Fantasy, explained Klein, consists of a psychic life of the child which moves from the inner self towards the outside world. This process constitutes a developmental movement towards an ever-increasing complexity of the child's mental life. This unconscious fantasy, suggested Klein, within the infant's own emerging mental life is inevitably adjusted and modified by the social environment of parental interaction. According to Klein, this process of movement towards the outside world occurs much earlier in the infant's maturation process than was recognized or allowed by Freud. The infant finds himself "testing" the viability, relevance, and practicality of his experience and encounter with the world of reality. Fantasy-testing constitutes the fundamental agenda of the child's maturation process. The relationship between the child's thought processes and the fantasies which he has developed constitutes the maturing process resulting from this reality-fantasy interactive evaluation. Thought processes within the child are actually based upon the more primordial fantasies and, indeed, actually derive from them. Reality constitutes the corrective for these *instinctually-generated* fantasies which are, in turn, used to test the real world.

Here Klein has made one of her most profound and long-lasting contributions to psychoanalytic theory, namely, the recognition that the role of these unconscious fantasies is essential for the development of cognitive processes within the child. Thinking, simply stated, is based upon unconscious fantasy in the testing process related to the world of reality. Image creation within the child's psyche (Klein's description of the unconscious fantasy world) is both a prerequisite and a precondition for the creation of a thought, a mental image, resulting from the convergence of experience and imagination. Thought, then, is a derivative of this mental convergence of fantasy and experience, the latter serving as a corrective to the former. The real world of experience essentially serves to modify the fantasy world of imagination. The brilliance of this insight into "thought formation" was recognized far and wide as a significant contribution to both cognitive process studies and psycho-linguistics. The convergence of fantasy and reality, of "preconception and realization" constitutes the matrix within which thought occurs. Illustrative of this process is that of the nipple-rooting infant which Klein understood to be the instinctual rooting as the "preconception" and the finding of the nipple (or mother's presenting the nipple) constitutes the realization from the world of experience. Through repeating this process over and over again, preconception and realization coalesce to create the concept. Maturation, then, occurs as these two counter-balancing components of preconception and realization interact thereby producing thought complexes and constellations of packaged experiences. This process, Klein explained, then produces first memories and these external experiences of the real world are meshed into the complex of fantasies such that eventually and ever progressively faster and faster the child's fantasies are able to conjure images as well as experiential sensations such as visual, audible, taste, touch, smells thereby producing an increasingly accurate encounter with the external and real world.

Both the brilliance of Melanie Klein's version of psychoanalysis is not open to dispute. Her courage in venturing out into unchartered waters as both a novice therapist trained in the psychoanalytic school of Freudian psychotherapy and a woman in a man's world speak for themselves. Her contribution to the study of children, her work within the confines of psychoanalysis in her bold application of that analytical school of therapy in the treatment of children, and her formulation of a play therapy that has stood the test of time and clinical practice all bespeak both a genius of intellect and a monumental personality. Jewish, divorced, alienated from her own daughter, facing the demands of an immigrant's life in a new country, all of these things converged in her life and conspired, even unwittingly, to make her the giant she became in the field of child psychology. Today, too often overlooked and too quickly discounted, Melanie Klein has earned her place among the leading voices in psychoanalytic psychotherapy in the treatment of children even though the general population is unaware of her greatness and the professional community is too easily distracted with their own aspirations for acknowledgment to give to her that which she has so profoundly earned, namely, respect and admiration as a pioneer in her field of study, research, and the clinical practice of child psychopathology.

SELECTED PRIMARY SOURCES OF MELANIE KLEIN

The Collected Writings of Melanie Klein

Volume 1 – *Love, Guilt and Reparation: And Other Works 1921–1945*, London: Hogarth Press.

Volume 2 – *The Psychoanalysis of Children*, London: Hogarth Press.

Volume 3 – *Envy and Gratitude*, London: Hogarth Press.

Volume 4 – *Narrative of a Child Analysis*, London: Hogarth Press.

CHAPTER TWELVE

ANNA FREUD and the Neo-Classical Approach to Child Psychoanalysis

True to her commitment to orthodox psychoanalytic theory, Anna Freud emphasized the need for effective nurturing of the child's ego development and functionality. The healthy child with a strong ego developmental history is identified as one with the acute ability to handle creatively the balancing of both internal factors and external factors in the social environment of home. A key point Anna Freud frequently made was the realization that the nature of the child's experience in the social environment consists of both the experience and the interpretation of that experience, not just what happens to a child but how that child then chooses to interpret and explain that experience. One does not just have experiences; one has experiences which then require description, explanation, and interpretation from within the individual's own cognitive conceptualization of their meaning. The processing of these experiences and their explanations constitute the maturation indicators Anna Freud observed in her therapeutic interviews with the child patient. Anna Freud was able to provide a comprehensive developmental theory of personality formation by showing how that the compilation of experiential, maturational, environmental, and ego processing went well beyond those of even her father as well as the behaviorists. Furthermore, she demonstrated with clinical documentation how paying attention to the contextualization of experience, maturation, and the child's ego development constituted the matrix within which emotional health or illness occurs.

There is little question within the medical community but what Anna Freud is fundamentally responsible for the launching of a monumental movement within psychiatry and psychotherapy towards the clinical study and treatment in child psychopathology. We have already seen that others preceded her and in their own right made significant contributions to the study of child behavioral disorders. Nevertheless, and that being acknowledged, Anna Freud's movement from within the ranks of classical psychoanalysis towards the application of traditional categories of diagnosis and treatment in a new mode of utility constituted the appearance of what would eventuate into a grand school of thought called neo-Freudian psychoanalysis. Never leaving the fundamental tenets and building blocks of classical psychoanalysis as she learned it from her father, she quite clearly and with intentionality adapted these building blocks to suit her own clinical experience in working with children suffering from behavioral disorders. Her 1927 series of lectures, later published as *The Psychoanalytical Treatment of Children,* unquestionably established both the field of child psychiatry and Anna Freud as the founder of child psychoanalysis. Though this recognition came early in her professional life, it did not come easily owing to the uniqueness of her medical and academic training, such as it was. But it did come and stayed with her throughout her life and even today there is no question of the centrality of her work in the current clinical practice of child psychoanalysis and psychiatry.

Born in Vienna on 3 December 1895, Anna Freud was the sixth and youngest of Sigmund Freud's children. Eventually and reluctantly sharing the recognition with Melanie Klein as the founder of the psychoanalytic treatment of child psychopathology, Anna embraced fully the classical theories of psychoanalysis developed by her father but focused most specifically upon the development of the ego with particular interest in child psychology. Being forced to leave Vienna in 1938 for London, all of the Freud family departed Austria to escape the Nazi regime destined to take over their country and in doing so Anna was poised to engage in her pioneering work in child psychopathology where she eventually established the Hampstead Child Therapy Course and Clinic in 1952 which was later renamed the Anna Freud National Centre for

Children and Families as an institution for therapy, training, and research work employing Anna's approach and interpretation of the psychoanalytic practice of psychotherapy.

Apparently growing up relatively unhappy as a child, she nevertheless was raised in a comfortable middleclass home where she was particularly close to her father of whom she was the favorite of his children but not so close to her mother but rather closer to her Catholic nurse named Josephine. Jealous of her older sister Sophie due to her greater beauty and the competition for their father's affections, the daughters worked a compromised living arrangement in which Sophie was called the beauty and Anna the brains of the family. It has been suggested based on her personal letters to her father that Anna suffered from depression and an eating disorder not unrelated to her competitive confrontations with all of her siblings, not just Sophie. Disinclined to focus her intellectual energies on the formal schooling which the family provided her, she rather focused her attention upon learning from her father and his professional practice, picking up Hebrew, German, English, French and Italian in the process. The formal study of her father's psychoanalytic theories began at age 15 with particular attention to Sigmund Freud's now classic text *The Interpretation of Dreams* (1899). Anna completed her institutional education at the Cottage Lyceum in Vienna in 1912 during which time she continued to suffer severely from both depression and anorexia due in part to the uncertainty of her future life after schooling as a young single woman.

A near domestic disaster was avoided owing to Sigmund Freud's quick and astute intervention when Ernest Jones, the eventual author of the authorized biography of Sigmund Freud, took Anna in 1914 for a visit in England during which time it became apparent that Jones had romantic intentions towards Anna. Freud wrote Jones pointing out that Anna was immature in such matters and that an extended delay in considering marriage was an agreed upon pact between Anna and her father. Nothing subsequently came of Jones' intentions, and in that year of 1914 Ann passed the required test validating her right to serve as a teaching apprentice at her alma mater, the Cottage Lyceum, where she worked with third, fourth, and fifth grade children. She was judged a professional success as a teacher at the Lyceum, becoming a head teacher for the second-grade students and eventually receiving a four-year contract in 1918 but resigned two years later owing to a debilitating illness, assumed to be depression. During two periods of her early life, 1918-1921 and 1924-1929, she was in formal psychoanalysis with her father having shown a special enduring interest in his work in psychiatry in the development of his newly created form of psychotherapy called psychoanalysis.

Her formal recognition as a promising professional practitioner of psychoanalysis came in 1922 when she presented a paper dealing with fantasies and daydreams before the Vienna Psychoanalytical Society at which time she was elected a member of that august body of professionals. The following year, at the age of 28, she began her own psychoanalytic practice working with children as a specialization and within two more years, in 1925 until 1934, she began teaching at the Vienna Psychoanalytic Training Institute on the practice of psychoanalysis applied to child psychopathology. She became Secretary of the International Psychoanalytical Association during this time, contributing scholarly papers based on her clinical research and teaching in the field of child psychoanalysis. Her career became well established and she continued to climb in international recognition as a leading theoretician as well as clinician in the practice of psychoanalysis. In 1935, she was elected Director of the Vienna Psychoanalytical Training Institute followed the next year with the publication of her now recognized classic dealing with ways and means whereby the ego wards off depression, displeasure and anxiety in her book titled *The Ego and the Mechanisms of Defense.* It quickly became the major textbook in the field of ego psychology and established her as an international authority in the field.

The launching of her private practice as a child psychoanalyst was greatly facilitated by her father's international reputation and her growing recognition as an authority in the treatment of children with behavioral disorders. Anna's career was greatly aided with the treatment in 1925 of Dorothy Burlingham's children, the heiress to the Tiffany fortune who had come to Vienna from New York with her four children where she herself had entered into analysis with the then well-established psychoanalyst Theodore Reik followed by treatment from Sigmund Freud himself. As the Burlingham family became increasingly close to the Freud family, they moved into the same apartment building and Anna became a sort of godmother to Dorothy's children. In 1938, the Gestapo arrested Anna for questioning regarding the nature and activities of the International Psychoanalytical Association of which she was an officer. In anticipation of the Nazi invasion of Austria, both Anna and her brother Martin had obtained a lethal poison, Veronal, to be used in case they were tortured or interned in a prison camp. Fortunately, Anna was released following extensive and exhaustive questioning with further consequences. Many of Sigmund Freud's friends had been eagerly admonishing him and his family to flee Austria to England where an enthusiastic following of psychoanalysis under the leadership of Ernest Jones eagerly awaited his decision to immigrate. Jones, the current President of the International Psychoanalytic Association at the time, made all of the arrangements for the journey which was made successfully in spite of Sigmund Freud's severe health conditions due to mouth cancer. He died within 15 months of arrival in London where he made his home at 20 Maresfield Gardens, Hampstead, which Anna occupied until her own death in 1982.

Three years after the Freuds arrival in London, Anna and Dorothy Burlingham set up the Hampstead War Nursery for the children of London who had been traumatized by the German bombings. They secured a splendid facility in Hampstead where both educational and residential psychotherapeutic treatment was made available to children and their mothers. Many of the staff were themselves refugees from Austria and Germany. Educational programs consisting of lectures and seminars in the field of psychoanalysis – both theory and practice – were offered for training of the staff. The two collaborated in the publishing of a series of data-based studies of children focusing upon developmental features identified and tracked as part of the work of the Hampstead Nursery with special attention to stress and traumatized depression. Eventually following the Second World War, they established what was called the Bulldog Banks Home designed and run specifically for traumatized children who had survived the Nazi concentration. The final developmental stage of their collaboration was the creation of the Hampstead Child Therapy Course and Clinic in 1952 which was subsequently re-named the Anna Freud National Centre for Children and Families focusing upon therapy, training, and research in the field of child care.

The creation of these entities for educational training as well as therapeutic practice was not without complications owing to the dominance of Melanie Klein's work in England prior to Anna Freud's arrival. Klein was the recognized authority in the use of psychoanalysis in the treatment of children in England and Anna Freud's arrival with her very different and strongly established approach to the psychoanalytic treatment of children created a serious division in the practice of psychoanalysis. The result was the eventual creation of three different approaches to the definition and practice of psychoanalysis as understood and embraced by the British psychoanalytic community, i.e., the Freudian, Kleinian, and the Independent approaches. Klein's approach differed significantly from the Freudian establish procedure in both methodology as well as theoretical foundations and treatment practices particularly as related to the therapeutic care of children, what Klein and her followers called *object relations theory*. Whereas Anna Freud and her loyal followers within the professional practice of psychoanalysis did not believe that children experience the superego or that their therapist should function as the object of the child's transference, Klein and company were insistent upon the idea that a child does have a developing superego and, therefore, should be treated therapeutically just as an adult is treated. Clearly, these differences in theory and clinical practice were sufficiently significant as to potentially jeopardize the collaboration of the various schools of psychoanalysis in England. Happily, and in the grand tradition of British compromise and accommodation, by the end of the World War, there was the formal recognition of both schools of theory and practice to the satisfaction of all professionals in England involved in the practice of psychoanalysis. Coincidentally, this *modus vivendi* occurred just as Anna Freud was being naturalized as a British subject in the summer of 1946.

On the heels of her father's death and her collaborative efforts during and following the War years to create institutional settings for the teaching and training of psychoanalysts, Anna Freud's star continued to rise. Beginning early in the 1950s, she would regularly travel to the United States on lecture tours and was elected Vice-President of the International Association of Psychoanalysts as well as a Foreign Honorary Member of the American Academy of Arts and Sciences in 1959, eventually being elected in 1973 as President of the International Association of Psychoanalysis. During the decade of the 1970s, she focused her research attention upon the behavioral issues of emotionally deprived and socially disadvantaged children as well as paying special attention to both deviate behavior and developmental delays in personality among deprived children. A collaboration eventuated with Joseph Goldstein and Albert J. Solnit at the Yale Law School where Anna Freud was teaching a seminar on crime and the family in the publishing of a three-volume set of books titled *Beyond the Best Interests of the Child, Before the Best Interests of the Child*, and *In the Best Interests of the Child*.

Anna Freud died in London on the 9th of October in 1982 at the age of 87 and was, like her parents, cremated at Golders Green Crematorium and placed next to her parents. Other family members as well as Dorothy Burlingham are buried there as well. The year following her death, Anna Freud's collected works were published in which she was described as a passionate and inspirational teacher. The Hampstead Clinic was renamed the Anna Freud Centre in 1984 and two years later her London home which she had shared with her father and mother was established as the Freud Museum dedicated specifically to Sigmund Freud and the British Psychoanalytical Society.

Anna Freud was, like her father, a prolific and dedicated researcher and author of scholarly articles as well as books in the field of psychoanalysis with special attention to the care and treatment of children. Her first book consisted of a collection of lectures she gave at various gatherings of professional teachers and caretakers of children in Vienna titled *An Introduction to Psychoanalysis: Lectures for Child Analysts and Teachers 1922-*

1935. The collection was acclaimed as a significant contribution to the study of children within the context of the psychoanalytic tradition as it dealt with fantasies and daydreaming on the part of children, a topic Sigmund Freud had addressed himself. Based on her own clinical studies of children, both his work and Anna's contributed substantially to the establishment of child psychopathology as a viable domain of classical psychoanalysis.

Following the success of this small collection of lectures published as a monograph in Vienna, she further developed her theory and practice of child psychoanalysis in her first major book in 1927 titled *An Introduction to the Technique of Child Analysis* which, alas, set the stage for a serious confrontation with Dr. Melanie Klein who, as a practicing psychoanalyst, was moving clearly and decidedly away from the classical tradition of psychoanalytic theory in the development of her own adaptations of Freud's foundational work. As a result of her work, Klein was considered a leader of a growing movement of what came to be known as *neo-Freudian.* Of particular relevance as a point of divergence was Anna Freud's contention, based on her own clinical practice, that in the analysis of children, the experience of classically described "transference" functions quite differently with children than with adults and, therefore, it is the responsibility of the analyst to function as the child patient's mother as well as represent a genuine "second mother" in the life experience of the child patient. This nuancing of the nature and function of transference in the treatment of children soon became a litmus test among orthodox psychoanalysts in determining one's loyalty to Anna Freud as the founder of this school of psychotherapy.

Nine years later, Anna Freud published in 1936 a major monograph based on her own extensive clinical practice dealing with issues in ego psychology with particular attention to the nature and function of defense mechanisms as had been substantially demonstrated in the work of Sigmund Freud, constituting one of the major building blocks of classical psychoanalysis. In this contribution to the furtherance of the theoretical foundations of ego psychology as defined and practiced within orthodox psychoanalysis, Anna Freud delineated a list of characteristics which became the basis for the relevance of the concept of defense mechanisms in therapeutic treatment. These characteristic categories included regression, repression, reaction formation, isolation, undoing, projection, introjection, turning against the self, reversal and sublimation. This listing facilitated the major focus upon ego development in the later theoretical stages of Sigmund Freud's concentration upon the ego. The trajectory of this line of research proved particularly relevant in the later childhood and early adolescent developmental stages in child psychopathology, even more so Anna thought than that of the latency period of the pre-Oedipal phases of personality development.

Anna Freud's early work in Vienna in this field of both theory and clinical practice of child psychopathology was becoming increasingly a point of international recognition and acclaim of her own original contributions to the development of psychoanalysis but her London years proved to be the most creative. By concentrating her research and clinical practice in the treatment of child psychopathology, she eventually established a substantial following of internationally recognized child developmental psychologists and psychoanalysts which included Erik Erikson, Edith Jacobson, and Margaret Mahler. This group consistently noted in their clinical studies that children suffering from behavioral disorders manifested their pathology in terms specifically of personality disorders which eventuated in their developmental appearances in early and young adulthood. Issues related to and descriptive of the damaged self-concept in children constituted a dominant focus of research and treatment. In 1965, Anna Freud publisher her book titled *Normality and Pathology in Childhood* which was considered a major contribution to developmental psychology as relates to personality maturation within children. The upshot of this creative work was the recognition of the central importance of the parental role in child developmental processes combining both her father's idea of the drive model with that of the developing concept of object relations thereby utilizing both orthodox psychoanalytic theory and Klein's notion of object relations theory.

Clearly, Anna Freud's commitment to her father's orthodox psychoanalytic theory and practice was unwavering and she was always insistent upon her continuing loyalty to classical psychoanalysis within the context of her awareness, with Sigmund's blessings, that she was broadening the application of traditional concepts to include her growing interest and clinical work in child psychopathology. She would inevitably yet not with her own ready acceptance of the term be labeled a "neo-Freudian" in the sense that her embracing of classical psychoanalysis led to her broadening of the tradition to reach beyond common practice without violating the accepted range of utility and application of the key concepts and theories. Neither her orthodoxy nor her creativity in the stretching of psychoanalytic theory and practice were ever questioned, not by her father and not by any of the members of the psychoanalytic community. More so than most other practicing orthodox psychoanalysts, Anna Freud was keen to emphasize the centrality of her father's place in the temple of understanding the human psyche and she never ceased emphasizing the foundational work upon which psychoanalysis was built which was discovered and not created by Sigmund Freud.

One of the distinguishing features of the Hampstead Child Therapy Course and Clinic (subsequently re-named the Anna Freud Centre) which she had established in 1959 mentioned earlier was the link she created with University College London. This link elevated her creative initiative in the development of child psychopathology to a national and eventually international recognition in which her threefold focus of the Clinic was emulated throughout the medical and psychiatric communities involved in treating children. This threefold focus addressed the crucial issue of training professionals in child psychoanalysis, in creating an actual child and adolescent clinic focused specifically upon youth, and very importantly for the perpetuation of her insights was the focus upon clinical research dealing with child psychopathologies. Her 1965 book titled *Normality and Pathology in Childhood* called attention to this institutional work she had created which illustrated clinically her theory dealing with the crucial importance of balancing all stages and components of a child's personality development from infancy through to adulthood. This child psychoanalytic perspective facilitated the therapist's ability to distinguish data from each of these various developmental stages and most importantly to understand the presenting psychopathologies within the context of developmental "normality," thereby contextualizing these symptoms within an overall assessment of the child's developmental stages in relationship to the presenting disorders.

Throughout her career which was by this time skyrocketing internationally, Anna Freud was able to demonstrate using her creativity in developing the now famous Anna Freud Centre her passionate dedication to the furtherance of the practice of child psychoanalysis within the professions of medicine and psychiatry but also sharing her clinical insights with teachers and parents, nurses and medical practitioners in pediatrics, and even with lawyers involved in child custody cases. A key concern of hers was studying the profoundly traumatic impact hospitalization of children away from parents which was clinically evidenced in her work. Remaining a loyal follower of orthodox psychoanalysis and the theoretical foundations of her father's work, unlike what occurred with both Jung and Adler to mention two of what eventually became many, Anna Freud was, nevertheless, actually more interested as a practitioner of child therapeutic treatment in the dynamic development of the psyche and the central importance of the emergence of maturity of the ego within the growing child. Less interested in theoretical discussions of the structure of the psyche, her father's interest, she felt that the ego was the justified focus of clinical research wherein the development of both the id and the superego within the context of the unconscious itself could best be observed. Whereas Sigmund Freud had focused his attention upon id within the unconscious, Anna Freud focused upon the balancing of the id and superego as factors in the development of the ego within the maturation process operative within the growing child. Anna and Sigmund did not disagree in their theoretical work, they simply had different but complimenting emphases.

Best known for her now classic book, *The Ego and the Mechanisms of Defense,* Anna Freud came into her own as a research scientist within the tradition of psychoanalysis with this insightful and clinically based probing of the nature and function of defense mechanisms with particular emphasis upon the ego development of the child. She made real and identifiable contributions and advancements in the study of defense mechanisms beyond what her father had done himself. Today we realize that the emergence of what is known as "ego psychology" had its beginnings with Anna Freud and her work on the issues related to ego development within children. This focus upon the ego constitutes the primary distinguishing feature of the contemporary practice of Freudian psychoanalysis. Building upon the monumental work of Sigmund Freud in the area of ego studies, Anna Freud moved above and beyond his foundational constructs to include less esoteric and more commonly recognized ordinary practical evidence of ego formation and development. This elaboration and elevation of the classic understanding of the ego to include more than just psychopathology but also the social and developmental characteristics of ego maturation led to such major contributions in ego psychology as produced by Erik Erikson, a student himself of Anna Freud.

Though acutely interested in the theoretical foundations of orthodox and classical psychoanalysis developed by her father, Anna Freud was not, after all, primarily interested in theory development but rather focused her attention upon the clinical practice – teaching, therapy, research – of child psychopathology as a viable and legitimate enterprise of psychoanalysis as a therapeutic modality. The focus was from the outset upon the care and treatment of children and adolescents, the therapeutic address to the furtherance and enhancement of the analytical techniques of treatment. Whereas Sigmund Freud had dedicated his entire professional career to the treatment of adult patients, and primarily upper middleclass women, and recognizing his many literary contributions to the discussion of personality development, it was for him always from the adult perspective. Anna Freud was determined to take this same analytical tool into the clinical practice of treating children as well and was dedicated to demonstrating its effectiveness when adapted and modified to the child's world of ego development.

Though fully conversant with and loyal to her father's understanding of the dynamics of the ego and its relationship to the unconscious functioning of the psyche in the adult, Anna Freud was insistent that in the therapeutic encounter the relationship between the therapist and the child patient is quite different from that of the relationship between the therapist and the adult patient. Anna realized more so than apparently Sigmund Freud did the dynamically central role the parent of the child patient plays in the therapeutic process. This dynamic relationship between parent and child must not and cannot be dominated by the therapist while yet maintaining the therapeutic role of an interested adult rather than either as an authoritarian figure or just another child friend. The most effective approach to handling what in psychoanalytic terms is called a *problem of transference* was essentially a practical and matter-of-fact relationship with the child patient by the therapist as a genuinely caring and concerned adult rather than either a substitute parent or a pretending playmate.

Within this context, Anna Freud was eager to point out that the symbol system operative within the child's psyche is not developed fully, is in the process of maturing, and though symbolic abilities do exist in the child's consciousness these abilities are immature. The result, of course, is the verbal ineptitude of the child to formulate a fair and correct recitation of their emotional feelings such that behavioral difficulties are not easily articulated in speech the way, for instance, adults have developed the capacity to disguise their feelings with words and ideational symbols. Because the child patient's emotional difficulties are existentially immediate rather than having been formed over a number of years as with adults, these emotionally disturbing feelings and behaviors are much more readily accessible to the child, more to the surface and thus more easily and directly rather than symbolically expressed. Because most of Anna Freud's contributions to child psychopathology in the study of personality development grew out of her involvement in the Hampstead Child Therapy Clinic in London, her experience was that one of the biggest presenting problems in working with the child patient had to do with the communication between child and therapist. Adult patients use adult language to communicate with the therapist; the child patient was much less likely to have this level of linguistic acuity.

Recognizing as she did this immediate problem of communication, Anna Freud reformulated a therapeutic understanding of the relationship between therapist and child within the framework of a developmental approach to the maturation process. This constituted a major contribution to child psychoanalysis. This component of what eventuated into the field of developmental psychology was built upon Anna Freud's insights related to the natural, normal, healthy signs of development within children along a spectrum of maturational behaviors such as eating behaviors, personal hygiene, play styles, relationships with other children. When all went well, the therapist had reason to believe that each child manifesting such normal behavior was developing in a healthy fashion. However, when one or more of these developmental components failed to manifest themselves in the child's non-compliance or lapses in continued maturation, then the therapist could more easily and correctly pinpoint the area of difficulty in the child's otherwise normal maturational advance along the developmental lines of ego maturation.

As a pedagogically oriented researcher and committed psychoanalyst in the orthodox and classical sense, Anna Freud was able to foster and nurture on-going research in what is generally thought of as Freudian psychology. For instance, given her interest in documented research she was able to formalize the keeping of clinical records on child patients who manifested diagnostic symptoms recorded in their biographical profiles. She further facilitated the collaborative research based on the clinical observations of her staff and psychoanalysts training in her Centre, going so far as to encourage longitudinal studies of ego development among the child patients from late infancy to early adolescence. She pioneered the use of what is now recognized as a legitimate research modality, i.e., that of natural experiments in observing groups of children at play who are suffering from war trauma or abuse and even physical disabilities such as blindness and speech impairment. Considering the creativity and innovative contribution of these variants of research methodologies, it seems unfair to criticize Freudian psychology for lacking empirical foundation if by that one narrowly circumscribes only clinically gathered data as legitimate.

The distinctiveness of Anna Freud's teaching, research and treatment of children constituted a significant variant yet compliment to Sigmund Freud's singular concentration on the clinical therapeutic treatment of adults in which he focused on the probing of their unconscious repressions through dream analysis and word association. On the other hand, Anna Freud chose to embrace the fundamental principles and insights of psychoanalytic theory and practice all the while reconstructing the viability of this analytical treatment modality to the needs of children who are less verbal, less symbolic, and less reflective than an adult. Though a psychoanalyst trained in classical Freudian psychology named Hermine von Hug-Hellmuth had written a clinically-based article titled "Play Therapy" as early as 1913, it was clearly Anna Freud who addressed herself as a clinical researcher and therapist of children to the systematization of concepts and theory into a *bona fide* sub-discipline within orthodox psychoanalysis in the care and treatment of children. Though others recognized the need for the elevation of child psychopathology to an established specialization within psychotherapy and psychiatry, it was Anna Freud herself who gets the credit for making it happen. She contended early, intensely, and continuously that the analysis of children in the psychoanalytic tradition could and should only occur when the child reaches the latency period of maturation (around 6 years of age) and before that stage the orientation of the therapist's analysis should focus upon the child patient's social and physical environment. The development of neurosis in the child until the latency period should be upon the child's psychosexual and emotional developmental environment in the home.

Recognized by Sigmund Freud himself and the many psychoanalysts with which she worked and came in contact with as a gifted therapist in the treatment of children, Anna Freud was known for her amazing talent of establishing a bonding relationship in therapeutic treatment of children as a relationship alliance. Acknowledging the reality that whereas adults take the initiative in seeking therapeutic help, children never do for that initiative is left to the concerned parent. Therefore, even before anything like therapeutic treatment of the child patient could commence, Anna Freud realized and utilized the necessity of establishing a relationship bond with the child such that confidence, trust, and a relationship without fear or suspicion could be established. This, she contended, can only occur when the child is genuinely convinced that they are being treated in the relationship as an independent person with feelings and insights of their own worthy of attention by the therapist.

What was called a "therapeutic alliance" constituted the central core of her treatment style. For instance, unlike with the adult patient who is expected to sit or lie still on the couch during the therapeutic interview, Anna Freud realized that this is an unreasonable expectation in dealing with children. Therefore, she was keen to permit the child patient to remain as active as they felt inclined during the interview interaction going so far as to allow the child, as it spoke and responded to the therapist, to roam around the room, write or color in a book, play with a toy, and most commonly draw pictures of whatever the child felt inclined to do such. These visual salvos, she contended, were as relevant to the child psychotherapist as word association with the adult patient. Within this context, it is clear that Anna Freud's contribution the child psychanalysis consists of two significant developments in both theory and practice, viz., the contention that analytic assessment of the child patient must be an on-going and developmental process drawing from a multiplicity of data sources such as listed above, and the necessity of creating a diagnostic profile of the child patient based on these developmental processes documented clinically for periodic reference in the assessment agenda. This should, of course, include the child's medical and physical history, information regarding the family background and home environment, and on-going documentation of maturation developments through the recognized stages of ego development from infancy to adolescence.

Among the many and varied components of child psychoanalytic theory and practice of which Anna Freud is considered the master, her clinically sophisticated documentation in the treatment of attachment/separation issues is considered among her most important contribution to the field. Until she formally addressed the topic of childhood attachment theory, little formally or systematically had been done in the clinical setting but she changed all of that. First, she emphasized the significance of the differentiation between psychological attachment and biological attachment with emphasis upon the realization that changes in the mental state and development of the child patient over time had a major impact upon the child's perception and interpretation of the experience of loss and separation. Anna Freud refined these insights by pointing out the need to describe with precision the temperamental, maturational, and environmental factors which impact the experience of attachment and its loss with special attention to the radically important developmental issues affecting the child during the second year of life. She furthermore introduced the idea of the family grouping of infants and small children in the caring agenda of the Centre designed to promote and nurture attachment between the child and the caregiver and, finally, she was particularly astute as a researcher with a gift for writing in her description of the multiplicity of reasons why attachment within the life of the young child is centrally important to personality, cognitive, and emotional development. Without doubt, these insights constitute the basis upon which Anna Freud is rightfully considered the founder of child psychoanalysis recognized as a *bona fide* treatment modality with theoretical infrastructures well in place.

Decidedly not the first to become immersed in the treatment of children and the development of a theoretical and treatment-based understanding of child psychopathology, Anna Freud's work came on the heels of three well established schools of theory and practice consisting of her father's own work in psychoanalytic theory, Arnold Gesell's salvos into the development of a maturational theory of child development, and certainly the behavioral theories of both J. B. Watson and B. F. Skinner, all recognized giants in the field of psychological research. Whereas Sigmund Freud viewed emotional development as the inevitable outcome of unconscious drives within the infant, Gesell contended, on the other hand, that psychological development within the child was reliant fundamentally upon biological factors disregarding or minimizing the relevance of the social and physical environment, context, and interactional relationships surrounding the child. The behavioral school of thought developed by Watson and Skinner assessed the child as essentially a *tabula rasa,* a blank tablet, and therefore the child's maturation process were totally dependent upon the full scope of environmental factors.

Never accused of abandoning orthodox psychoanalysis or her father, Anna Freud nevertheless was creative in her continued development of theories and therapeutic practices designed specifically for the treatment of child psychopathology, clearly and understandably going beyond (but not against) her father's own work in developmental psychology and well beyond and away from Gesell, Watson, and Skinner's behaviorism. Her system was comprehensive, not adjacent to a broader school of thought as with these psychologists, for she was singularly dedicated to child psychopathology with an emphasis in theory and practice on the child. One can identify four significant factors in child development upon which she focused in her book, *Normality and Pathology in Childhood: Assessments of Development*, published in1965. Her first concern and eventually a key component in the building blocks of her developmental psychology was that of the "experience" of the child, contextualized and documented based on the accounts provided by the parents or caregivers of the child as well as the child's own recitation especially and particularly if trauma was a factor in the presenting symptoms of psychopathological behavior. These factors of experience, Anna Freud explained, may have a profound impact upon the emotional as well as even physical development of the child and must be taken fully into consideration in the assessment and treatment of the child patient.

Another key factor was that of the maturation indicators in the child's development as reported by the parents or caregivers of the child as well as the therapist's own observations of the child undergoing treatment. Tracking these indicators of maturity on the part of the child constituted a major focus of the assessment process in therapy. Environmental contextualization of the child's life experiences constituted for Anna Freud an indispensable composite of data needed in the assessment process. Such factors in the home environment as parental support and encouragement, affectionate expressiveness, foster of self-confidence and assurance of affirmation all constitute indispensable components in the positive development of the child. The creative balance, Anna Freud emphasized, in the home environment of both guidance and discipline with nurture and encouragement was crucial in the healthy child.

A consummate scholar with the advantage of having grown up under the influence of her scientist father, Anna Freud was keenly aware of the interplay between theory and practice in her work as a practicing psychoanalyst and researcher/author in developmental psychology. The Hampstead Clinic (subsequently the Anna Freud Centre) provided just the clinical environment and opportunity for her and her colleagues to observe, experiment, and publicize their work. The focus of the Clinic's primary care was for children traumatized by war. Anna Freud became a leading voice and spokesperson in the call for more extensive research and quality of treatment and care for those who had suffered emotional stress due to the London bombings. Two key insights and contributions her research produced had to do with the recognition of the central importance of the parents' contact with and guidance of the child particularly during times of great stress and trauma and the fundamentally important realization that the family grouping is so very important to stabilize the maturation process of the developing child particularly in unusual situations such as war time when children are often necessarily separated from parents. Her primary focus upon the developmental assessment of the child patient constituted one of her major overall contributions to both the field of child psychopathology and developmental psychology.

At the Hampstead Clinic, for instance, she and her clinical colleagues created a template for the tracking of a developmental profile for diagnostic purposes of the child patient effective from infancy to adolescence. This diagnostic profile template was comprehensive in its data classification of each child under treatment at the Clinic. The profile collected data on the child patient from a variety of sources from the social worker involved in the case to the parents of the child to the child's own randomized recitation of experience and emotional feelings about life. The uniqueness of each child's profile is both recognized and held sacrosanct yet all profiles consist of several standardized categories of data including, for instance, the reasons for referral in the first place, a physical description of the child and its parents, an overarching history and background of the family itself including employment, residences, schooling, etc., a recitation of environmental factors and influences in the child's life, and a keen delineation of reported data by the parents or caregiver related to the child patient's developmental traits and characteristics, all such data being used in the on-going assessment and diagnostic agenda.

A strong and unique characteristic of this diagnostic profile created by Anna Freud and colleagues was the insistence that the data gathered through the use of this research instrument must be an on-going affair of continual observation and reporting rather than a onetime event for assessment purposes commonly employed in adult therapy but absolutely discounted in child therapy. The continual documentation of the child parent's activities, behaviors, stories, creative endeavors all must be perpetually kept in the diagnostic profile in order to understand the relationship between developmental issues and pathological behavior. The effective utilization of this comprehensive data organization and collection in the diagnostic profile was Anna Freud's key contribution to the field of child psychopathology, not in the creation of any particularly form of testing devices. This diagnostic profile functions to organizes, integrate, and report on the data being collected in a fashion clear enough for a developmental psychologist to assess and treat the child patient.

Essentially, Anna Freud's contributions to this field which she herself is credited for having established to a recognized sub-specialization within general psychiatric practice consisted of the contention that the assessment of the child patient must be an ongoing agenda filling in and drawing from the diagnostic profile created for this purpose. Recognition that a developmental approach to the assessment of the child patient is crucial in order to embrace the whole picture of the child's world including, as well as recited above, reasons for the referral in the first place, description physically of the child, a recounting of the family background and personal history of the parents as well as the child, accounting for environmental factors in the child's living space at home and in community, and an overarching observation by the therapist of the current behavioral situation of the child patient.

SELECTED PRIMARY SOURCES OF ANNA FREUD

Freud, Anna (1966–1980). The Writings of Anna Freud: 8 Volumes. New York: Indiana University of Pennsylvania (These volumes include most of Freud's papers.)

Vol. 1. *Introduction to Psychoanalysis: Lectures for Child Analysts and Teachers* (1922–1935)

Vol. 2. *Ego and the Mechanisms of Defense* (1936); (Revised edition: 1966 (US), 1968 (UK))

Vol. 3. *Infants Without Families Reports on the Hampstead Nurseries*

Vol. 4. *Indications for Child Analysis and Other Papers* (1945–1956)

Vol. 5. *Research at the Hampstead Child-Therapy Clinic and Other Papers* (1956–1965)

Vol. 6. *Normality and Pathology in Childhood: Assessments of Development* (1965)

Vol. 7. *Problems of Psychoanalytic Training, Diagnosis, and the Technique of Therapy* (1966–1970)

Vol. 8. *Psychoanalytic Psychology of Normal Development*

Freud in collaboration with Sophie Dann: "An Experiment in Group Upbringing", in: *The Psychoanalytical Study of the Child*, VI, 1951.

CONCLUSION

As we have seen, the social and psychological as well as the physical environment within which the self can be damaged often leads to the diminishment of an individual's potential for a meaningfully fulfilling life. The self-concept in its concomitant components of self-image, self-esteem, and the ideal self has been studied by leading behavioral and social scientists within the framework of the *interpersonal theory of psychotherapy* developed by Harry Stack Sullivan and subsequent theorists such as Anna Freud, Melanie Klein, and Karen Horney have explicated the insightful approach of this theory in the study of child psychopathology. The development of the self-concept, as we have discussed, is composed of a balancing integration of self-image and self-esteem and these are directly developed and nurtured through the maturation process in childhood. Such leading research behavioral scientists as Freud, Adler, Maslow, Rogers, and Erikson have provided us with a psychological perspective designed to explicate the complexities of this phenomenon relevant to the tracing of the etiology of mental illness in adulthood. Social scientists such as Cooley and Mead have demonstrated the integration of psychopathological insights into the self-concept such that the psychotherapeutic efficacy of this deeper and broader understanding of the damaged self in childhood can be more effective analyzed. In clinical cases of a diminished sense of self (demeaned self-image and/or self-esteem), there is evidence of a failure within the family matrix of nurturing the child's sense of self, whether that failure is due to a self-conscious disregard of the child or an inadvertent failure to assume parental oversight in the child's development. Whether indifference or inattentive parenting constitutes the matrix of maturation, a diminished life is the result of this failure to foster a positive and healthy self-concept in childhood and it has been our intention in this study to explore the psychopathology resulting from this failure in what we have labeled the *damaged self.*

GENERAL REFERENCE BIBLIOGRAPHY

(relevant to child psychopathology)

Abel, Kathryn M. (2010). "Birth weight, schizophrenia, and adult mental disorder: is risk confined to the smallest babies?". *Archives of General Psychiatry. 67 (9): 923–930.*

Adams, Henry E., Sutker, Patricia B. (2001). *Comprehensive Handbook of Psychopathology. Third Edition.* Springer.

Adler, David A., ed. (1990). *Treating Personality Disorders.* San Francisco: Jossey-Bass.

Akhtar, Salman (1987). "Schizoid Personality Disorder: A Synthesis of Developmental, Dynamic, and Descriptive Features." *American Journal of Psychotherapy. 41: 499–518.*

Akhtar, S. (1990). "Paranoid Personality Disorder: A Synthesis of Developmental, Dynamic, and Descriptive Features." *American Journal of Psychotherapy*, 44, 5-25.

Akiskal HS, Yerevanian BI, Davis GC, King D, Lemmi H (February 1985). "The nosologic status of borderline personality: clinical and polysomnographic study." *Am J Psychiatry. 142 (2): 192–8.*

Alam C.M.; Merskey H. (1992). "The development of hysterical personality." *History of Psychiatry. 3: 135–165.*

Alarcón RD, Sarabia S (2012). "Debates on the narcissism conundrum: trait, domain, dimension, type, or disorder?" *J Nerv Ment Dis (200): 16–25.*

Allday, Erin (November 26, 2011). "Revision of psychiatric manual under fire". *San Francisco Chronicle.*

Allen DM, Farmer RG (1996). "Family relationships of adults with borderline personality disorder." *Compr Psychiatry. 37 (1): 43–51.*

Alexander, Brian (May 22, 2008). "What's 'normal' sex? Shrinks seek definition: Controversy erupts over creation of psychiatric rule book's new edition". *MSNBC. Retrieved June 14, 2008.*

Alterman, AI; Rutherford, MJ; Cacciola, JS; McKay, JR; Boardman, CR (1998). "Prediction of 7 months methadone maintenance treatment response by four measures of antisociality." *Drug and Alcohol Dependence. 49 (3): 217–23.*

Aluja, Anton; Garcia, Luis F.; Blanch, Angel; De Lorenzo, D.; Fibla, Joan (1 July 2009). "Impulsive-disinhibited personality and serotonin transporter gene polymorphisms: association study in an inmate's sample." *Journal of Psychiatric Research. 43 (10): 906– 914.*

Amad, A; Ramoz, N; Thomas, P; Jardri, R; Gorwood, P (March 2014). "Genetics of borderline personality disorder: systematic review and proposal of an integrative model." *Neuroscience and biobehavioral reviews. 40: 6–19.*

American Psychiatric Association Practice Guidelines (October 2001). "Practice guideline for the treatment of patients with borderline personality disorder. American Psychiatric Association." *Am J Psychiatry. 158 (10 Suppl): 1–52.*

Anderluh MB, et al. (2003). "Childhood obsessive–compulsive personality traits in adult women with eating disorders: defining a broader eating disorder phenotype." *Am J Psychiatry. 160 (2): 242– 47.*

Anglina, Deidre M., Patricia R. Cohenab, and Henian Chena (2008). "Duration of early maternal separation and prediction of schizotypal symptoms from early adolescence to midlife." *Schizophrenia Research,* Volume 103, Issue 1, Pages 143-150.

Aoki, Yuta; Inokuchi, Ryota; Nakao, Tomohiro; Yamasue, Hidenori (25 February 2017). "Neural bases of antisocial behavior: a voxel-based meta-analysis." *Social Cognitive and Affective Neuroscience. 9 (8): 1223–1231.*

Aragona M. (2014) "Epistemological reflections about the crisis of the DSM-5 and the revolutionary potential of the RDoC project Dialogues."*Philosophy, Mental and Neuro Sciences* 7: 11-20

Arntz, Arnoud (September 2005). "Introduction to special issue: cognition and emotion in borderline personality disorder." *Journal of Behavior Therapy and Experimental Psychiatry. 36 (3): 167–72.*

Aronson TA (August 1985). "Historical perspectives on the borderline concept: a review and critique." *Psychiatry. 48 (3): 209–22.*

Atwell Irene; Azibo Daudi A (1991). "Diagnosing personality disorder in Africans (Blacks) using the Azibo nosology: Two case studies". *Journal of Black Psychology. 17 (2): 1–22.*

Aviram, RB; Brodsky, BS; Stanley, B (2006). "Borderline personality disorder, stigma, and treatment implications." *Harvard Review of Psychiatry. 14 (5): 249–56.*

Ayduk O, Zayas V, Downey G, Cole AB, Shoda Y, Mischel W (February 2008). "Rejection Sensitivity and Executive Control: Joint predictors of Borderline Personality features." *J Res Pers. 42 (1): 151–168.*

Azibo, Daudi Ajani ya (November 2014). "The Azibo Nosology II: Epexegesis and 25th Anniversary Update: 55 Culture-focused Mental Disorders Suffered by African Descent People" (PDF). *Journal of Pan African Studies. 7 (5): 32–176.*

Baca-Garcia, E.; Perez-Rodriguez, M. M.; Basurte-Villamor, I.; Del Moral, A. L. F.; Jimenez-Arriero, M. A.; De Rivera, J. L. G.; Saiz-Ruiz, J.; Oquendo, M. A. (March 2007). "Diagnostic stability of psychiatric disorders in clinical practice". *The British Journal of Psychiatry*. 190 (3): 210–6.

Baer, Lee. (1998). "Personality Disorders in Obsessive–Compulsive Disorder." *In Obsessive–Compulsive Disorders: Practical Management. Third edition*. Jenike, Michael et al. (eds.). St. Lou is: Mosby.

Baker, Laura A.; Bezdjian, Serena; Raine, Adrian (1 January 2006). "Behavioral Genetics: The Science of Antisocial Behavior." *Law and Contemporary Problems. 69 (1–2): 7–46.*

Bakkevig J.F.; Sigmund K. (2010). "Is the diagnostic and statistical manual of mental disorders, fourth edition, histrionic personality disorder category a valid construct?" *Comprehensive Psychiatry. 51: 462–470.*

Ball JS, Links PS (February 2009). "Borderline personality disorder and childhood trauma: evidence for a causal relationship." *Curr Psychiatry Rep. 11 (1): 63–8.*

Barlow, H.D. & Durand, V.M. (2005). "Personality Disorders." *Abnormal Psychology: An Integrative Approach (4th ed.)*. Belmont, CA: Thomas Wadsworth.

Battle, Cynthia L.; Shea, M. Tracie; Johnson, Dawn M.; Yen, Shirley; Zlotnick, Caron; Zanarini, Mary C.; Sanislow, Charles A.; Skodol, Andrew E.; et al. (2004). "Childhood Maltreatment Associated With Adult Personality Disorders: Findings From the Collaborative Longitudinal Personality Disorders Study." *Journal of Personality Disorders. 18 (2): 193–211.*

Bayer, Ronald (1981). *Homosexuality and American Psychiatry: The Politics of Diagnosis*. Princeton University Press p. 105.

Beck, Aaron T; Freeman, Arthur (1990). *Cognitive Therapy of Personality Disorders.* New York: Guilford Press.

Becker D (October 2000). "When she was bad: borderline personality disorder in a posttraumatic age." *Am J Orthopsychiatry. 70 (4): 422–32.*

Benazzi F (January 2006). "Borderline personality-bipolar spectrum relationship." *Prog. Neuropsychopharmacol. Biol. Psychiatry. 30 (1): 68–74.*

Bender, Donna S.; Skodol, Andrew E.; Dyck, Ingrid R.; Markowitz, John C.; Shea, M. Tracie; Yen, Shirley; Sanislow, Charles A.; Pinto, Anthony; Zanarini, Mary C.; McGlashan, Thomas H.; Gunderson, John G.; Daversa, Maria T.; Grilo, Carlos M. (2007). "Ethnicity and Mental Health Treatment Utilization by Patients with Personality Disorders." *Journal of Consulting and Clinical Psychology. 75 (6): 992–999.*

Bender, D; Dolan R; Skodol A (2001). "Treatment utilization by patients with personality disorders." *Am J Psychiatry. 158. 158 (Am J Psychiatry 2001): 295–302.*

Bender, D.; Skodol, A. E.; Pagano, M. E.; Dyck, I. R.; Grilo, C. M.; Shea, M. T.; Sanislow, C. A.; Zanarini, M. C.; Yen, S.; McGlashan, T. H.; Gunderson, J. G. (2006). "Prospective assessment of treatment use by patients with personality disorders." *Psychiatr Serv. 57. 2 (Psychiatr Serv): 254–257.*

Benjamin, Lorna Smith (1993). *Interpersonal Diagnosis and Treatment of Personality Disorders.* Guilford Press.

Benjamin, Lorna Smith (1996). "Dependent Personality Disorder." *Interpersonal Diagnosis and Treatment of Personality Disorders.* Guilford Press. pp. 221–39.

Benjamin, Lorna Smith (1996). "Dependent Personality Disorder." *Interpersonal Diagnosis and Treatment of Personality Disorders.* Guilford Press. *pp. 221–39.*

Bentall, R. (2006). "Madness explained : Why we must reject the Kraepelinian paradigm and replace it with a 'complaint-orientated' approach to understanding mental illness". *Medical Hypotheses.* 66 (2): 220–233.

Berenbaum, Howard, Eve M. Valera and John G. Kerns (2003). "Psychological Trauma and Schizotypal Symptoms," *Schizophrenia Bulletin*, Volume 29, Number 1 Pp. 143-152.

Bernstein, David P.; Arntz, Arnoud; Vos, Marije de (2007). "Schema Focused Therapy in Forensic Settings: Theoretical Model and Recommendations for Best Clinical Practice." *International Journal of Forensic Mental Health. 6 (2): 169–183.*

Berger, Fred K. (29 July 2016). "Antisocial personality disorder: MedlinePlus Medical Encyclopedia." *MedlinePlus.*

Bernstein, D. P., Useda, D., Siever, L. J. (1995). "Paranoid Personality Disorder." In: J. W. Livesley (Ed.). *The DSM-IV Personality Disorders.* (pp. 45-57). New York: Guilford.

Bhugra, D. & Munro, A. (1997). Troublesome Disguises: Underdiagnosed Psychiatric Syndromes. *Blackwell Science Ltd.*

Binks CA, Fenton M, McCarthy L, Lee T, Adams CE, Duggan C (2006). Binks C, ed. "Pharmacological interventions for people with borderline personality disorder." *Cochrane Database of Systematic Reviews (1): CD005653.*

Black DW, Gunter T, Allen J, et al. (2007). "Borderline personality disorder in male and female offenders newly committed to prison." *Compr Psychiatry. 48 (5): 400–5.*

Blais M.A.; Hilsenroth M.; Fowler C. (1998). "Rorschach correlates of the DSM-IV histrionic personality disorder." *Journal of Personality Assessment. 70 (2): 355–365.*

Blaney, Paul H. (2014). *Oxford Textbook of Psychopathology.* Oxford University Press.

Blechner, Mark J. (July 1994). "Projective identification, countertransference, and the 'maybe-me'." *Contemporary Psychoanalysis. 30 (3): 619–30.*

Bleuler, Eugen (1924). *Textbook of Psychiatry*, New York: Macmillan.

Blom, Jan Dirk (2010). *A Dictionary of Hallucinations (1 ed.).* New York: Springer.

Bolton S, Gunderson JG (September 1996). "Distinguishing borderline personality disorder from bipolar disorder: differential diagnosis and implications." *Am J Psychiatry. 153 (9): 1202–7.*

Bornstein, Robert F. (1996-01-01). "Sex Differences in Dependent Personality Disorder Prevalence Rates." *Clinical Psychology: Science and Practice. 3 (1).*

"Borderline Personality Disorder". NIMH, 16 March 2016.

"BPD Awareness Month – Congressional History". (2010). *BPD Today. Mental Health Today. Retrieved 1 November 2010.*

Bradley R, Jenei J, Westen D (January 2005). "Etiology of borderline personality disorder: disentangling the contributions of intercorrelated antedents." *J. Nerv. Ment. Dis. 193 (1): 24–31.*

Breedlove, S. Marc (2015). *Principles of Psychology.* Oxford University Press.

Brock, Michael (2020). *Journeys of Faith: Religion, Spirituality, and Humanistic Psychology.*

Brown MZ, Comtois KA, Linehan MM (February 2002). "Reasons for suicide attempts and nonsuicidal self-injury in women with borderline personality disorder." *J Abnorm Psychol. 111 (1): 198–202.*

Brown, Serena-Lynn; Botsis, Alexander; Van Praag; Herman M. (1994). "Serotonin and Aggression." *Journal of Offender Rehabilitation. 3–4. 21 (3): 27–39.*

Cain, Nicole; Ansell, Emily B.; Simpson, H. Blair; Pinto, Anthony (2014). "Interpersonal Functioning in Obsessive–Compulsive Personality Disorder." *Journal of Personality Assessment. 97 (1): 1–10.*

Caligor, E; Levy, KN; Yeomans, FE (May 2015). "Narcissistic personality disorder: diagnostic and clinical challenges." *The American Journal of Psychiatry. 172 (5): 415–22.*

Callaghan G. M.; Summers C. J.; Weidman M. (2003). "The treatment of histrionic and narcissistic personality disorder behaviors: A single-subject demonstration of clinical improvement using functional analytic psychotherapy." *Journal of contemporary psychotherapy. 33 (4): 321–339.*

Calvo, Rosa; Lázaro, Luisa; Castro-Fornieles, Josefina; Fonta, Elena; Moreno, Elena; Toro, J. (April 2009). "Obsessive-compulsive personality disorder traits and personality dimensions in parents of children with obsessive-compulsive disorder." *European Psychiatry. 24 (3): 201–206.*

Carey, Benedict (December 17, 2008). "Psychiatrists Revise the Book of Human Troubles". *The New York Times.*

Carey, Benedict (May 8, 2012), "Psychiatry Manual Drafters Back Down on Diagnoses", *The New York Times, nytimes.com, retrieved May 12, 2012*

Carlson, Neil R.; Heth, C. Donald (2010). *Psychology: The Science of Behavior.* Pearson Canada.

Cassels, Caroline (2 December 2012). "DSM-5 Gets APA's Official Stamp of Approval". *Medscape.* WebMD, LLC. Retrieved 2012-12-05.

Caspi A, McClay J, Moffitt TE, Mill J, Martin J, Craig IW, et al. (Aug 2002). "Role of genotype in the cycle of violence in maltreated children." *Science. 297 (5582): 851–4.*

Chafos VH, Economou P (July 2014). "Beyond Borderline Personality Disorder: The Mindful Brain." *Social Work. 59 (4): 297–302.*

Chanen, Andrew M; Thompson, Katherine N (1 April 2016). "Prescribing and borderline personality disorder." *Australian Prescriber. 39 (2): 49–53.*

Chen, C. K., Lin, S. K., Sham, P. C.; et al. (2005). "Morbid risk for psychiatric disorder among the relatives of methamphetamine users with and without psychosis." *American Journal of Medical Genetics. 136: 87–91.*
Lou Chibbaro, Jr. (May 30, 2008). "Activists alarmed over APA: Head of psychiatry panel favors 'change' therapy for some trans teens". *Washington Blade.*

Chodoff, P. (2005) "Psychiatric Diagnosis: A 60-Year Perspective," *Psychiatric News* June 3, 2005 Volume 40 Number 11, p17

Cleary M, Siegfried N, Walter G (September 2002). "Experience, knowledge and attitudes of mental health staff regarding clients with a borderline personality disorder." *Int J Ment Health Nurs. 11 (3): 186–91.*

Cohen P (September 2008). "Child development and personality disorder." *Psychiatr Clin North Am. 31 (3): 477–93.*

Comer, Ronald (2014). *Fundamentals of abnormal psychology (PDF).* New York, NY: Worth Publishers.

Compton, Michael T. (2007) Recovery: Patients, Families, Communities Conference Report, *Medscape Psychiatry & Mental Health*, October 11–14, 2007.

Connors, Mary E. (1997). "The Renunciation of Love: Dismissive Attachment and its Treatment." *Psychoanalytic Psychology. 14: 475–493.*

Connolly, Adrian J. (2008). "Personality disorders in homeless drop-in center clients." *Journal of Personality Disorders. 22 (6): 573–588.*

Coolidge, Frederick L. (2012). "Are alexithymia and schizoid personality disorder synonymous diagnoses?" *Comprehensive Psychiatry. 54 (2): 141–148.*

Cooper, JE; Kendell, RE; Gurland, BJ; Sartorius, N; Farkas, T (April 1969). "Cross-national study of diagnosis of the mental disorders: some results from the first comparative investigation". *The American Journal of Psychiatry.* 10 Suppl: 21–9.

Corbitt, E., Widiger, T. (1995). "Sex differences among the personality disorders: An exploration of the data." *Clinical Psychology: Science and Practice. 2 (3): 225–238.*

Cordier, Thomas A. (2016). "The Creation and Implementation of the Interpersonal-Cognitive-Behavioral Treatment System (I-CBT)," in *Foundation Theology 2016,* edited by John H. Morgan. South Bend, IN: GTF Books.

Cosgrove, Lisa; Krimsky, Sheldon; Vijayaraghavan, Manisha; Schneider, Lisa (April 2006), "Financial Ties between DSM-IV Panel Members and the Pharmaceutical Industry", *Psychotherapy and Psychosomatics,* 75 (3): 154–160.

Cosgrove, Lisa; Drimsky Lisa (March 2012). "A comparison of DSM-iv and DSM-5 panel members' financial associations with industry: A pernicous problem persisits". *PLoS Medicine.* 9 (3): 1–5.

Cosmides, Leda; John Tooby (1999). "Toward an Evolutionary Taxonomy of Treatable Conditions" (PDF). *Journal of Abnormal Psychology.* 108 (3): 453–464.

Crimlisk H.; Ron M. (1999). "Conversion hysteria: history, diagnostic issues, and clinical practice." *Cognitive Neuropsychiatry. 4 (3): 165–180.*

Dalal PK, Sivakumar T (2009). "Moving towards ICD-11 and DSM-5: Concept and evolution of psychiatric classification". *Indian Journal of Psychiatry. 51 (4): 310–319.*

Daley SE, Burge D, Hammen C (August 2000). "Borderline personality disorder symptoms as predictors of 4-year romantic relationship dysfunction in young women: addressing issues of specificity." *J Abnorm Psychol. 109 (3): 451–60. PMID 11016115.*

Diagnostic and Statistical Manual of Mental Disorders (DSM-5), (New York: American Psychiatric Association, 2013, 5th edition).

Darke, S; Finlay-Jones, R; Kaye, S; Blatt, T (1996). "Anti-social personality disorder and response to methadone maintenance treatment." *Drug and alcohol review. 15 (3): 271–6.*

Deans C, Meocevic E (2006). "Attitudes of registered psychiatric nurses towards patients diagnosed with borderline personality disorder." *Contemp Nurse. 21 (1): 43–9.*

Demazeux, Steeves and Singy, Patrick (2015). *Perspective: Philosophical Reflections on the Psychiatric Babel.* Springer.

De Reus, Rob J.M.; Paul M.G. Emmelkamp (February 2012). "Obsessive–compulsive personality disorder: A review of current empirical findings." *Personality and Mental Health. 6 (1): 1–21.*

Derefinko, Karen J.; Thomas A. Widiger (2008). "Antisocial Personality Disorder." *The Medical Basis of Psychiatry: 213–226.*

DeSoto, M. Catherine (2007). "Borderline Personality Disorder, Gender and Serotonin: Does Estrogen Play a Role?" *In Czerbska, Martina T. Psychoneuroendocrinology Research Trends. Nova Biomedical.* Nova Science Publishers. pp. 149–60.

DeSoto MC, Geary DC, Hoard MK, Sheldon MS, Cooper L (August 2003). "Estrogen fluctuations, oral contraceptives and borderline personality." *Psychoneuroendocrinology. 28 (6): 751–66.*

Dhawan N, Kunik ME, Oldham J, Coverdale J (2010), "Prevalence and Treatment of Narcissistic Personality Disorder in the Community: A Systematic Review." *Comprehensive Psychiatry, 51 (4): 333–339.*

Diagnostic and Statistical Manual-5. Arlington, VA: American Psychiatric Association.
Millon, Théodore and Grossman, Seth (2004). Personality Disorders in Modern Life. Wiley.

Disney, K.L., Weinstein, Y., & Oltmanns, T.F. (2012). "Personality disorder symptoms are differentially related to divorce frequency." *Journal of Family Psychology. 26: 959–965.*

Domino, George (2002). "Creativity and Ego Defense Mechanisms: Some Exploratory Empirical Evidence." *Creativity Research Journal. 14 (1): 17–25.*

Dozier, Mary; Stovall-McClough, K. Chase; Albus, Kathleen E. (1999*). "Attachment and psychopathology in adulthood". In Cassidy, Jude; Shaver, Phillip R. Handbook of attachment.* New York: Guilford Press. pp. 497–519.

DSM-5 Overview: The Future Manual | APA DSM-5 Archived December 17, 2009, at the *Wayback Machine.*

DSM-5 Ignores Biology of Mental Illness (2013). "The latest edition of psychiatry's standard guidebook neglects the biology of mental illness. New research may change that." May 5, 2013 *Scientific American.*

Ducasse, Déborah; Courtet, Philippe; Olié, Emilie (2014). "Physical and Social Pains in Borderline Disorder and Neuroanatomical Correlates: A Systematic Review." *Current Psychiatry Reports. 16 (5): 443.*

Eggum, Natalie D.; Eisenberg, Nancy; Spinrad, Tracy L.; Valiente, Carlos; Edwards, Alison; Kupfer, Anne S.; Reiser, Mark (2009). "Predictors of withdrawal: Possible precursors of avoidant personality disorder." *Development and Psychopathology. 21 (3): 815–38.*

Ehret, Anna M.; Berking, Matthias (2013). Translated by Welsh, Susan. "From DSM-IV to DSM-5: What Has Changed in the New Edition?." *Verhaltenstherapie. Karger. 23 (4): 258–266.*

Ekleberry, Sharon (2014). "Dependent Personality Disorder (DPD)." *Treating Co-Occurring Disorders. pp. 63–4.*

Ekleberry, Sharon C. (2008). "Cluster A - Schizoid Personality Disorder and Substance Use Disorders." in *Integrated Treatment for Co-Occurring Disorders: Personality Disorders and Addiction.* Routledge.

Ellison, J. M.; Adler, D. A. (1990). "A strategy for the pharmacotherapy of personality disorders." In *Adler, David A. Treating Personality Disorders. San Francisco: Jossey-Bass. pp. 43–63.*

Esterberg, Michelle L. (2010). "Cluster A Personality Disorders: Schizotypal, Schizoid and Paranoid Personality Disorders in Childhood and Adolescence." *Journal of Psychopathology and Behavioral Assessment 32 (4): 515–528.*

Fallon P (August 2003). "Travelling through the system: the lived experience of people with borderline personality disorder in contact with psychiatric services." *J Psychiatr Ment Health Nurs. 10 (4): 393–401.*

Fancher, R.E. & Rutherford, A. (2012). *Pioneers of Psychology.* New York, NY: W. W. Norton & Company.

Farrington, David P. and Coid, Jeremy (2004). *Early Prevention of Adult Antisocial Behavior.* Cambridge University Press. p. 82.

Fazel, Seena; Danesh, John (2002). "Serious mental disorder in 23 000 prisoners: A systematic review of 62 surveys." *The Lancet. 359 (9306): 545–550.*

Ferrer M, Andión O, Matalí J, et al. (December 2010). "Comorbid attention-deficit/hyperactivity disorder in borderline patients defines an impulsive subtype of borderline personality disorder." *J. Pers. Disord. 24 (6): 812–22.*

Ficks CA, Waldman ID (Sep 2014). "Candidate genes for aggression and antisocial behavior: a meta-analysis of association studies of the 5HTTLPR and MAOA-uVNTR". *Behavioral Genetics. 44 (5): 427–44.*

Fineberg, N. A., Sharma, P., Sivakumaran, T., Sahakian, B., & Chamberlain, S. (2007). "Does Obsessive-Compulsive Personality Disorder Belong Within the Obsessive-Compulsive Spectrum." *CNS Spectrum. 12 (6): 467–474, 477–482.*

Fitzgerald, Michael; Aiden Corvin (2001-07-01). "Diagnosis and differential diagnosis of Asperger syndrome." *Advances in Psychiatric Treatment. 7 (4): 310–318.*

Foa, EB; Kozak MJ; Goodman WK; Hollander E; Jenike MA; Rasmussen SA (1995). "obsessive-compulsive disorder." *DSM-IV field trial. 152 (Am J Psychiatry): 90–96.*

Fogelson, David L. ; Keith Nuechterlein (2007). "Avoidant personality disorder is a separable schizophrenia-spectrum personality disorder even when controlling for the presence of paranoid and schizotypal personality disorders." *Schizophrenia Research. 91: 192–199.*

Frances, Allen (17 May 2013). "The New Crisis in Confidence in Psychiatric Diagnosis". *Annals of Internal Medicine.*

Frances, Allen (11 May 2012). "Diagnosing the D.S.M.". *New York Times* (New York ed.). p. A19.

Frances, Allen (June 26, 2009). "A Warning Sign on the Road to DSM-V: Beware of Its Unintended Consequences". *Psychiatric Times.* Retrieved September 6, 2009.

Frances, Allen; Mack, Avram H.; Ross, Ruth; First, Michael B. (2000) [1995]. "The DSM-IV Classification and Psychopharmacology". In Bloom, Floyd E.; Kupfer, David J. *Psychopharmacology: The Fourth Generation of Progress.* American College of Neuropsychopharmacology.

Frances, Allen J. (December 2, 2012). "DSM 5 Is Guide Not Bible—Ignore Its Ten Worst Changes: APA approval of DSM-5 is a sad day for psychiatry". *Psychology Today.* Retrieved 2013-03-09.

Freedman, Robert; Lewis, David A.; Michels, Robert; Pine, Daniel S.; Schultz, Susan K.; Tamminga, Carol A.; Gabbard, Glen O.; Gau, Susan Shur-Fen; Javitt, Daniel C.; Oquendo, Maria A.; Shrout, Patrick E.; Vieta, Eduard; Yager, Joel (January 2013). "The Initial Field Trials of DSM-5: New Blooms and Old Thorns". *American Journal of Psychiatry.* 170 (1): 1–5.

Friedheim, Donald K., Editor (1992). *History of Psychotheraphy: A Century of Change* (Washington, DC: American Psychological Association).

Freud, S. (1959, original work published 1908).*Character and Anal Eroticism*, in The Standard Edition of the Complete Psychological Works of Sigmund Freud, 9, 170–71. James Strachey, ed. London: Hogarth.

Frazzetto G, Di Lorenzo G, Carola V, Proietti L, Sokolowska E, Siracusano A, et al. (2007). "Early trauma and increased risk for physical aggression during adulthood: the moderating role of MAOA genotype." *PLOS ONE. 2 (5): e486.*

Gabbard, Glen O., Gunderson John G. (2000). *Psychotherapy for Personality Disorders. First Edition.* American Psychiatric Publishing.

Gabbard, G.O. (2014). *Psychodynamic psychiatry in clinical practice. 5th Edition.* American Psychiatric Publishing: Washington, D.C.

Galarza M, Merlo A, Ingratta A, Albanese E, Albanese A (2004). "Cavum septum pellucidum and its increased prevalence in schizophrenia: a neuroembryological classification." *The Journal of neuropsychiatry and clinical neurosciences. 16 (1): 41–6.*

Ghaemi, S. Nassir; Knoll, James L., IV; Pearlman, Theodore (14 October 2013). "Why DSM-III, IV, and 5 are Unscientific". *Psychiatric Times*: Couch in Crisis Blog.

Gillberg, C.; Billstedt, E. (November 2000). "Autism and Asperger syndrome: coexistence with other clinical disorders." *Acta Psychiatrica Scandinavica. 102 (5): 321–330.*

Gjerde, L. C.; Czajkowski, N.; Røysamb, E.; Ørstavik, R. E.; Knudsen, G. P.; Østby, K.; Torgersen, S.; Myers, J.; Kendler, K. S.; Reichborn-Kjennerud, T. (2012). "The heritability of avoidant and dependent personality disorder assessed by personal interview and questionnaire." *Acta Psychiatrica Scandinavica. 126 (6): 448–57.*

Grijalva E, Newman DA, Tay L (2015), "Gender differences in narcissism: A meta-analytic review." *Psychological Bulletin, 141 (2): 261.*

Glenn, Andrea L. (January 2011). "The other allele: Exploring the long allele of the serotonin transporter gene as a potential risk factor

for psychopathy: A review of the parallels in findings."
Neuroscience & Biobehavioral Reviews. 35: 612–620.

Golomb, Elan (1992). *Trapped in the Mirror,* New York: Morrow.

Gooding DC; Tallent KA; Matts CW (2005). "Clinical status of at-
risk individuals 5 years later: Further validation of the psychometric
high-risk strategy." *Journal of Abnormal Psychology. 114: 170–175.*

Goodman, M; New, A; Siever, L (December 2004). "Trauma, genes,
and the neurobiology of personality disorders." *Annals of the New
York Academy of Sciences. 1032: 104–16.*
Bibcode:2004NYASA1032..104G.

Grady-Weliky, TA (January 2003). "Premenstrual dysphoric
disorder." *N. Engl. J. Med. 348 (5): 433–8.*

Grant BF, Chou SP, Goldstein RB, et al. (April 2008). "Prevalence,
correlates, disability, and comorbidity of DSM-IV borderline
personality disorder: results from the Wave 2 National
Epidemiologic Survey on Alcohol and Related Conditions."*J Clin
Psychiatry. 69 (4): 533–45.*

Grant, Bridget F.; Hasin, Deborah S.; Stinson, Frederick S.;
Dawson, Deborah A.; Chou, S. Patricia; Ruan, W. June; Pickering,
Roger P. (2004). "Prevalence, Correlates, and Disability of
Personality Disorders in the United States." *The Journal of Clinical
Psychiatry. 65 (7): 948–58.*

Grob, GN. (1991) "Origins of DSM-I: a study in appearance and
reality," *Am J Psychiatry.* April;148(4):421–31.

Grossman R, Yehuda R, Siever L (June 1997). "The dexamethasone
suppression test and glucocorticoid receptors in borderline
personality disorder." *Annals of the New York Academy of Sciences.
821: 459–64.*

Grant, Chou, Goldstein, Huang, Stinson, Saha, Smith, Dawson,
Pulay, Pickering, Ruan (April 2008). "Prevalence, correlates,

disability, and comorbidity of DSM-IV borderline personality disorder: Results from the Wave 2 National Epidemiologic survey on alcohol and related conditions." *Journal of Clinical Psychology (69): 533–545.*

Greenberg, S; Shuman, DW; Meyer, RG (2004). "Unmasking forensic diagnosis". International *Journal of Law and Psychiatry*. 27 (1): 1–15.

Greenberg, Gary (January 29, 2012). "The D.S.M.'s Troubled Revision". *The New York Times.*

Grilo CM. (2004). "Diagnostic efficiency of DSM-IV criteria for obsessive compulsive personality disorder in patients with binge eating disorder." *Behaviour Research and Therapy* 42(1) January,57–65.

Gunderson JG, Kolb JE, Austin V (July 1981). "The diagnostic interview for borderline patients." *Am J Psychiatry. 138 (7): 896–903.*

Gunderson, John G. (26 May 2011). "Borderline Personality Disorder." *The New England Journal of Medicine. 364 (21): 2037–2042.*

Gunderson, JG; Sabo, AN (1993). "The phenomenological and conceptual interface between borderline personality disorder and PTSD". *Am J Psychiatry. 150 (1): 19–27.*

Gunderson JG, Elliott GR (March 1985). "The interface between borderline personality disorder and affective disorder." *Am J Psychiatry. 142 (3): 277–88.*

Gunderson, John G.; Links, Paul S. (2008). *Borderline Personality Disorder: A Clinical Guide (2nd ed.).* American Psychiatric Publishing, Inc.

Guntrip, Harry (1969). *Schizoid Phenomena, Object-Relations, and The Self.* New York: International Universities Press.

Guo, Guang; Ou, Xiao-Ming; Roettger, Michael; Shih, Jean C. (May 2008). "The VNTR 2 repeat in MAOA and delinquent behavior in adolescence and young adulthood: associations and MAOA promoter activity." *European Journal of Human Genetics. Nature Publishing Group. 16 (5): 626–34.*

Guo G, Roettger M, Shih JC (August 2008). "The integration of genetic propensities into social-control models of delinquency and violence among male youths." *American Sociological Review. 73 (4): 543–568.*

Hales E and Yudofsky JA, eds. (2003). *The American Psychiatric Press Textbook of Psychiatry.* Washington, DC: American Psychiatric Publishing, Inc.

Hales, E. (1 February 1996). "Psychopathy and Antisocial Personality Disorder: A Case of Diagnostic Confusion," *Psychiatric Times. UBM Medica. 13 (2).*

Halmi, KA; et al. (December 2005). "The relation among perfectionism, obsessive–compulsive personality disorder, and obsessive–compulsive disorder in individuals with eating disorders." *Int J Eat Disord. 38 (4): 371–4.*

Halpern, L, Trachtman, H. and Duckworth, K. "From Within: A Consumer Perspective on Psychiatric Hospitals," in Textbook of *Hospital Psychiatry*, S. Sharfstein, F. Dickerson and J. Oldham eds. American Psychiatric Publishing, 2009, pp.237-244.

Hands, D. Wade (December 2004). "On Operationalisms and Economics". Journal of Economic Issues. 38 (4): 953–968.

Harbinger, New (May 22, 2013). "Goodbye to the DSM-V". *Huffington Post. Retrieved May 23, 2013.*

Haznedar, M. M.; Buchsbaum, M. S.; Hazlett, E. A.; Shihabuddin, L.; New, A.; Siever, L. J. (2004). "Cingulate gyrus volume and metabolism in the schizophrenia spectrum." *Schizophrenia Research. 71 (2–3): 249–262.*

Healy D (2006) The Latest Mania: Selling Bipolar Disorder *PLoS Med* 3(4): e185.

Herman, Judith Lewis; Judith Herman MD (1992). *Trauma and recovery.* New York: BasicBooks.

Herbert JD, Hope DA, Bellack AS (1992). "Validity of the distinction between generalized social phobia and avoidant personality disorder." *J Abnorm Psychol. 101 (2): 332–9.*

Herpertz SC, Dietrich TM, Wenning B, et al. (August 2001). "Evidence of abnormal amygdala functioning in borderline personality disorder: a functional MRI study." *Biol. Psychiatry. 50 (4): 292–8.*

Hesse M, Schliewe S, Thomsen RR; Schliewe; Thomsen (2005). "Rating of personality disorder features in popular movie characters." *BMC Psychiatry. London: BioMed Central. 5: 45.*

"Highlights of Changes from DSM-IV-TR to DSM-5" (PDF). *American Psychiatric Association.* 17 May 2013. Archived from the original (PDF) on 2015-02-26.

Hinshaw, Stephen P.; Lee, Steve S. (2003). "Conduct and Oppositional Defiant Disorders" (PDF). *In Mash, Eric J.; Barkely, Russell A. Child Psychopathology* (2 ed.). New York: Guilford Press. pp. 144–198.

Hinshelwood RD (March 1999). "The difficult patient. The role of 'scientific psychiatry' in understanding patients with chronic schizophrenia or severe personality disorder." *Br J Psychiatry. 174 (3): 187–90.*

Hirsh JB, Quilty LC, Bagby RM, McMain SF (August 2012). "The relationship between agreeableness and the development of the working alliance in patients with borderline personality disorder." *J. Pers. Disord. 26 (4): 616–27.*

Hofvander, Björn; Delorme, Richard; Chaste, Pauline; Nydén, Agneta; Wentz, Elisabet; Stahlberg, Ola; Herbrecht, Evelyn; Stopin, Astrid; Anckarsäter, Henrik; Gillberg, Christopher; et al. (2009). "Psychiatric and psychosocial problems in adults with normal-intelligence autism spectrum disorders." *BMC Psychiatry. 9 (1): 35.*

Holden C (2010). "Psychiatry. APA seeks to overhaul personality disorder diagnoses." *Science. 327 (5971): 1314.*

Horesh N, Sever J, Apter A (July–August 2003). "A comparison of life events between suicidal adolescents with major depression and borderline personality disorder." *Compr Psychiatry. 44 (4): 277–83.*

Horney, Karen (1999). "Resignation: The Appeal of Freedom". In *Neurosis and Human Growth: The Struggle Towards Self-Realization.* Routledge.

Houts A.C. (2000). "Fifty years of psychiatric nomenclature: Reflections on the 1943 War Department Technical Bulletin, Medical 203". *Journal of Clinical Psychology. 56 (7): 935–967.*

"How Using the Dsm Causes Damage: A Client's Report" *Journal of Humanistic Psychology,* Vol. 41, No. 4, 36-56 (2001).

Huizinga, David; Haberstick, Brett C.; Smolen, Andrew; Menard, Scott; Young, Susan E.; Corley, Robin P.; Stallings, Michael C.; Grotpeter, Jennifer; Hewitt, John K. (October 2006). "Childhood Maltreatment, Subsequent Antisocial Behavior, and the Role of Monoamine Oxidase A Genotype." *Biological Psychiatry. 60 (7): 677–683.*

Huppert, Jonathan D.; Strunk, Daniel R.; Ledley, Deborah Roth; Davidson, Jonathan R. T.; Foa, Edna B. (2008). "Generalized social anxiety disorder and avoidant personality disorder: structural analysis and treatment outcome." *Depression and Anxiety. 25 (5): 441–8.*

ICD-9-CM Codes for Selected General Medical Conditions and Medication-Induced Disorders, Appendix G.

ICD-10 Classification of Mental and Behavioural Disorders: *"Blue Book"* (Clinical descriptions and diagnostic guidelines) und "Green Book" (Diagnostic criteria for research)

Ike, Michael. (1998). "Psychotherapy of Obsessive–compulsive Personality". In *Obsessive–Compulsive Disorders: Practical Management. Third edition*. Jenike, Michael et al. (eds.). St. Louis: Mosby.

Insel, Thomas (29 April 2013). "Transforming Diagnosis". Director's Blog. *National Institute of Mental Health*. Retrieved 2013-09-02.

Jamison, Kay R.; Goodwin, Frederick Joseph (1990). *Manic-depressive illness*. Oxford: Oxford University Press.

Jayson, Sharon (12 May 2013). "Books blast new version of psychiatry's bible, the DSM". USA Today. Retrieved 2013-05-21.

Jefferys, Don; Moore, KA (2008). "Pathological hoarding." *Australian Family Physician. 37 (4): 237–41.*

Jenkins, R. L. and S. Glickman (April 1946). "The Schizoid Child." *American Journal of Orthopsychiatry. 16 (2): 255–61.*

Johnson, Stephen M. 1987). *Humanizing the Narcissistic Style.* W.W. Norton.

Johnson, JG; Smailes, EM; Cohen, P; Brown, J; Bernstein, DP (2000). "Associations between four types of childhood neglect and personality disorder symptoms during adolescence and early adulthood: findings of a community-based longitudinal study." *Journal of personality disorders. 14 (2): 171–87.*

Johnson, J. G.; Cohen, P; Brown, J; Smailes, EM; Bernstein, DP (1999). "Childhood Maltreatment Increases Risk for Personality Disorders During Early Adulthood." *Archives of General Psychiatry. 56 (7): 600–6.*

Joseph, Sonny (1997). "Chapter 3, Schizoid Personality Disorder". Personality Disorders: New Symptom-Focused Drug Therapy. *Psychology Press.*

Joyce, Peter R.; McKenzie, Janice M.; Luty, Suzanne E.; Mulder, Roger T.; Carter, Janet D.; Sullivan, Patrick F.; Cloninger, C. Robert (2003). "Temperament, childhood environment and psychopathology as risk factors for avoidant and borderline personality disorders." *Australian and New Zealand Journal of Psychiatry. 37 (6): 756–64.*

Kantor, M. (1993, revised 2003). *Distancing: A Guide to Avoidance and Avoidant Personality Disorder*. Westport, Conn: Praeger Publishers.

Kay, Jerald et al. (2000). "Obsessive–Compulsive Disorder". In *Psychiatry: Behavioral Science and Clinical Essentials.* Jenike, Michael et al. Philadelphia: W. B. Saunders.

Karterud, Sigmund (September 2011). "Validity aspects of the Diagnostic and Statistical Manual of Mental Disorders, Fourth Edition, narcissistic personality disorder construct." *Comprehensive psychiatry. 52 (5): 517–526.*

Kendell, R.; Jablensky, A (January 2003). "Distinguishing Between the Validity and Utility of Psychiatric Diagnoses". *American Journal of Psychiatry. 160 (1): 4–12.*

Kendler KS, Czajkowski N, Tambs K, et al. (2006). "Dimensional representations of DSM-IV cluster A personality disorders in a population-based sample of Norwegian twins: a multivariate study." *Psychological Medicine 36 (11): 1583–91.*

Kendler Kenneth S.; Muñoz Rodrigo A.; George Murphy M.D. (2009). "The Development of the Feighner Criteria: A Historical Perspective." *Am J Psychiatry. 167: 134–142.*

Khalifa, N., Duggan, C., Stoffers, J., Huband, N., Völlm Birgit, A., Ferriter, M., & Lieb, K. (2010). "Pharmacological interventions for antisocial personality disorder." *Cochrane Database of Systematic Reviews*, (8).

Khan, Masud (1974). "The Role of phobic and counterphobic mechanisms and separation anxiety in schizoid character formation." *The Privacy of the Self - Papers on Psychoanalytic Theory and Technique.* New York: International Universities Press.

Kinderman, Peter (20 May 2013). "Explainer: what is the DSM?". The Conversation Australia. *The Conversation Media Group.* Retrieved 2013-05-21.

Kinney, Dennis K.; Richards, Ruth (2001). "Creativity in Offspring of Schizophrenic and Control Parents: An Adoption Study." *Creativity Research Journal. 13 (1): 17–25.*

Kirk, Stuart A.; Kutchins, Herb (1994). "The Myth of the Reliability of DSM". *Journal of Mind and Behavior.* 15 (1&2): 71–86. Archived from the original on 2008-03-07. Retrieved 2008-03-04.

Klein, Melanie (1932). *The Psychoanalysis of Children.* London: Hogarth Press.

Kleinman A (1997). "Triumph or pyrrhic victory? The inclusion of culture in DSM-IV". *Harv Rev Psychiatry.* 4 (6): 343–4.

Kluft, Richard P. (1990). *Incest-Related Syndromes of Adult Psychopathology.* American Psychiatric Pub, Inc.

Kluft, Richard; Goodwin, Jean (1985). *Childhood Antecedents of Multiple Personality Disorder: Credibility Problems in Multiple Personality Disorder Patients and Abused Children.* American Psychiatric Publishing, Inc.

Koenigsberg HW, Harvey PD, Mitropoulou V, et al. (May 2002). "Characterizing affective instability in borderline personality disorder." *Am J Psychiatry. 159 (5): 784–8.*

Korzekwa MI, Dell PF, Links PS, Thabane L, Webb SP (2008). "Estimating the prevalence of borderline personality disorder in psychiatric outpatients using a two-phase procedure." *Compr Psychiatry. 49 (4): 380–6.*

Kraepelin, E. (1906). *Uber Sprachstorungen im Traume.* Leipzig: Engelmann.

Krawitz R (July 2004). "Borderline personality disorder: attitudinal change following training." *Aust N Z J Psychiatry. 38 (7): 554–9.*

Kreisman J, Strauss H (2004). *Sometimes I Act Crazy. Living With Borderline Personality Disorder.* Wiley & Sons.

Kress, Victoria (July 2014). "The Removal of the Multiaxial System in the DSM-5: Implications and Practice Suggestions for Counselors". *The Professional Counselor Journal.* 4 (3): 191–201.

Kretschmer, Ernst (1931). *Physique and Character.* London: Routledge (International Library of Psychology,1999).

Krueger, RF.; Watson, D.; Barlow, DH.; et al. (2005). "Introduction to the Special Section: Toward a Dimensionally Based Taxonomy of Psychopathology". *Journal of Abnormal Psychology.* 114 (4): 491–493.

Kupfer, David and D. A. Regier (2011). "DSM-V Task Force Member Disclosure Report: David J Kupfer, MD" (PDF). American Psychiatric Association. and "DSM-V Task Force Member Disclosure Report: Darrel Alvin Regier M.D" (PDF). American Psychiatric Association. May 2, 2011. Retrieved May 5, 2011.

Kupfer, David; Regier, Darrell, eds. (2013). *Diagnostic and Statistical Manual of Mental Disorders (5 ed.).* Washington, DC: American Psychiatric Association.

Laing, R. D. (1965). "The Inner Self in the Schizoid Condition". The Divided Self: an Existential Study," in *Sanity and Madness.* Harmondsworth, Middlesex; Baltimore: Penguin Books.

Lane, Christopher. *"The NIMH Withdraws Support for DSM-5".* *Psychology Today.*

Lane, Christopher (2007). *Shyness: How Normal Behavior Became a Sickness.* Yale University Press. p. 263.

Lane, Christopher (July 24, 2009). "The Diagnostic Madness of DSM-V". *Slate.*

Lazzaretti, Matteo; Morandotti, Niccolò; Sala, Michela; Isola, Miriam; Frangou, Sophia; De Vidovich, Giulia; Marraffini, Elisa; Gambini, Francesca; et al. (2012). "Impaired working memory and normal sustained attention in borderline personality disorder." *Acta Neuropsychiatrica. 24 (6): 349–55.*

Lehnhardt, Fritz-Georg, Astrid Gawronski, Kathleen Pfeiffer, Hanna Kockler, Leonhard Schilbach, and Kai Vogeley (2013). "The investigation and differential diagnosis of Asperger syndrome in adults." *Deutsches Ärzteblatt International. 110 (45): 760.*

Leichsenring, F; Leibing, E; Kruse, J; New, AS; Leweke, F (1 January 2011). "Borderline personality disorder." *Lancet (London, England). 377 (9759): 74–84.*

Lenzenweger, Mark F.; Clarkin, John F. (2005). *Major Theories of Personality Disorder.* Guilford Press.

Levy KN, Meehan KB, Weber M, Reynoso J, Clarkin JF (2005). "Attachment and borderline personality disorder: implications for psychotherapy." *Psychopathology. 38 (2): 64–74.*

Lieb K, Zanarini MC, Schmahl C, Linehan MM, Bohus M (2004). "Borderline personality disorder." *Lancet. 364 (9432): 453–61.*

Linehan MM, Comtois KA, Murray AM, et al. (July 2006). "Two-year randomized controlled trial and follow-up of dialectical behavior therapy vs therapy by experts for suicidal behaviors and borderline personality disorder." *Arch. Gen. Psychiatry. 63 (7): 757–66.*

Links, Paul S.; Shah, Ravi; Eynan, Rahel (2017). "Psychotherapy for Borderline Personality Disorder: Progress and Remaining Challenges." *Current Psychiatry Reports. 19 (3): 16.*

Lock, M. P. (2008). "Treatment of antisocial personality disorder." *The British Journal of Psychiatry. 193 (5): 426.*

Loeber, Rolf; Keenan, Kate; Lahey, Benjamin B.; Green, Stephanie M.; Thomas, Christopher (August 1993). "Evidence for developmentally based diagnoses of oppositional defiant disorder and conduct disorder." *Journal of Abnormal Child Psychology. International Society for Research in Child and Adolescent Psychopathology. 21 (4): 377–410.*

Livesley, John W. (2001). *Handbook of Personality Disorders: Theory, Research, and Treatment.* The Guilford Press.

Lubke, GH; Laurin, C; Amin, N; Hottenga, JJ; Willemsen, G; van Grootheest, G; Abdellaoui, A; Karssen, LC; Oostra, BA; van Duijn, CM; Penninx, BW; Boomsma, DI (August 2014). "Genome-wide analyses of borderline personality features.." *Molecular Psychiatry. 19 (8): 923–9.*

Lynskey, Michael T.; Fergusson, David M. (June 1995). "Childhood conduct problems, attention deficit behaviors, and adolescent alcohol, tobacco, and illicit drug use." *Journal of Abnormal Child Psychology. International Society for Research in Child and Adolescent Psychopathology. 23 (3): 281–302.*

MacFarlane, Malcolm M. (ed.) (2004). *Family Treatment of Personality Disorders. Advances in Clinical Practice*. Binghamton, NY: The Haworth Press.

Mackinnon DF, Pies R (February 2006). "Affective instability as rapid cycling: theoretical and clinical implications for borderline personality and bipolar spectrum disorders." *Bipolar Disord. 8 (1): 1–14.*

MacManus, Deirdre; Fahy, Tom (August 2008). "Personality disorders." *Medicine 36 (8): 436–441.*

Magnavita, Jeffrey J. (1997). Restructuring Personality Disorders: A Short-Term Dynamic Approach. *New York: The Guilford Press.*

Maher, Alicia R. (June 2012). "Summary of the comparative effectiveness review on off-label use of atypical antipsychotics". *J Manag Care Pharm. 18 (5 Suppl B): S1–20.*

Manfiel Maj, Mario (2005). *Personality Disorders.* Chichester: J. Wiley & Sons.

Maj, Mario (2005). *Personality Disorders.* Chichester: J. Wiley & Sons.

Manfield, Philip (1992). *Split Self/Split Object: Understanding and Treating Borderline, Narcissistic, and Schizoid Disorders. N.Y.:* Jason Aronson.

Martens, Willem H. J. (2010). "Schizoid personality disorder linked to unbearable and inescapable loneliness." *The European Journal of Psychiatry. 24 (1).*

Maser, JD. & Patterson, T. (2002). "Spectrum and nosology: implications for DSM-5." *Psychiatric Clinics of North America,* December, 25(4)p855-885.

Maser, JD & Akiskal, HS. et al. (2002). "Spectrum concepts in major mental disorders." *Psychiatric Clinics of North America,* Vol. 25, Special issue 4.

Masterson, James F. and Ralph Klein (1995). *Disorders of the Self - The Masterson Approach.* New York: Brunner / Mazel.

Mather, Amber A. (2008). "Associations Between Body Weight and Personality Disorders in a Nationally Representative Sample." *Psychosomatic Medicine. 70 (9): 1012–1019.*

Matsui M., Sumiyoshi T., Kato K.; et al. (2004). "Neuropsychological profile in patients with schizotypal personality disorder or schizophrenia." *Psychological Reports. 94 (2): 387–397.*

May F, Chen Q, Gilbertson M, Shenton M, Pitman R (2004). "Cavum septum pellucidum in monozygotic twins discordant for combat exposure: relationship to posttraumatic stress disorder." *Biol. Psychiatry. 55 (6): 656–8.*

Mayes, Rick; Bagwell, Catherine; Erkulwater, Jennifer L. (2009). "The Transformation of Mental Disorders in the 1980s: The DSM-III, Managed Care," and "Cosmetic Psychopharmacology"". *Medicating Children: ADHD and Pediatric Mental Health.* Harvard University Press.

Mayo Clinic Staff (2 April 2016). "Overview- Antisocial personality disorder". *Mayo Clinic.*

McCommon, B. (2006). "Antipsychiatry and the Gay Rights Movement." *Psychiatr Serv* 57:1809, December.

McGlashan T.H., Grilo C.M., Skodol A.E., Gunderson J.G., Shea M.T., Morey L.C.; et al. (2000). "The collaborative longitudinal personality disorders study: Baseline axis I/II and II/II diagnostic co-occurrence." *Acta Psychiatrica Scandinavica. 102: 256–264.*

McHugh Paul R (2005). "Striving for Coherence: Psychiatry's Efforts Over Classification". *JAMA.* 293 (20): 2526–2528.

McNally, RJ (March 2001). "On Wakefield's harmful dysfunction analysis of mental disorder". *Behaviour Research and Therapy.* 39 (3): 309–14.

McWilliams, Nancy (2011). *Psychoanalytic Diagnosis: Understanding Personality Structure in the Clinical Process (2nd ed.).* New York: Guilford Press.

Mellsop, Graham (1973). "Antecedents of Schizophrenia." *Australian and New Zealand Journal of Psychiatry 7 (3): 208–211.*

Menelaos L. Batrinos (2012). "Testosterone and Aggressive Behavior in Man." *Int J Endocrinol Metab. 10 (3): 563–568.*

Mezzich, Juan E. (2002). "International Surveys on the Use of ICD-10 and Related Diagnostic Systems" (guest editorial, abstract). *Psychopathology.* 35 (2–3): 72–75.

Miller AL, Muehlenkamp JJ, Jacobson CM (July 2008). "Fact or fiction: diagnosing borderline personality disorder in adolescents." Clin Psychol Rev. 28 (6): 969–81.

Millon, Theodore (1981). *Disorders of Personality: DSM-III, Axis II.* New York: Wiley.

Millon, Theodore (2004). *Personality Disorders in Modern Life.* John Wiley & Sons, Inc., Hoboken, New Jersey.

Millon, Theodore; Martinez, Alexandra (1995). "Avoidant Personality Disorder." *In Livesley, W. John. The DSM-IV Personality Disorders.* Guilford Press.

Millon, Theodore (2004). *The Schizoid Personality (Chapter 11).* In: *Personality Disorders in Modern Life.* Wiley, 2nd Edition.

Millon, Theodore; Davis, Roger Dale (1996). *Disorders of Personality: DSM-IV and Beyond.* New York: Wiley.

Millon, Theodore; Millon, Carrie M.; Meagher, Sarah; Grossman, Seth; Ramnath, Rowena (2004). *Personality Disorders in Modern Life*. Wiley.

Moffitt, Terrie E. (October 1993). "Adolescence-limited and life-course-persistent antisocial behavior: A developmental taxonomy." *Psychological Review. American Psychological Association. 100 (4): 674–701.*

Moore TM, Scarpa A, Raine A (2002). "A meta-analysis of serotonin metabolite 5-HIAA and antisocial behavior." *Aggressive Behavior. 28 (4): 299–316.*

Morgan, John H. (2019). *An Encyclopedic Dictionary of Interpersonal Psychotherapy: Concepts and Terms* (Elkhart, IN: MacBain & Boyd, Publishers).

Morgan, John H. (2019). *Child Psychopathology in Clinical Practice: The Psychoanalytic Theories of Karen Horney, Melanie Klein, and Anna Freud* (Elkhart, IN: MacBain & Boyd, Publishers).

Morgan, John H. (2018). *Psychopathology: A Clinical Guide to Personality Disorders.* South Bend, IN: GTF Books.

Morgan, John H. (2017a). "Geriatric Narcissism: The Psychotherapeutics of Self-Regard among the Elderly (a literature review)," Chapter 12 in John H. Morgan, *Geriatric Psychotherapy: Essays in Clinical Studies and Counseling Psychology* (Mishawaka, IN: GTF Books, 2017).

Morgan, John H. (2017b). "Geriatric Health and Social Values: Exploring the Practical Range of Sociopharmacology (with particular attention to health care practices among the eldery), Chapter 8 in John H. Morgan, *Geriatric Psychotherapy: Essays in Clinical Studies and Counseling Psychology* (Mishawaka, IN: GTF Books, 2017).

Morgan, John H. (2017c, 2nd edition). *Clinical Psychotherapy: A History of Theory and Practice (from Sigmund Freud to Aaron*

Beck). South Bend, IN: GTF Books.

Morgan, John H. (2016). *Clinical Psychotherapy: A History of Theory and Practice (from Sigmund Freud to Aaron Beck).* South Bend, IN: GTF Books.

Morgan, John H. (2015a). "Palliative Psychotherapy in the Treatment of Geriatric Depression: A Review of Evidence-Based Psychogenic Options," *Innovative Issues and Approaches in Social Sciences* (Vol. 8, No. 1:46-59, 2015).

Morgan, John H. (2015b). "Cognitive Behavioral Therapy and Reminiscence Therapy in the Treatment of Depression: A Convergent Palliative Care Methodology in Geriatric Psychotherapy," *The Online Journal of Counseling and Education* 2015, 4(2):51-67.

Morgan, John H. (2014a). "The Interpersonal Psychotherapy of Harry Stack Sullivan: Remembering the Legacy," *Journal of Psychology and Psychotherapy* (Volume 4, Issue 6, 2014).

Morgan, John H. (2014b). "The Deep Structure of Human Nature: Probing the Psycho-Social Propensities in Behavioral Matrices (with special reference to E. O. Wilson)," *Journal of Academic Emergency Medicine Case Reports* / Akademik A;Oct, 2014, Vol. 5 Issue 10, p112.

Morgan, John H. (2013a). "What to Do When There is Nothing to Do: The Psychotherapeutic Value of Meaning Therapy in the Treatment of Late Life Depression," *Health, Culture and Society,* Vol. 5, #1 (2013), pp.52-59.

Morgan, John H. (2013b). "Late-Life Depression and the Counseling Agenda: Exploring Geriatric Logotherapy as a Treatment Modality," *International Journal of Psychological Research*, Vol. VI, #1 (2013).

Morgan, John H. (2012a). "The Personal Meaning of Social Values in the Work of Abraham Maslow," *Interpersona: International*

Journal of Interpersonal Relationships Vol. 6 (1) June, 2012: 1-19.

Morgan, John H. (2012b). "Geriatric Logotherapy: Exploring the Psychotherapeutics of Memory in Treating the Elderly," *Psychological Thought, Vol. 5, #2,* 2012:99-105.

Morgan, John H. (2012c). "Pastoral Nurture of the Elderly: The 'Happy Memory' in Geriatric Logotherapy"in *Clinical Pastoral Psychotherapy: A Practitioner's Handbook for Ministry Professionals* Expanded 2nd Edition (Mishawaka, IN: GTF Books, 2012).

Morgan, John H. (2012d). "Medication and Counseling in Psychiatric Practice: Biogenic Psychopharmacology and Psychogenic Psychotherapy (Partnering in the Treatment of Mental Illness)," in *Clinical Pastoral Psychotherapy: A Practitioner's Handbook for Ministry Professionals* (Expanded 2nd Edition, Mishawaka, IN: GTF Books, 2012).

Morgan, John H. (2012e). "A Tribute to Carl Rogers," in *Clinical Pastoral Psychotherapy: A Practitioner's Handbook for Ministry Professionals* Expanded 2nd Edition (Mishawaka, IN: GTF Books, 2012).

Morgan, John H. (2011). "*On Becoming a Person* (1961) Carl Rogers' Celebrated Classic in Memoriam," *Journal of Psychological Issues in Organizational Culture* (II, #3, 95-105, Oct. 2011).

Morgan, John H. (2010). "Harry Stack Sullivan and Interpersonal Psychotherapy: The Father of Modern Social Psychiatry," in *Foundation Theology 2010* (Mishawaka, IN: GTF Books). .

Morgan, John H. (2006). "Personal Meaning as Psychotherapy: The Interpretive Hermeneutic of Viktor Frankl," In *Foundation Theology 2006* (Mishawaka, IN: GTF Books).

Morgan, John H. (1983). "Personal Meaning as Therapy: The Roots and Branches of Frankl's Psychology," *Pastoral Psychology*, Fall Issue, 1983.

Morgan, John H. (1978). "The Theology of Medicine: The Political-Philosophical Foundations of Medical Ethics," *Journal of the American Academy of Religion,* Vol. 46, #2, pp. 250ff., 1978.

Morgan, John H. (1976). "Pastoral Ecstasy and the Authentic Self: Theological Meanings in Symbolic Distance," *Pastoral Psychology,* XXV, #2 (Winter, 1976), 128-137.

Morgan, John H. (1975). "Silence as Creative Therapy: A Contemplative Approach to Pastoral Care," *Journal of Pastoral Care,* XXIX, 4 (Dec., 1975): 248-253.

Morgan, John H. (1973). "The Psychotherapeutics of Silence," *Spiritual Frontiers,* V, #2 (Spring, 1973).

Murphy, Dominic; Stich, Stephen (16 December 1998). "Darwin in the Madhouse: Evolutionary Psychology and the Classification of Mental Disorders". Archived from the original on 5 December 2013. Retrieved 2013-12-03.

Murphy, Michael; Cowan, Ronald; Sederer, Lloyd I., eds. (2009). "Personality Disorders." *Blueprints Psychiatry (5th ed.).* Wolters Kluwer/Lippincott Williams & Wilkins.

Murray, Robin M. et al (2008). *Psychiatry. Fourth Edition.* Cambridge University Press.
Nannarello, Joseph J. (1953). "Schizoid." *The Journal of Nervous and Mental Disease. 118 (3): 237–249.*

Nedic, Aleksandra; Zivanovic, Olga; Lisulov, Ratomir (2011). "Nosological status of social phobia: contrasting classical and recent literature." *Current Opinion in Psychiatry. 24 (1): 61–6.*

Nehls N (1998). "Borderline personality disorder: gender stereotypes, stigma, and limited system of care." *Issues Ment Health Nurs. 19 (2): 97–112.*

Nehls N (August 1999). "Borderline personality disorder: the voice of patients." *Res Nurs Health. 22 (4): 285–93.*

Nenadic, Igor; Güllmar, Daniel; Dietzek, Maren; Langbein, Kerstin; Steinke, Johanna; Gader, Christian (February 2015). "Brain structure in narcissistic personality disorder: A VBM and DTI pilot study." *Psychiatry Research Neuroimaging. Elsevier Ireland. 231 (2): 184–186.*

Netherton, S.D.; Holmes, D.; Walker, C.E. (1999). *Child and Adolescent Psychological Disorders: Comprehensive Textbook.* New York, NY: Oxford University Press.

New, Antonia; Triebwasser Joseph; Charney Dennis (October 2008). "The case for shifting borderline personality disorder to Axis I" (PDF). *Biol. Psychiatry. 64 (8): 653–9.*

Nolen-Hoeksema, S. (2014). "Personality Disorders. (pp. 266–267)." *Abnormal Psychology* (6th ed.). New York, NY: McGraw-Hill.

Nordgaard, Julie; Louis A. Sass (June 2013). "The psychiatric interview: validity, structure, and subjectivity". European archives of *Psychiatry and Clinical Neuroscience.* 263 (4): 353–364.

Nussbaum, Abraham (2013). The Pocket Guide to the DSM-5 Diagnostic Exam. *Arlington: American Psychiatric Association.*

O'Donohue, William (2007). *Personality Disorders : Toward the DSM-V.* Los Angeles: SAGE Publications.

Oldham, John M.; Morris, Lois B. (1990). *The Personality Self-portrait: Why You Think, Work, Love, and Act the Way You Do.* Bantam.

Oldham, John M., Skodol, Andrew E., Bender, Donna S. (2005) *The American Psychiatric Publishing Textbook of Personality Disorders.* American Psychiatric Publishing.

Oldham, John M., Skodol, Andrew E., Bender, Donna S. (2005). *Textbook of Personality Disorders.* American Psychiatric Publishing.

Oldham, John M. (2005). "Personality Disorders". *FOCUS.* 3: 372–382.

O'Neil, Aisling; Thomas Frodl (18 January 2012). "Brain structure and function in borderline personality disorder." *Brain Structure and Function. 217: 767–782.*

Osborne, Duncan (May 15, 2008). "Flap Flares Over Gender Diagnosis". *Gay City News. Archived from the original on October 24, 2008. Retrieved June 14, 2008.*

Oscar-Berman M; Valmas M; Sawyer K; Kirkley S; Gansler D; Merritt D; Couture A (April 2009). "Frontal brain dysfunction in alcoholism with and without antisocial personality disorder." *Neuropsychiatric Disease and Treatment. 5: 309–326.*

Oumaya, M; Friedman, S; Pham, A; Abou Abdallah, T; Guelfi, JD; Rouillon, F (October 2008). "[Borderline personality disorder, self-mutilation and suicide: literature review]." *L'Encephale. 34 (5): 452–8.*

Overholser, J. C. (November 1989). "Differentiation between schizoid and avoidant personalities: an empirical test". *Canadian Journal of Psychiatry. 34 (8): 785–90.*

Panagiotis, Parpottas (2012). "A critique on the use of standard psychopathological classifications in understanding human distress: The example of 'Schizoid Personality Disorder'." *Counselling Psychology Review 27 (1): 44–52.*

Parens, Henri (2014). *War Is Not Inevitable: On the Psychology of War and Aggression.* Lexington Books.

Paris, Joel (2014). "Modernity and narcissistic personality disorder." *Personality Disorders: Theory, Research, and Treatment, 5 (2): 220.*

Paris J (2008). *Treatment of Borderline Personality Disorder. A Guide to Evidence-Based Practice.* The Guilford Press.

Paris J (2004). "Borderline or bipolar? Distinguishing borderline personality disorder from bipolar spectrum disorders." *Harv Rev Psychiatry. 12 (3): 140–5.*

Paris J (June 2004). "Is hospitalization useful for suicidal patients with borderline personality disorder?". *J. Pers. Disord. 18 (3): 240–7.*

Paris J (February 2010). "Effectiveness of different psychotherapy approaches in the treatment of borderline personality disorder." *Curr Psychiatry Rep. 12 (1): 56–60.*

Parker, AG; Boldero, JM; Bell, RC (September 2006). "Borderline personality disorder features: the role of self-discrepancies and self-complexity." *Psychol Psychother. 79 (Pt 3): 309–21.*

Patrick, Christopher J. (2005). *Handbook of Psychopathy.* Guilford Press.

Pearson, Catherine (20 May 2013). "DSM-5 Changes: What Parents Need To Know About The First Major Revision In Nearly 20 Years". *The Huffington Post.* Retrieved 2013-05-21.

Penzel, Fred. (2000). *Obsessive–Compulsive Disorders: A Complete Guide to Getting Well and Staying Well.* Oxford University Press, USA.

Perry, J. C. (1996). "Dependent personality disorder." In *Gabbard, Glen O.; Atkinson, Sarah D. Synopsis of Treatments of Psychiatric Disorders. American Psychiatric Press. pp. 995–8.*

Phillips, James; Frances, Allen; Cerullo, Michael A; Chardavoyne, John; Decker, Hannah S; First, Michael B; Ghaemi, Nassir; Greenberg, Gary; et al. (January 13, 2012). "The Six Most Essential Questions in Psychiatric Diagnosis: A Pluralogue. Part 1: Conceptual and Definitional Issues in Psychiatric Diagnosis" (PDF). Philosophy, Ethics, and Humanities in Medicine. *BioMed Central.* 7 (3): 1–51.

Pilkonis PA, Frank E (1988). "Personality pathology in recurrent depression: nature, prevalence, and relationship to treatment response." *Am J Psychiatry. 145: 435–41.*

Pincus AL, Ansell EB, Pimentel CA, Cain NM, Wright AG, Levy KN; Ansell; Pimentel; Cain; Wright; Levy (2009). "Initial construction and validation of the Pathological Narcissism Inventory." *Psychol Assess. 21 (3): 365–79.*

Pincus, H. A.; Zarin, DA; First, M (1998). "'Clinical Significance' and DSM-IV". *Arch Gen Psychiatry.* 55 (12): 1145; author reply 1147–8.

Pinkofsky, HB (1997). "Mnemonics for DSM-IV personality disorders." *Psychiatric Services. Washington, D.C. 48 (9): 1197–8.*

Pinto, Anthony (2014). "Capacity to Delay Reward Differentiates Obsessive-Compulsive Disorder and Obsessive-Compulsive Personality Disorder." *Biol Psychiatry. 75 (8): 653–659.*

Pinto, Anthon y; Eisen, Jane L.; Mancebo, Maria C.; Rasmussen, Steven A. (2008). "Obsessive-Compulsive Personality Disorder." In Abramowitz, Jonathan S.; McKay, Dean; Taylor, Steven. *Obsessive-Compulsive Disorder: Subtypes and Spectrum Conditions. Elsevier. pp. 246–263.*

Poland, JS. (2001) Review of Volume 1 of DSM-IV sourcebook Archived May 1, 2005, at the *Wayback Machine.*

Poland, JS. (2001) Review of vol 2 of DSM-IV sourcebook Archived September 27, 2007, at the *Wayback Machine.*

Posner MI, Tang YY, Lynch G (2014). "Mechanisms of white matter change induced by meditation training." *Frontiers in Psychology. 5 (1220): 297–302.*

"Professor co-authors letter about America's mental health manual". *Point Park University.* Retrieved 6 February 2017.

"Professor co-authors letter about America's mental health manual". *Point Park University.* December 12, 2011.

Pulay, A. J., Stinson, F. S., Dawson, D. A., Goldstein, R. B., Chou, S. P., Huang, B.; et al. (2009). "Prevalence, correlates, disability, and comorbidity of DSM-IV schizotypal personality disorder: results from the wave 2 national epidemiologic survey on alcohol and related conditions." *Primary Care Companion to the Journal of Clinical Psychiatry. 11 (2): 53–67.*

Quadrio, C (December 2005). "Axis One/Axis Two: A disordered borderline." *Australian and New Zealand Journal of Psychiatry. 39: A107.*

Raine, A. (2006). "Schizotypal personality: Neurodevelopmental and psychosocial trajectories." *Annual Review of Psychology. 2: 291–326.*

Raine, Adrian; Lydia Lee; Yaling Yang; Patrick Colletti (2010). "Neurodevelopmental marker for limbic maldevelopment in antisocial personality disorder and psychopathy." *BJPsych. the British Journal of Psychiatry. 197 (3): 186–192.*

Raja M, Azzoni A (2007). "The impact of obsessive–compulsive personality disorder on the suicidal risk of patients with mood disorders." *Psychopathology. 40 (3): 184–90.*

Ralevski, E.; Sanislow, C. A.; Grilo, C. M.; Skodol, A. E.; Gunderson, J. G.; Tracie Shea, M.; Yen, S.; Bender, D. S.; et al. (2005). "Avoidant personality disorder and social phobia: distinct

enough to be separate disorders?." *Acta Psychiatrica Scandinavica.*
112 (3): 208–14.

Rapkin, AJ; Lewis, EI (November 2013). *"Treatment of
premenstrual dysphoric disorder."* Womens Health (Lond Engl). 9
(6): 537–56.

Rautiainen, M.-R.; Paunio, T.; Repo-Tiihonen, E.; Virkkunen, M.;
Ollila, H. M.; Sulkava, S.; Jolanki, O.; Palotie, A.; Tiihonen, J. (6
September 2016). "Genome-wide association study of antisocial
personality disorder." *Translational Psychiatry. Macmillian
Publishers Limited. 6 (9): e883.*

Reber, Arthur S. (2009) [1985]. *The Penguin Dictionary of
Psychology (4th ed.).* London; New York: Penguin Books.

Reichborn-Kjennerud, Ted (1 March 2010). "The genetic
epidemiology of personality disorders." *Dialogues in Clinical
Neuroscience. 12 (1): 103–114.*

Reichborn-Kjennerud, T.; Czajkowski, N.; Torgersen, S.; Neale, M.
C.; Orstavik, R. E.; Tambs, K.; Kendler, K. S. (2007). "The
Relationship Between Avoidant Personality Disorder and Social
Phobia: A Population-Based Twin Study." *American Journal of
Psychiatry. 164 (11): 1722–8.*

Retzlaff, P. D. (1995*). Tactical Psychotherapy of the Personality
Disorders: An MCMI-III-Based Approach.* Boston: Allyn & Bacon.

Reich, James (2009). "Avoidant personality disorder and its
relationship to social phobia." *Current Psychiatry Reports. 11 (1):
89–93.*

Rheaume, J; Freeston, MH; Dugas, MJ; Letarte, H; Ladouceur, R
(1995). "Perfectionism, responsibility and obsessive-compulsive
symptoms." *Behav Res Ther. 33. 33 (7): 785–794.*

Richards, Henry Jay (1993). *Therapy of the Substance Abuse Syndromes.* New York: Jason Aronson.

Rissmiller, DJ, D.O., Rissmiller, J. (2006) "Letter in reply." *Psychiatr Serv* 57:1809-a-1810, December.

Robinson, David J. (2005). *Disordered Personalities.* Rapid Psychler Press.

Robinson, David J. (1999). *The Field Guide to Personality Disorders.* Rapid Psychler Press.

Robinson, David J. (2003). *Reel Psychiatry: Movie Portrayals of Psychiatric Conditions.* Port Huron, Michigan: Rapid Psychler Press.

Ronningstam, Elsa (2016). "New Insights Into Narcissistic Personality Disorder." *Psychiatric Times, 33 (2): 11.*

Ronningstam, Elsa (19 January 2016). "Pathological Narcissism and Narcissistic Personality Disorder: Recent Research and Clinical Implications." *Current Behavioral Neuroscience Reports. Springer International Publishing. 3 (1): 34–42.*

Ronningstam E (2010). "Narcissistic personality disorder: a current review." *Curr Psychiatry Rep. 12 (1): 68–75.*

Rosenthal, MZ; Cheavens, JS; Lejuez, CW; Lynch, TR (September 2005). "Thought suppression mediates the relationship between negative affect and borderline personality disorder symptoms." *Behav Res There. 43 (9): 1173–85.*

Rossi A; et al. (2000). "Pattern of comorbidity among anxious and odd personality disorders: the case of obsessive–compulsive personality disorder." *CNS Spectr. 5 (9): 23–6.*

Ruocco, Anthony C.; Amirthavasagam, Sathya, Choi-Kain, Lois W.; McMain, Shelley F. (2013). "Neural Correlates of Negative Emotionality in Borderline Personality Disorder: An Activation-

Likelihood-Estimation Meta-Analysis." *Biological Psychiatry. 73 (2): 153–160.*

Rydén, Göran; Rydén, Eleonore; Hetta, Jerker (2008). "Borderline personality disorder and autism spectrum disorder in females: A cross-sectional study." *Clinical Neuropsychiatry. 5 (1): 22–30.*

Ryle, A. & Kerr, I. B. (2002). *Introducing Cognitive Analytic Therapy: Principles and Practice.* Chichester: John Wiley & Sons.

Sachdeva S.; Goldman G.; Mustata G.; Deranja E.; Gregory R. J. (2013). "Naturalistic outcomes of evidence-based therapies for borderline personality disorder at a university clinic: A quasi-randomized trial." *Journal of the American Psychoanalytic Association. 61: 578–584.*

Sachse S, Keville S, Feigenbaum J (Jun 2011). "A feasibility study of mindfulness-based cognitive therapy for individuals with borderline personality disorder." *Psychology and Psychotherapy. 84 (2): 184–200.*

Sadock, Benjamin J. (October 1999). "DSM-IV Sourcebook, vol. 4 (Book Forum: Assessment and Diagnosis)". *American Journal of Psychiatry.* 156 (10): 1655.

Salekin, R. (2002). "Psychopathy and therapeutic pessimism: Clinical lore or clinical reality?." *Clinical Psychology Review. 22: 169–183.*

Salzman, Leon. (1995).*Treatment of Obsessive and Compulsive Behaviors*, Jason Aronson Publishers.

Samuels J et al. (2000). "Personality disorders and normal personality dimensions in obsessive–compulsive disorder." *Br J Psychiatry.* Nov. 177: 457–62.

Samuels, Jack; Costa, Paul T. (2012). "Obsessive-Compulsive Personality Disorder." In Widiger, Thomas. *The Oxford Handbook of Personality Disorders. Oxford University Press. p. 568.*

Sansone, Randy A.; Sansone, Lori A. (1 May 2011). "Gender Patterns in Borderline Personality Disorder." *Innovations in Clinical Neuroscience. 8 (5): 16–20.*

Sansone, R.A.; Hendricks, C. M.; Gaither, G. A.; Reddington, A. (2004). "Prevalence of anxiety symptoms among a sample of outpatients in an internal medicine clinic: a pilot study." *Depress Anxiety. 19. 19 (2): 133–136.*

Sansone, R.A.; Hendricks, C. M.; Sellbom, M.; Reddington, A. (2003). "Anxiety symptoms and healthcare utilization among a sample of outpatients in an internal medicine clinic." *Int J Psychiatry Med. 33. 33 (2): 133–139.*

Sauer, SE; Baer, Ruth A.; Baer, RA (February 2009). "Relationships between thought suppression and symptoms of borderline personality disorder." *J. Pers. Disord. 23 (1): 48–61.*

Sciencedaily.com (2008). "Possible Genetic Causes Of Borderline Personality Disorder Identified." 20 December.

Schaffer, David (1996). "A Participant's Observations: Preparing DSM-IV" (PDF). *Can J Psychiatry.* 41: 325–329.

Schatzberg, Alan and Francis (2010). Psychiatrists Propose Revisions to Diagnosis Manual. via *PBS Newshour,* interview February 10.

Schmahl CG, Elzinga BM, Vermetten E, Sanislow C, McGlashan TH, Bremner JD (July 2003). "Neural correlates of memories of abandonment in women with and without borderline personality disorder." *Biol. Psychiatry. 54 (2): 142–51.*

Schuldberg, David (2001). "Six subclinical spectrum traits in normal creativity." *Creativity Research Journal. 13 (1): 5–16.*

Schulze L, Dziobek I, Vater A, Heekeren HR, Bajbouj M, Renneberg B, Heuser I, Roepke S; Dziobek; Vater; Heekeren; Bajbouj; Renneberg; Heuser; Roepke (2013). "Gray matter abnormalities in patients with narcissistic personality disorder." *J Psychiatr Res. 47 (10): 1363–9.*

Scoriels, Linda (2013). "Modafinil effects on cognition and emotion in schizophrenia and its neurochemical modulation in the brain." *Neuropharmacology. 64: 168–184.*

Sederer, Lloyd I. (2009). *Blueprints Psychiatry (5th ed.).* Philadelphia: Wolters Kluwer/Lippincott Williams & Wilkins.

Seinfeld, Jeffrey (1991): *The Empty Core: An Object Relations Approach to Psychotherapy of the Schizoid Personality.* Jason Aronson.

Selby EA (October 2013). "Chronic sleep disturbances and borderline personality disorder symptoms." *J Consult Clin Psychol. 81 (5): 941–7.*

Seligman, Martin E.P. (1984). "Chapter 11." *Abnormal Psychology.* W. W. Norton & Company.

Semple, David; Smyth, Roger; Burns, Jonathan; Darjee, Rajan; McIntosh, Andrew (2005). *The Oxford Handbook of Psychiatry.* New York: Oxford University Press.

Sharfstein, SS. (2005) "Big Pharma and American Psychiatry: The Good, the Bad, and the Ugly" *Psychiatric News* August 19, 2005 Volume 40 Number 16.

Shea MT; et al. (1992). "Comorbidity of personality disorders and depression; implications for treatment." *J Consult Clin Psychol. 60: 857–68.*

Shedler J, Beck A, Fonagy P, Gabbard GO, Gunderson J, Kernberg O, Michels R, Westen D; Beck; Fonagy; Gabbard; Gunderson; Kernberg; Michels; Westen (September 2010). "Personality Disorders in DSM-5." *American Journal of Psychiatry. 167 (9): 1026–1028.*

Siegel JP (2006). "Dyadic splitting in partner relational disorders." *J Fam Psychol. 20 (3): 418–22.*

Siever, L.J. (1992). "Schizophrenia spectrum disorders." *Review of Psychiatry. 11: 25–42.*

Simonoff E, Elander J, Holmshaw J, Pickles A, Murray R, Rutter M (2004). "Predictors of antisocial personality Continuities from childhood to adult life. *The British Journal of Psychiatry. 184 (2): 118–127.*

Skeem, J. L.; Polaschek, D. L. L.; Patrick, C. J.; Lilienfeld, S. O. (15 December 2011).
"Psychopathic Personality: Bridging the Gap Between Scientific Evidence and Public Policy". *Psychological Science in the Public Interest. 12 (3): 95–162.*

Skodol AE, Bender DS (2003). "Why are women diagnosed borderline more than men?". *Psychiatr Q. 74 (4): 349–60.*

Skodol AE; et al. (2002). "Functional Impairment in Patients With Schizotypal, Borderline, Avoidant, or Obsessive–Compulsive Personality Disorder." *Am J Psychiatry. 159: 276–83.*

Sperry, Len (1995). *Psychopharmacology and Psychotherapy: Strategies for Maximizing Treatment Outcomes.* Psychology Press.

Sperry, Len (2003). "Avoidant Personality Disorder." *Handbook of diagnosis and treatment of DSM-IV-TR personality disorders.* Philadelphia: Brunner-Routledge. pp. 59–79.

Sperry, Lynn (1999). *Narcissistic Personality Disorder, Cognitive Behavior Therapy of DSM-IV Personality Disorders: Highly Effective Interventions for the Most Common Personality Disorders.* Ann Arbor, MI: Edwards Brothers.

Spiegel, Alix (3 January 2005). "The Dictionary of Disorder: How one man revolutionized psychiatry". *The New Yorker.* Archived from the original on 12 December 2006.

Spiegel, Alix; Glass, Ira (18 January 2002). "81 Words". *This American Life*. Chicago: WBEZ Chicago Public Radio.

Spitzer, Robert L.; Fleiss, Joseph L. (1974). "A re-analysis of the reliability of psychiatric diagnosis". *British Journal of Psychiatry*. 125 (4): 341–347.

Spitzer, R.L. (1981). "The diagnostic status of homosexuality in DSM-III: a reformulation of the issues". *Am J Psychiatry*. 138 (2): 210–215.

Spitzer, First (2005). "Classification of Psychiatric Disorders". *JAMA*. 294 (15): 1898–1899.

Spitzer, Robert L.; Williams, Janet B.W.; First, Michael B.; Gibbon, Miriam. "Biometric Research". *Psychiatric Institute* 2001-2002. New York State Psychiatric Institute. Archived from the original on 7 March 2003.
Spitzer, RL; Wakefield, JC. (December 1999). "DSM-IV diagnostic criterion for clinical significance: does it help solve the false positives problem?". *Am J Psychiatry*. 156 (12): 1856–64.

Startup, M.; B. Jones; H. Heard; M. Swales; J.M.G. Williams; R.S.P. Jones (November 1999). "Autobiographical memory and dissociation in borderline personality disorder." *Psychological Medicine. 29 (6): 1397–1404.*

Steinglass, Joanna (2012). "Increased Capacity to Delay Reward in Anorexia Nervosa.*" Journal of the International Neuropsychological Society. 18: 1–8.*

Stern, Adolf (1938). "Psychoanalytic investigation of and therapy in the borderline group of neuroses." *Psychoanalytic Quarterly. 7: 467–489.*

Stiglmayr CE, Grathwol T, Linehan MM, Ihorst G, Fahrenberg J, Bohus M (May 2005). "Aversive tension in patients with borderline personality disorder: a computer-based controlled field study." *Acta Psychiatr Scand. 111 (5): 372–9.*

Stoffers, JM; Völlm, BA; Rücker, G; Timmer, A; Huband, N; Lieb, K (15 August 2012). "Psychological therapies for people with borderline personality disorder." *The Cochrane database of systematic reviews. 8: CD005652.*

Stone, Michael H. (1993). *Abnormalities of Personality: Within and Beyond the Realm of Treatment.* Norton.

Stone MH (2005). "Borderline Personality Disorder: History of the Concept." In Zanarini MC. *Borderline personality disorder. Boca Raton, FL: Taylor & Francis. pp. 1–18.*

Suinn, Richard M. (1984). *Fundamentals of Abnormal Psychology (Updated ed.).* Chicago: Nelson-Hall.

Sullivan, Harry Stack (1953). *The Interpersonal Theory of Psychiatry.* (N.Y.: W.W. Norton).

"Summary of Practice-Relevant Changes to the DSM-IV-TR". *American Psychiatric Association.* Archived from the original on 13 May 2012.

Sutker, Patricia B., and Albert N. Allain, Jr. (2002). "Antisocial Personality Disorder." Comprehensive Handbook of Psychopathology. Vol. III. : Springer, pp. 445-90.

Sutker, P. B. (2002). *Histrionic, Narcissistic, and Dependent Personality Disorders. Comprehensive handbook of psychopathology (3rd ed.).* New York: Kluwer Academic.

Swartz, Marvin; Blazer, Dan; George, Linda; Winfield, Idee (1990). "Estimating the Prevalence of Borderline Personality Disorder in the Community." *Journal of Personality Disorders. 4 (3): 257–272.*

Szeszko PR, Robinson D, Alvir JM, et al. (October 1999). "Orbital frontal and amygdala volume reductions in obsessive-compulsive disorder." *Arch. Gen. Psychiatry. 56 (10): 913–9.*

Tang YY, Posner MI (Jan 2013). "Special issue on mindfulness neuroscience." *Social Cognitive & Affective Neuroscience. 8 (1): 1–3.*

"TARA Association for Personality Disorder". *tara4bpd.org. Archived from the original on October 20, 2014. Retrieved January 29, 2015.*

Tasca C.; Rapetti M.; Carta M.G.; Fadda B. (2012). "Women and hysteria in the history of mental health." *Clinical Practice & Epidemiology in Mental Health. 8: 110–119.*

Tasman, Allan et al (2008). *Psychiatry. Third Edition.* John Wiley & Sons, Ltd.

Torgersen, S; Lygren, S; Oien, PA; Skre, I; Onstad, S; Edvardsen, J; Tambs, K; Kringlen, E (December 2000). "A twin study of personality disorders." *Comprehensive psychiatry. 41 (6): 416–25.*

Torgersen, S (March 2000). "Genetics of patients with borderline personality disorder." *Psychiatr. Clin. North Am. 23 (1): 1–9.*

Torgersen, S; Lygren, S; Oien, PA; et al. (2000). "A twin study of personality disorders". *Compr Psychiatry. 41 (6): 416–25.*

Urnes, O (30 April 2009). "[Self-harm and personality disorders]." *Tidsskrift for den Norske laegeforening : tidsskrift for praktisk medicin, ny raekke. 129 (9): 872–6.*

Vaillant, George E. (1985). "Maturity of Ego Defenses in Relation to DSM-III Axis II Personality Disorder". *Archives of General Psychiatry. 42 (6): 597.*

Vaillant GE (1992). "The beginning of wisdom is never calling a patient a borderline; or, the clinical management of immature

defenses in the treatment of individuals with personality disorders."
J Psychother Pract Res. 1 (2): 117–34.

van Heeringen K, Audenaert K, Van de Wiele L, Verstraete A
(November 2000). "Cortisol in violent suicidal behaviour:
association with personality and monoaminergic activity." *J Affect
Disord. 60 (3): 181–9.*

Van Velzen, C. J. M. (2002). *Social Phobia and Personality
Disorders: Comorbidity and Treatment Issues.* Groningen:
University Library Groningen.

Vedantam, Shankar (June 26, 2005). "Psychiatry's Missing
Diagnosis: Patients' Diversity Is Often Discounted". *The Washington
Post.*

Villemarette-Pittman, Nicole R; Matthew Stanford; Kevin Greve;
Rebecca Houston; Charles Mathias (2004). "Obsessive-Compulsive
Personality Disorder and Behavioral Disinhibition." *The Journal of
Psychology. 138 (1): 5–22.*

Wakefield, Jerome C.; PhD, MF; PhD, MB; PhD, DSW; Schmitz,
Mark F.; First, Michael B.; MD; Horwitz, Allan V. (2007).
"Extending the Bereavement Exclusion for Major Depression to
Other Losses: Evidence From the National Comorbidity Survey".
Arch Gen Psychiatry. 64 (4): 433–440.

Waldinger, Robert J. (1 August 1997). "Psychiatry for Medical
Students." *American Psychiatric.*

Walker, E., Kestler, L., Bollini, A.; et al. (2004). "Schizophrenia:
etiology and course." *Annual Review of Psychology. 55: 401–430.*

Wedding D, Boyd MA, Niemiec RM (2005). *Movies and Mental
Illness: Using Films to Understand Psychopathology.* Cambridge,
MA: Hogrefe.

West, Malcolm L. and A. E. Sheldon-Keller (1994). *Patterns of Relating An Adult Attachment Perspective.* New York: Guilford Press.

Widiger, T. (1998). "Sex biases in the diagnosis of personality disorders." *Journal of Personality Disorders. 12 (2): 95–118.*

Widiger TA, Sankis LM (2000). "Adult psychopathology: issues and controversies". *Annu Rev Psychol.* 51 (1): 377–404.

Wilson, M. (March 1993). "DSM-III and the transformation of American psychiatry: a history". *Am J Psychiatry.* 150 (3): 399–410.

Wing, Peter C. (1997). "Patient or Client? If in Doubt, Ask." *Canadian Medical Association, 157:287-89.*

Winnicott, Donald (1965): *The Maturational Process and the Facilitating Environment.* Karnac Books.
Winnicott, Donald (2006). *The Family and Individual Development.* Routledge.

Winnicott, Donald (2012). *Playing and Reality.* Routledge Classics.

Wolff, Sula (1995). *Loners - The Life Path of Unusual Children.* Routledge.

Woodbury-Smith, MR and F. R. Volkmar (2008). "Asperger syndrome." *Eur Child Adolesc Psychiatry. 18 (1): 2–11.*

Yang, Yaling; Raine, Adrian (30 November 2009). "Prefrontal Structural and Functional Brain Imaging findings in Antisocial, Violent, and Psychopathic Individuals: A Meta-Analysis." *Psychiatry Research. 174 (2): 81–88.*

Yildirim, Bariş O. (August 2013). "Systematic review, structural analysis, and new theoretical perspectives on the role of serotonin and associated genes in the etiology of psychopathy and sociopathy." *Neuroscience & Biobehavioral Reviews. 37: 1254–1296.*

Zanarini, MC; Frankenburg, FR (1997). "Pathways to the development of borderline personality disorder." *J. Pers. Disord.* 11 (1): 93–104.

Zanarini MC, Frankenburg FR, DeLuca CJ, Hennen J, Khera GS, Gunderson JG (1998). "The pain of being borderline: dysphoric states specific to borderline personality disorder." *Harv Rev Psychiatry. 6 (4): 201–7.*

Zanarini MC, Frankenburg FR, Dubo ED, et al. (December 1998). "Axis I comorbidity of borderline personality disorder." *Am J Psychiatry. 155 (12): 1733–9.*

Zanarini MC, Frankenburg FR, Reich DB, et al. (2000). "Biparental failure in the childhood experiences of borderline patients." *J Personal Disord. 14 (3): 264–73.*

Zanarini MC, Frankenburg FR, Khera GS, Bleichmar J (2001). "Treatment histories of borderline inpatients." *Compr Psychiatry. 42 (2): 144–50.*

ABOUT THE AUTHOR

John H. Morgan, Ph.D., D.Sc.(London), Psy.D. (FH/Oxford), is the retired Senior Fellow in Behavioral Science at Foundation House/Oxford (UK) and *Emeritus* Research Professor of Clinical Psychopathology. He has been Postdoctoral Visiting Scholar at Harvard University (1998, 2011, 2015) as well as a National Science Foundation Science Faculty Fellow at the University of Notre Dame. For 20 years he taught a doctoral-level seminar in the International Summer Program at Oxford University and is the author of over 25 books in the social sciences.

Books by John H. Morgan
Published by Wyndham Hall Press
related to Child Psychology

https://www.amazon.com/John-H.-
Morgan/e/B001JOYD54%3Fref=dbs_a_mng_rwt_scns_share

*Sigmund Freud Comprehensive Reference Dictionary of
    Psychoanalysis*
*Harry Stack Sullivan Encyclopedic Dictionary of Interpersonal
    Psychotherapy*
*Psychopathology: A Clinical Guide to Personality Disorders
    Clinical Psychotherapy: A History of Theory and Practice*
*Understanding Ourselves: Essays in the History & Philosophy of the
    Social Sciences*
*Child Psychopathology in Clinical Practice: The Psychoanalytic
    Theories of Karen Horney, Melanie Klein, and Anna Freud*
*The Learning Spectrum in Child Development: Developmental
    Psychology in Maria Montessori, Jean Piaget, and Erik
    Erikson*
*Geriatric Psychotherapy: Essays in Clinical Practice and
    Counseling Psychology*
*The Scope of Modern Psychiatry: Treatment Options in Clinical
    Practice*